Feminist Visions and Queer Futures in Postcolonial Drama

Routledge Advances in Theatre and Performance Studies

1. **Theatre and Postcolonial Desires**
Awam Amkpa

2. **Brecht and Critical Theory**
Dialectics and Contemporary Aesthetics
Sean Carney

3. **Science and the Stanislavsky Tradition of Acting**
Jonathan Pitches

4. **Performance and Cognition**
Theatre Studies after the Cognitive Turn
Edited by Bruce McConachie and F. Elizabeth Hart

5. **Theatre and Performance in Digital Culture**
From Simulation to Embeddedness
Matthew Causey

6. **The Politics of New Media Theatre**
Life®™
Gabriella Giannachi

7. **Ritual and Event**
Interdisciplinary Perspectives
Edited by Mark Franko

8. **Memory, Allegory, and Testimony in South American Theater**
Upstaging Dictatorship
Ana Elena Puga

9. **Crossing Cultural Borders Through the Actor's Work**
Foreign Bodies of Knowledge
Cláudia Tatinge Nascimento

10. **Movement Training for the Modern Actor**
Mark Evans

11. **The Politics of American Actor Training**
Edited by Ellen Margolis and Lissa Tyler Renaud

12. **Performing Embodiment in Samuel Beckett's Drama**
Anna McMullan

13. **The Provocation of the Senses in Contemporary Theatre**
Stephen Di Benedetto

14. **Ecology and Environment in European Drama**
Downing Cless

15. **Global Ibsen**
Performing Multiple Modernities
Edited by Erika Fischer-Lichte, Barbara Gronau, Christel Weiler

16. **The Theatre of the Bauhaus**
The Modern and Postmodern Stage of Oskar Schlemmer
Melissa Trimingham

17. **Feminist Visions and Queer Futures in Postcolonial Drama**
Community, Kinship, and Citizenship
Kanika Batra

Feminist Visions and Queer Futures in Postcolonial Drama

Community, Kinship, and Citizenship

Kanika Batra

LONDON AND NEW YORK

First published 2011
by Routledge
52 Vanderbilt Avenue, New York, NY 10017

Simultaneously published in the UK
by Routledge
2 Park Square, Milton Park, Abingdon, Oxon OX14 4RN

Routledge is an imprint of the Taylor & Francis Group, an informa business

First issued in paperback 2012

© 2011 Taylor & Francis

The right of [Editor/Author name] to be identified as author of this work has been asserted by [him/her/them] in accordance with sections 77 and 78 of the Copyright, Designs and Patents Act 1988.

Typeset in Sabon by IBT Global.

All rights reserved. No part of this book may be reprinted or reproduced or utilised in any form or by any electronic, mechanical, or other means, now known or hereafter invented, including photocopying and recording, or in any information storage or retrieval system, without permission in writing from the publishers.

Trademark Notice: Product or corporate names may be trademarks or registered trademarks, and are used only for identification and explanation without intent to infringe.

Library of Congress Cataloging in Publication Data
Batra, Kanika, 1972-
  Feminist visions and queer futures in postcolonial drama : community, kinship, and citizenship / by Kanika Batra.
     p. cm. -- (Routledge advances in theatre and performance studies ; 17)
  Includes bibliographical references and index.
  1. Feminist drama—History and criticism. 2. Feminism and theater. 3. Feminist theater—Jamaica. 4. Feminist theater—India. 5. Feminist theater—Nigeria.
  6. Feminism in literature. 7. Women in literature. 8. Sex role in literature.
  9. Postcolonialism in literature. 10. Postcolonialism—Commonwealth countries. I. Title.
  PN1590.W64B38 2010
  792.082—dc22
                                          2010018517

ISBN13: 978-0-415-87591-2 (hbk)
ISBN13: 978-0-203-83985-0 (ebk)
ISBN13: 978-0-415-81817-9 (pbk)

*For my parents, Kimshuk, Puneet
and for Rich*

Contents

List of Illustrations ix
Permissions xi
Acknowledgments xiii

Introduction: Feminist Visions and Queer Futures   1

PART I
Jamaica

1   Making Citizens: Community, Kinship, and the National Imaginary in Dennis Scott's *An Echo in the Bone* (1974) and *Dog* (1978)   29

2   "We Shouldn't Shame to Talk": Postcolonial Sexual Citizenship in Sistren Theatre Collective's *Bellywoman Banagarang* and *QPH*   47

PART II
India

3   A People's Theatre from Delhi in Alliance with the Women's Movement   69

4   Queering the Subaltern: Postcolonial Performativity in Mahesh Dattani's *Seven Steps around the Fire* and Mahasweta Devi and Usha Ganguli's *Rudali*   92

PART III
Nigeria

5 Resistant Citizenship: Reading Feminist Praxis and
   Democratic Renewal in Nigeria through Femi
   Osofisan's *Morountodun*   113

6 "Daughters Who know the Languages of Power:"
   Community, Sexuality, and Postcolonial Development
   in Tess Onwueme's *Tell It to Women*   130

   Epilogue   146

Notes   151
Bibliography   163
Index   175

Illustrations

2.1	Sistren founding members, Lorna Burrell and Bev "Didi" Elliot, stand to attention in a performance of *Domestick*.	49
2.2	Queenie addresses her flock in the collective creation of *QPH*.	53
2.3	Miss Freeman and Goddy spy on Yvonne and her boyfriend in *Bellywoman Bangarang*.	54
2.4	Didi listens as her mother expresses concern over her pregnancy in *Bellywoman Bangarang*.	55
3.1	Moloyashree Hashmi amid the circle of actors in a performance of *Aurat*.	74
3.2	The woman worker holds up a red flag in Janam's 1981 performance of *Aurat* for a working class audience in Haryana.	75
3.3	The girl slowly rises up after being raped by thugs in Janam's performance of *Police Charitram*.	79
3.4	A street vendor is surrounded by the police in Janam's performance of *Police Charitram*.	80
3.5	Janam actors enter the central area wearing masks and scarves in the opening scene of *Aartanaad*.	84
3.6	One of the narrators throws her *chunni* (scarf) to indicate the rape of the child, who never appears on stage in *Aartanaad*.	85
6.1	Idu women raise their voices and gesticulate in protest at the showcasing of development in *Tell It to Women*.	143
6.2	Idu women dance their resistance in a new dance step in the last movement of *Tell It to Women*.	144

Permissions

1. Sections of Chapter 1 were published as an article titled "Bread, Blood, and Bones: Democratic Socialism and Jamaican Drama" in Sumanyu Satpathy (ed.), *Southern Postcolonialisms: The Global South and the 'New' Literary Representations,* New Delhi: Routledge, 2008, 184–95.

2. Sections of Chapter 4 were published in "Pulling the Coat: Postcolonial Performativity in Black British Women's Drama" in *African and Black Diaspora: An International Journal* 1.2 (2009): 85–95.

3. Sections of Chapter 6 were published as "'Daughters Who Know the Languages of Power': Community, Sexuality, and Postcolonial Development in Tess Onwueme's *Tell It to Women*" in *Interventions: International Journal of Postcolonial Studies* 9.1 (2007): 124–38.

4. Quotes from Sistren Theatre Collective's *Bellywoman Bangarang* in *Contemporary Drama of the Caribbean,* eds. Erika J. Waters and David Edgecombe, Kingshill, St. Croix: Caribbean Writer Research Publications, 2001.

5. Quotes from Jana Natya Manch's plays *Aurat, Police Charitram,* and *Aatranad,* published in *Nukkad Janam Samvad* [*Street Theatre Performance*], Special issue on Women and Performance, March 2008, Delhi, India.

6. Quotes from Mahesh Dattani's *Seven Steps around the Fire* in *Collected Plays,* New Delhi: Penguin, India, 2000, 1–42.

7. Quotes from Mahasweta Devi and Usha Garguli's *Rudali: From Fiction to Performance,* Calcutta: Seagull, India, 1997, 93–156.

8. Quotes from Femi Osofisan's *Morountodun* in Abiola Irele (ed.), *Oriki of a Grasshopper and Other Plays,* Washington: Howard UP, 1995, 127–95.

9. Quotes from Tess Onwueme's *Tell It to Women,* Detroit: Wayne State UP, 1997.

Acknowledgments

The idea for this book originated when I was enrolled in the Master's in Philosophy program at the Department of English, University of Delhi. Delhi provided a dynamic and energetic academic environment where the politics of literary studies is constantly being debated. The governing body and principals, Dr. Aruna Chakravarty and Dr. Indu Anand, of Janki Devi Memorial College kindly granted me leave to undertake this research. My senior colleagues at the Department of English, in particular, Jitender Gill, Swati Pal Sinha, Rita Sinha, Vani Subbanna, G. K. Taneja, and Geeta Wadhwa, deserve a special mention for their support and encouragement, as do my young colleagues Bharti, Nidhi, Shikha, and Ruchi for reconnecting me to Delhi University after a five-year absence. During the time away from home Professor Vinod Sena's work for students with special needs reminded me of my responsibility towards my country. His friendship and timely assistance have marked my intellectual pursuits over the past fifteen years. I only wish he had lived long enough to see the results of his influence. My friends Prity Joshi, Purabi Panwar, and Sumita Sharma made the effort to keep in touch with e-mails, cards, and the few meetings we could manage over the years I was away from home.

I also acknowledge with gratitude the financial and academic support offered by the Graduate School and the Department of English, Loyola University Chicago, my home for six years, where the availability of academic resources for cross-cultural work was matched by wonderful teachers and colleagues. Special thanks to Harveen Mann, who has been adviser, friend, and confidante since my move to the US over a decade ago. Paul Jay and Christopher Castiglia encouraged me at all stages in this work above and beyond their call of duty. Ayana Karanja and Pamela Caughie inspired with their commitment to interdisciplinary programs in Black Studies and Women's Studies. I am grateful for having had the opportunity to work closely with them. The Department of Modern Languages and Literatures, especially Professors Paulo Giordano, Andrew McKenna, and Susana Cavallo, offered timely employment, a welcoming space, and the freedom to develop courses on South Asian Literature in Translation.

xiv *Acknowledgments*

I was blessed with a kinship of heart and mind in Chicago. Thank you Tapati, Abhishek, Janet, and Neha for always being around to tempt me away from the library and for keeping me company on the long days spent at home writing these chapters. Steven and Tripthi helped with their advice and interest in my work. A very special thanks to Roger for his kindness, generosity, and friendship over the years. I could not have managed without his unflagging patience and amazing sense of humor during an intensely stressful period. From Chicago I was also connected to friends from Delhi on their own research endeavors in the US. Anuradha Ramanujan, Sangeeta Mediratta, and Renuka Bisht were just a telephone call or a short flight away when I needed to talk about my life or my work. My continued connection with Chicago is in large measure due to Richa Sharma and Francis Scolt, who opened their homes to me and provided a wonderfully congenial base for my research excursions and holidays to this amazing city.

I am grateful to have found a new community and kin in Lubbock, Texas, my home for the past three years. The Department of English at Texas Tech University has provided a collegial environment and funding in the form of a College of Arts and Sciences Fellowship for this work. Among the many colleagues who are also my closest friends I would like to mention in particular Priscilla Ybarra, kindred spirit and wonderful listener. Priscilla Ybarra, Karen Clark, Angela Eaton, and Jennifer Snead form the best group of "sistahs" a girl could hope for. Ann Daghistany Ransdell, Yuan Shu, and Rich Rice were there when I needed someone to talk to and hesitated to reach out. Rich's support, generosity, laughs, stories, e-mails, impromptu celebrations, and late-night conversations have enriched my life in ways too numerous to name. If I can call Lubbock home it is also in no small measure because of Laura and Ken Baake's friendship. Thank you Laura for drawing people to you in an ever-widening but always close circle, including Karen Brehm, Jen and Zuzu Shelton, Jean Tripp, Anisa and Paul Zvonkovick, among others. Weekly meetings, food, and conversations with these dear friends keep me happy.

I owe thanks Moloyashree Hashmi, Constance Kuriyama, Roger McNamara, Jen Shelton, Yuan Shu, Honor Ford-Smith, and Rich Rice for reading sections of this book. Their encouragement, perceptive comments, and awareness of recent events connected to the book helped refine my ideas at various stages from the proposal submission to the final revisions.

Grateful thanks are also due to Honor Ford-Smith, former Artistic Director of the Sistren Theatre Collective in Jamaica; Marc Epprecht from York University, Toronto; Moloyshree Hashmi of Jana Natya Manch in New Delhi; and Tess Onwueme at the University of Wisconsin, Eau Claire, for sharing their ideas, unpublished manuscripts, archival material, and performance recordings. Their commitment to gender and class concerns continues to inspire me. Thanks also to Professor Malashri Lal of the Department of English and formerly of the Women's Studies and Development Center,

Acknowledgments xv

University of Delhi for access to the Center's archive. Joseph McLaren's perceptive input has influenced the chapters on African literature; I thank him for facilitating connections with the African Literatures Association. Maureen Eke encouraged me to forge closer bonds with the Association. I thank her for support and belief in my capabilities.

Professor Sumanyu Satpathy kindly granted me permission to reprint a version of Chapter 1 of this book which first appeared in his edited anthology *Southern Postcolonialisms* published by Routledge, New Delhi. Thanks also to the editors of the Taylor and Francis journal *Interventions* for allowing me to reprint my article on Tess Onwueme as Chapter 6 of this book. Jana Natya Manch, Sistren Theatre Collective, and Tess Onwueme generously allowed me to reprint photographs of productions of their plays.

Thanks also to Caroline Rooney for expressing initial interest in this work, to the two anonymous readers whose suggestions helped shape it, and to my editors at Routledge, in particular, Erica Wetter and Elizabeth Levine, for their patience and promptness in replying to queries.

This book is for my parents, my aunt Raj Rani Batra, my brothers, Kimshuk and Puneet, and my spouse Rich who understand how important this work is for me. Their unstinting support, encouragement, and love have made it possible.

Introduction
Feminist Visions and Queer Futures

> The postulate of a founding heterosexuality must also be read as part of the operation of power—and I would add fantasy—such that we can begin to ask how the invocation of such a foundation works in the building of a certain fantasy of state and nation.
>
> (Judith Butler, "Is Kinship Always Already Heterosexual" 124)

The scene is a gathering of about two hundred students seated in tiered rows in an open-air auditorium. There is a hushed silence as the performers dressed in black shirts circle the stage chanting rhythmically. The performance is by Jana Natya Manch (People's Theatre Forum), a street theatre group invited to perform in a women's college at the University of Delhi, India. The play, *Hinsa Parmo Dharm* (*Violence as Supreme Religion*), based on a short story by India's foremost progressive writer, Munshi Premchand, depicts economic and gendered violence perpetrated by the nexus between religious fundamentalism and capitalism. I remember walking away amid groups of excited students animatedly discussing the performance wondering if classroom teaching ever generated such a response. Much like the play I saw performed that day, postcolonial Indian drama takes the social as the primary reason for its existence. This is evident not only in the themes central to contemporary drama written in various Indian languages but also in the goals of the state-funded National School of Drama, the country's premier institute of theatre training and performance studies.[1]

A little known fact about theatre in India is the noncommercial basis of activities of the National School of Drama (NSD) which sometimes works in close collaboration with other state-supported organizations such as the Sangeet Natak Akademi or the Academy for Music and Dance and has followed "a consistent program of publication, preservation, and patronage, especially in relation to the 'traditional' theatre arts" even when "funds for new theatres, amateur companies, and theatre education have not materialized on the scale imagined in the first decade of independence" (Dharwardker 43–44). In keeping with these noncommercial aims the NSD and other cultural institutions such as the Shriram Arts Center and the Nehru Youth Centre in New Delhi conduct free summer theatre workshops for children. One of my most vivid memories of these activities is of a summer workshop conducted by the NSD in the mid-1990s. I remember the workshop director telling a boisterous group of children to enact a situation they cared about, and looked on in amazement as a twelve-year-old boy lay on the ground

2 *Feminist Visions and Queer Futures in Postcolonial Drama*

writhing in soundless agony. Asked to explain, he said that he was playing an old woman in pain, a person who had been abandoned by her family or perhaps did not have one to take care of her in her old age. Learning about the Jamaican theatre group, Sistren Theatre Collective many years later, the implicit connection between the enactment of an old woman in pain by a twelve-year-old child in India and Honor Ford-Smith's description of making plays dealing with real-life situations of poor, destitute, and old women in Jamaica provided the impetus for the transnational connections I was seeking.

My summer experiences at the children's theatre workshops over the course of a decade, the all-female audiences at performances such as the one by Jana Natya Manch in a Delhi University college, and my work with students-actors in women-centered plays, brought to the fore connections between social drama, performers, and their audiences. In many ways this book is an attempt to answer the questions I began asking about these experiences over a decade ago. As I read about and saw contemporary postcolonial drama in various metropolitan and nonmetropolitan settings I began to think about how drama, one of the most powerful mediums of conveying social concerns, has been deployed in India and other postcolonial nations to articulate gender justice. How do cultural and educational institutions such as schools of drama, colleges, and universities contribute performers and performance venues for socially progressive dramaturgy in postcolonial locations? What is the role of the postcolonial state in encouraging or curtailing the possibilities of socially inflected dramaturgy particularly if it explicitly critiques the state's gender policies? Is it possible to examine these performances as a form of 'citizenship education' that impacts on students and other audiences by shaping their views on pressing political issues of our times, among them the postcolonial state's reneged promise of gender justice to its citizens? How does the idea of the 'political' as gender justice connect feminist activism and postcolonial drama? In what ways and forms do postcolonial dramatists reflect on economic, gendered, and sexual violence and initiate a discussion on the situation of alternative sexualities, a contentious issue facing postcolonial feminists?

This book thinks through these some of these questions from a theoretical perspective informed by feminist, queer, and postcolonial studies. The comparisons charted in this book resonate with the key terms of Gayatri Spivak's call for "planetarity"—responsibility, community, citizenship, and pedagogy—as a model enabling the renewal of comparative literature in opposition to what is assumed to be self-explanatory globalization (*Death*). Encompassing a range of post-independence political, social, and cultural processes that may be analyzed comparatively, there is a productive tension between the various national contexts of my study and the implications for a particularly postcolonial mode of inquiry. I see the value of locally directed analyses as well as their implications within a comparative, cross-cultural framework. To this end, the first rationale for bringing together

Jamaican, Indian, and Nigerian contexts is chronological. The focus is on cultural activism and feminist organization in connection with specific forms of postcolonial governance between the 1970s and the 1990s, roughly corresponding with second- and third-wave feminist movements in these countries. This is a period also marked by theatre and feminist activists' engagement with the economic liberalization policies of neocolonial governments in India, Jamaica, and Nigeria.

The second rationalization for my selection of contexts and plays is a pedagogical imperative to examine similarities and differences in concerns addressed by cultural activists in nations that were often grouped together as the 'third world.' These are the basis of course offerings such as 'Twentieth Century Anglophone Drama', 'The Family in Postcolonial Literature', or even as general as topic as 'Contemporary Non-Western Literature' in the Euro-American academy. There are obvious cultural connections between Africa and the African Diaspora in the Americas; less recognized are campaigns to secure economic, gender, caste, class, and racial justice that connect social and cultural movements in Africa and the Caribbean to those in Asia and Latin America. These connections are often overshadowed by what Aijaz Ahmad calls the hegemony of literary translation and critical reception of Western texts in non-Western contexts and a concomitant neglect of the literary and political interfaces between non-Western literatures. While postcolonial studies has gone a long way in redressing this neglect, transnational connections between less studied genres, such as poetry and drama, can facilitate this interface.

Finally, the literary and political validation for this project is drawn from Helen Gilbert's summation of the *form* of recent postcolonial drama that "provokes the readers to consider how stylistic devices can articulate postcoloniality" since "the bias against naturalism is, in fact, fairly typical of the broader field from which these scripts are drawn." Gilbert argues, quite correctly, that "non-naturalistic theatre presumes a specific kind of relationship with its audience, one that avoids illusionism in favor of more explicit engagement with its interpretive community" (5). The plays analyzed in this book use structural devices associated with non-naturalistic drama to ensure critical engagement with spectatorial interpretive communities. Many of the playwrights also use rituals to comment on the inherently dramatic nature of everyday life and to disrupt the illusion of the theatrical experience by encouraging a critical mode of thinking. Of the non-naturalistic drama discussed in the book, some of the plays were created collectively while others were published under the name of individual playwrights. All the plays, whether collectively or individually conceptualized, are, I claim, 'performance events' that refer to political, economic, and social conditions of the times. Even the work published and performed under the names of an individual author rather than a collective carries the stamp of research collaboration. And in some cases the authors directly acknowledge the communities with whom they interacted during the process of play making. The plays reference various subaltern groups: rural farming communities facing poverty and destitution demanding their rights through revolutionary action; professional mourners hired by wealthy patrons to mourn at funerals of family members; transsexual or transgendered men earning a living through performance and prostitution; and all-female households in uncertain economic conditions sharing obligations of kinship and support.

My argument about the cause-and-effect relationship between hegemonic gender ideologies and a normative citizenship impacting on subaltern groups considers the possibility of postcolonial drama generating a dialogue on citizenship. Such a dialogue takes into account the material and sexual aspects of the lives of women and sexual minorities with the awareness that drama has a limited reach and appeal, although still a tremendous impact, in these times of mass-mediated production and consumption of images. I introduce the key terms of this study—community, kinship, and citizenship—through two modes of analysis that are seldom conjoined due to a perception of theoretical discordance: postcolonial historical, political, and cultural analysis suggests new ways of looking at these concepts; feminist-oriented gay, lesbian, and queer studies from various disciplinary perspectives provide a methodology of grounding these in concrete gendered and sexual practices. Connecting this discussion to feminist and incipient queer activism in India, Jamaica, and Nigeria, my focus is on drama by groups and individuals who work in close conjunction with these efforts. Finally, I delineate key ideas in performance theory that have impacted postcolonial theatre and drama practitioners, and theorize the gendered and sexually marked body in performance and among audiences.

COMMUNITY, KINSHIP, AND POSTCOLONIAL CITIZENSHIP

Analyzing the representation of gender, sexuality, and citizenship in postcolonial drama involves examining ideas that subsume public discussions of women's sexual and material autonomy. Primary among these are 'kinship', 'community', 'citizenship', and implicitly 'development'. Under patriarchal state structures community relations replicate the power relations evinced in political structures at large. However, community and kinship structures can also work in opposition to patriarchal state apparati. For instance, the specific form of democracy in Jamaica has been defined by Carl Stone as "clientelistic" or as one marked by "predation politics" according to Obika Gray. This situation is similar to that in India where political patronage often enables citizens to secure their legal and extra-legal rights in a domain existing between the state and civil society, described by Partha Chatterjee as "political society." In the Nigerian context, characterized by the collapse of democracy, a resurgence of militarism, followed by restoration of democracy, Richard Joseph describes this phenomenon as "prebendalism" or "machine politics," whereby rights are obtained through a process of personal and piecemeal negotiation including trading favors with and bribing various levels of the governmental machinery. Within such systems women's negotiating power is largely reliant on their class position, association with men, or trade-offs between sexual favors and material gain. Various forms of the postcolonial state are depicted in the drama analyzed in the following chapters: pedagogic democratic socialism, a privatized and corrupt neocolonial regime, a feudal heteropatriarchy, a disciplinary apparatus, and anti-resource redistributive. The female citizen's compromised citizenship under these structures makes her wary of excessive reliance on the state. This does not lead to her giving up her claims on the state, but, as I argue, encourages a reliance on non-biological kinship to ensure social, psychological, and emotional survival.

Some of the more useful definitions of community in relation to kinship have emerged from the subaltern school. Among these Chatterjee's and Gyan Pandey's implicit conjoining of community and kinship in India deserves special mention. Beginning with Benedict Andersen's famous theorization of the nation as an "imagined community," Chatterjee discusses how during the Indian nationalist struggle for independence from colonial rule, the concept of the nation "was made tangible in the concreteness of an imagined network of kinship extending outward from the local structures of community." This "fuzzy" notion of community, Chatterjee maintains, is retained in popular political discourse since the modern state, embedded as it is "within the universal narrative of capital, cannot recognize within its jurisdiction any form of community except the single, determinate, demographically enumerable form of the nation" (*Nation* 225, 238). Marking a slight departure from Chatterjee, Pandey speaks of the persistence of community as a "political project," much like class or nation. He also proposes that the political claim is effective because of "a moral, affective quality" inherent in notions of the community (410). It is the specific material consequences of this affective component that I emphasize by pointing to the conjunctions between community and kinship in contemporary Indian drama.

Caribbean historians and political scientists have also cogently discussed the political possibilities of community. From Jamaica, Carl Stone's phenomenal work on political formations in Jamaica proposes a three-tier model of community: urban populations with a minimum population size of five thousand residents; "main road" communities located close to main highways that connect to major populations, production, and commercial centers in Jamaica; and remote rural and hillside district communities (*Democracy* 139–41). In later work Stone modifies his theory to account for the powerlessness of certain groups in ways that suggest a conception of community based not merely on place but on levels of organization: "[P]oorer socioeconomic groupings have neither resources, leadership, nor motivation to organize on a community or other collective basis" (*Class* 50). David Scott proposes a nuanced adaptation of Stone's idea to "interrupt the

6 Feminist Visions and Queer Futures in Postcolonial Drama

liberal discourse of community" with the aim of reasserting "the primacy of the political, and with it, a *politics of settlements*" (*Refashioning* 183). The possibility of organized collectivities demanding their entitlements as citizens while forming kin-like associations with other dispossessed members of the community is embodied in the "politics of settlements" depicted in Jamaican drama of the 1970s and 1980s.

Examining the applicability of the subaltern paradigm to African colonial and postcolonial historiography, Frederick Cooper rightly cautions that a recourse to community as an antidote to one sort of oppression might very well ignore other forms of oppression that might well lie within communities (177). Speaking of the construction of community among the Ibo in Nigeria, Axel Harneit-Sievers clarifies that a local community is defined by a shared awareness of belonging to a specific place of residence or origin, sometimes labeled "village groups." However, Harneit-Sievers also emphasizes that the active process of the construction of community may involve competing notions of 'progress' and 'development' brought over by members of local groups who are part of larger contexts such as migration to foreign countries (12). Contemporary Nigerian drama by Femi Osofisan and Tess Onwueme depicts class and ethnic alignments as insufficient for membership within a community. Indeed, some members of the community may actively work to fracture the common goals even while drawing on a specious rhetoric of kinship.

Given the various connotations of community in these three contexts, I outline the broad contours of the discussion and connect it to citizenship with the acknowledgment that this is a schematic and provisional summarization and one which is being redefined even at the very moment of my writing. In India, community is often synonymous with religiously defined and caste-based groups so that Hindus and Muslims are coded as majority and minority and upper and lower castes as powerful and powerless communities respectively. In Jamaica the word often connotes "garrison" communities primarily in urban neighborhoods comprising supporters of the two major parties—the People's National Party and the Jamaica Labor Party—sometimes engaged in violence of the kind witnessed between Hindus and Muslims or the upper and lower castes in India. In Nigeria, community is invoked in relation to both ethnic group and geographical affiliations as an expression of indigeneity, often in opposition to urban, Westernized lifestyles. Used in these senses community can predicate an atavistic recourse to religion, combative politics, and non-modern forms of existence even while it points to the inadequacy of the hegemonic idea of citizenship forwarded by the nation-state. Clearly if there are groups of people who are not willing to let go of their religious, political, and traditional ways of life, they cannot be successfully enumerated as the model 'citizen-subjects' of the nation-state. In fact, their very existence throws the postcolonial project of development into a crisis of sorts particularly since gender and sexuality are often the test cases for inclusive and egalitarian conceptions of community in the contexts that are the subject of my investigation.

The project of a radical democracy forwarded by feminist political theorists is relevant to this discussion. Chantal Mouffe's thesis that "in the domain of politics, and as far as citizenship is concerned, sexual difference should not be a pertinent distinction" is articulated in opposition to feminist definitions of citizenship highlighting the political relevance of sexual difference. Mouffe argues eloquently that "an active conception of citizenship that emphasizes the value of political participation and the notion of a common good . . . [should be] prior to and independent of individual desires and interests" (377). Although the notion of a "common good" serves as a "social imaginary" and as a "grammar of conduct" for citizens marked by the awareness that "a fully inclusive political community can never be realized," Mouffe does not specify the contours of this "active conception of citizenship" (379). An incomplete realization of a political community and the minimal gains achieved by women and other feminized citizens on the horizon of the social imaginary are foils to alternative structures of kinship which interrogate normative postcolonial citizenship. This interrogation is framed by two contradictory ideas of community: as a differentially positioned structure that reinforces non-egalitarian social and gender relations and, as I argue in this book, as a non-biological support network that compensates for the state's neglect of the common good of all citizens.

Subscribing to the latter view of the community while interrogating whether kinship is always already heterosexual, Judith Butler mentions situations when "the relations of kinship arrive at boundaries that call into question the distinguishability of kinship from community." According to her, these constitute a 'breakdown' of traditional kinship that "displaces the central place of biological and sexual relations from its definition" to give sexuality a domain separate from that of kinship. In her opinion, this allows us to think of "durable tie[s] outside the conjugal frame and thus opens kinship to a set of community ties that are irreducible to family" ("Is Kinship" 127). Butler's connections between community and kinship draw on a long history of feminist-influenced gay and lesbian history and anthropology. Esther Newton's study of female impersonators in America was one of the earliest to account for the contested nature of the 'community' she studied. Newton demolished at the outset of her investigation the idea of a homogenous community based on sexual identity, stating that "the community is an on-going social reality in, around, and against which people align themselves according to their own self-definitions" (21). The community centered on voluntary associations such as organizations like the Mattachine Society and the Daughters of Bilitis, informal institutions such as bars and clubs, and informal social groups comprising parties and living arrangements with an acknowledgment that various "kinds and degrees of participation in the community are possible and available" (Newton 21). In his phenomenal history of the emergence of a "homosexual minority" in the United States, John D' Emilio writes of gay men and lesbian women's participation in an "urban subculture that sustained their sense of belonging to a group" concretized by venues of socialization such as bars and clubs and later by magazines (53). D'Emilio's account of the making of a homosexual community emphasizes place, specifically urban locations, as important to self-conceptualization.

The theoretical contours of the discussion of community are connected to kinship in Kath Weston's study where "community as a cultural category" is "implicated in the renegotiation of kinship relations" (18). Weston points to the imbrication of community and kinship and the abandonment of this model in the 1980s. The "nonerotic ties elaborated in terms of community and or friendship" were, in her opinion, succeeded by "chosen families" which introduced something novel into kinship relations within the United States (136). An interrogation of the family model and the reinstatement of community and kinship as inextricable have marked much recent theory on the subject. Judith Halberstam asks "what alternatives to family models and normative kinship are available to us as we try to produce feminist and queer models of politics and relation?" (319). Halberstam's call for narratives of "cooperation, affiliation, and the appeal of forgetting family" implicitly reinstates community into her argument (323).

In the light of this account of kinship and community from feminist-oriented gay and lesbian studies, let me go back to the political arguments with which I began. Many postcolonial political theorists mention that the invocation of community introduces a precapitalist structure into the dynamics of postcolonial modernity. Might we then think of the invocation and recourse to community as a way of resisting the worst effects of capitalism in postcolonial nation-states? Secondly, although this is not necessarily the direction in which political theory runs, there is ample scope to read community and kinship from the vectors of gender and sexuality particularly since postcolonial feminist and queer activists and theorists are evolving and describing non-Eurocentric ways of sociality and relationality. Finally, feminist collectives as well as theatre groups, and sometimes a fortuitous conjunction of the two, can be seen as political communities with an acknowledgment of the historical specificity of these efforts as described in the next section.

POSTCOLONIAL FEMINISMS

The first phase of the women's movement in the three contexts of this study, India, Jamaica, and Nigeria, is roughly coterminous with first-wave Euro-American feminism. It is connected to women's participation in anti-colonial nationalisms from the late nineteenth century to the 1930s. During this period middle class men and women modeled their plans for gender equity on Western feminists' demands for electoral, educational, and employment rights adapted to an indigenous program of social reform (French and Ford-Smith; Gandhi and Shah; Johnson-Odim and Mba). As formerly colonized nations attained independence, established postcolonial modes of governance, and moved on varying economic and political paths of democratically or militarily engineered socialism, capitalism, and globalization, the period from the 1940s to the 1980s was marked by interest in redressing women's socio-economic and legal standing as citizens (Cumper; Ojewusi; Agnes). The second-wave postcolonial feminist agenda often developed in conjunction with the newly independent nations' programs for women's development and included securing legislative and social security for women and children.[2] Besides the various political party-based women's development units working in collaboration with the state, this period witnessed the emergence of autonomous women's networks negotiating with the state not only to facilitate these changes but also to critique its policies when they perceived a discrepancy between proclaimed ideals and real achievements.

Networks such as Sistren in Jamaica, Women in Nigeria (WIN), and Manushi from India, emerging in the 1970s and 1980s, are often considered models of feminist organization for their threefold emphasis on social, cultural, and educational outreach. Although these groups understood the value of theatre and drama in furthering women's empowerment, the degree of their attention to the medium has varied widely. Sistren's cultural work in theatre and drama was the basis of a social and educational program that included a research component and later a journal on women in the Caribbean. WIN evolved a program of action through a series of conferences on legislative, religious, and economic factors affecting women's lives, later published as reports. While it has used drama in consciousness-raising, unlike Sistren this has not been a major activist strategy for WIN. Like WIN, the Indian feminist collective, Manushi, has relied largely on the publication of an independently run feminist journal on women and society to publicize violence against women combined with legislative action through public interest litigations. The core group has sporadically used street theatre to create public awareness about domestic and social violence in alliance with other feminist networks.

These organizations have been instrumental in pointing to and remedying the neglect of gender and sexuality as factors impacting citizenship in postcolonial nation-states. However, their attention to sexual minorities facing similar conditions of domestic and social violence is sporadic and, in some cases, nonexistent. One of the key ideas explored in M. Jacqui Alexander and Chandra Talpade Mohanty's introduction and some contributions to their anthology *Feminist Genealogies, Colonial Legacies, Democratic Futures*—which can be seen as articulating 'third-wave' postcolonial feminist concerns—is that nation and citizenship continue to be "premised within normative parameters of masculinity and heterosexuality" ("Introduction" xiv). It is crucial to distinguish third-wave concerns addressed primarily by US-based feminists such as Rebecca Walker and

Barbara Findlen from the different set of issues articulated by postcolonial feminists. In the US, this body of work has addressed second-wave feminists' lack of emphasis on specific demands of women of color, an exclusive focus on theoretical analyses to the neglect of women's lived experiences, positing of women as victims rather than survivors, and a compromised relation to institutions such as the university critiqued, yet inhabited by second-wave feminists. On the other hand, US third-wave feminists have themselves been found lacking in an analysis of class relations and global political and economic processes (Kinser; Diaz).

When analyzing the third wave of women's organizing in postcolonial locations, it is useful to remember that, as in the US context, there cannot be a neat disjuncture between this and the previous phase. However, postcolonial feminists have only recently echoed US second-wave politicization of alternative sexualities, especially the emphasis on intersectional identities by lesbians of color. In some contexts such as Nigeria, the contours of the discussion are still taking shape. Hence, a focus on lesbian, gay, bisexual, transsexual, and transgendered lives emerges as a specific (although not always explicit) third-wave postcolonial feminist concern. Rather than being reformist in its orientation, this stage is best characterized by a dual emphasis on material and identity-based claims of gendered and sexualized citizen-subjects, necessary because, according to Alexander and Mohanty, "these [postcolonial] states conflate heterosexuality with citizenship and organize a 'citizenship machinery' in order to produce a class of loyal heterosexual citizens and a subordinated class of sexualized, nonprocreative, noncitizens, disloyal to the nation" ("Introduction" xxiii). Postcolonial feminists' sporadic and, in some cases, sustained alliances with left-wing and socialist ideologies during the period 1970s to 1990s led to an interrogation of statist gender ideologies that I have conceptualized as 'national pedagogy' in the case of Jamaica, a term which is just as applicable to Nigeria and India, the other contexts of this study. I describe how postcolonial dramatists' involvement with gender issues has led to questioning the state's implicit conceptualization of the heterosexual male engaged in 'productive' occupations as the model citizen. This is achieved through dramatic representations of community and kinship contesting this model.

Of the many kin-like associations other than heterosexual monogamy, some are recognized by the community while others are invalidated, even stigmatized, in the contexts of my discussion. In the Caribbean, to take one example, anthropological research by Edith Clarke, Gloria Wekker, and Carla Freeman, among others, indicates that women's households share reciprocal obligations with those unrelated to them by blood or marriage through intangible relations of emotional support and caregiving as well as more tangible manifestations of material and economic sustenance. That these may translate into sexualized forms of intimacy is largely ignored in most accounts of socialities in the region. In Nigeria, these associations take the form of "clans" as described in Ifi Amadiume's ethnographic study of Nnobi, an Ibo village. Here the "daughters" and "wives" of the clan have mutual obligations towards each other, although the "wives" enjoy a lesser social status than the "daughters." Amadiume's analysis hints at but does not follow up on the possibility of sexual relations between women socially related to each other either by clan obligations or by the communally accepted tradition of "female husbands." Similar quasi-kinship associations exist in India, such as those among the *hijra* households (a community of transsexual and/or transgendered men who earn their living as performers), where the leader of the house is "mother" to all its members who relate to each other as "sisters." Yet theirs is a stigmatized identity that is not granted social recognition unlike other caste, religious, and ethnic identities. Same-sex relations remain proscribed, so that while there is vigorous debate about reserved representation for women in structures of parliamentary democracy in India, Jamaica, and Nigeria, there are few efforts towards granting sexual minorities their rights as citizens by decriminalizing homosexuality.[3]

One of the most common arguments used to dismiss the provision of sexual justice in these nations is that there are other more urgent developmental issues facing the nation-state. Whereas gender concerns are earmarked as developmental by women's groups and international agencies, attempts at collective assertion by sexual minorities are dismissed as mimicking the divisive identity politics of Western societies and cultures. Kinship and community obligations are pressed into service to try and suppress any form of sexual expression other than heterosexuality. The panic discourse on AIDS in India, Jamaica, and Nigeria also reveals lack of concern about the health and welfare of alternative sexualities. Cindy Patton writes that "postcolonial health managers' ideas about the state of nations' development" have led to public information campaigns that, in Africa (as in India and Jamaica), advocate safe-sex practices in a clinically detached manner along with warnings about needle sharing in drug use and moral messages about the dangers of sexual promiscuity (xxvii). These campaigns are the only way in which these nation-states indicate a minimal awareness of alternative sexual preferences and posit homosexuality as invidious to public health.

Additionally, the criminalization of homosexuality is a colonial legislative legacy that is endorsed by these states. The message is conveyed in popular cultural forms such as music and films, advocating misogyny, homophobic violence, or a comic tolerance of sexual minorities. There is as yet no clear move among feminists to articulate a vigorous politics of defense and justice for sexual minorities that is directly oppositional to the state. This serious political neglect reflects the two distinct understandings of injustice Nancy Fraser categorizes "socio-economic injustice" and "cultural and symbolic injustice," so that economic marginalization and exploitation are considered just issues on the feminist agenda but identity-based claims to recognition such as those by sexual minorities are considered secondary, echoing the state's hierarchy of developmental priorities (13–14). The absence of a coalition between feminist activism and the movement for rights of sexual minorities has not gone unnoticed or uncommented. This is rightly seen as a serious lack in the otherwise progressive agenda of the feminist movement in these nations (Vanita "Thinking"; Ogundipe-Leslie; Pike). *Feminist Visions and Queer Futures* forwards the claim that postcolonial feminist networks have worked towards (although not directly addressed) the bivalent claims of recognition and redistribution by highlighting socio-economic, physical, and sexual violence against women and sexual minorities. In this sense, postcolonial drama presents a progressive agenda, sometimes in advance of the feminist networks, by representing alternative forms of kinship offering material, social, and emotional sustenance to economically and sexually marginalized citizens.

METHODOLOGY OF POSTCOLONIAL DRAMA ANALYSIS

Taken individually, the chapters in this book look at the work of playwrights and groups insufficiently analyzed in postcolonial drama criticism, often defined by the canonized work of a few male dramatists. In contrast to critical accounts which either survey or further eulogize plays by celebrated postcolonial dramatists, some recent anthologies and critical commentaries examine canonized authors in conjunction with less well-known but equally important drama practitioners. However, drama by Dennis Scott, Jana Natya Manch, Mahasweta Devi, and Tess Onwueme often does not find a place in revisionist criticism supplementing the canon of postcolonial drama. Part of the feminist project of this book is to indicate the centrality of ideas of gender justice to postcolonial drama, neglected in available discussions of the field.

For Bruce King, one of the earliest commentators on this drama, the tension between the terms commonwealth and postcolonial seems to be resolved in favor of the former with a select focus on canonical male dramatists such as Athol Fugard, Wole Soyinka, and Derek Walcott. Colonial subjection and its impact on the language and culture of the colonized are key ideas in Brian Crow and Chris Banfield's account of postcolonial theatres through virtually the same dramatists. The authors argue that these playwrights' awareness of Western as well as indigenous forms of performance makes theatre and drama a medium of cultural reconnection in postcolonial times. Although Crow and Banfield do not dwell on the specific political impact of postcolonial drama, they suggest that politics is evident when practitioners "use the stage to define and affirm their people's cultural 'personality'—in the face of continuing cultural, economic, and political subjugation—by recovering the past, freed from the biases of metropolitan or mainstream history" and "expose the forces that still obstruct liberation" (17). The authors admit to have focused on male dramatists and

Introduction 13

acknowledge that "female playwrights are still seriously under-represented in the post-colonial context." At the same time they reject the vitality of women's drama as equitable with published playscripts:

> If there has been no breakthrough by women dramatists in Africa or India to compare with the striking emergence of women writers in much Western theatre, or with female prose writers, *there has nevertheless been an encouraging growth in theatre reflecting indigenous feminist 'movements'*. It is, difficult, internationally, to find published material by or about them, but we should at least be aware of the remarkable work achieved by such groups as the women's theatre collective Sistren in Jamaica, by playwrights such as Mahasweta Devi and Dolly Mehta in India, and by workshopped productions such as *You Strike the Woman, You Strike the Rock* in South Africa. (167, emphasis added)

This remark acknowledges the tradition of feminist postcolonial drama evidenced in street theatre traditions and its variants across Asia, Africa, and the Caribbean. The contrast between Western and non-Western women dramatists made by the authors ignores women's individual and collective contributions to postcolonial drama. The lack of published material noted by Crow and Banfield is a serious issue and one that makes it difficult to work on drama as a genre in postcolonial studies. This is particularly true when the focus is on locating and reading non-canonical drama that politicizes sexuality and citizenship in advance of "indigenous feminist 'movements'" focus on these issues.

The neglect of women's drama is analogous to drama being overlooked as a genre in postcolonial criticism. To cite a few instances: the Caribbean writers Dennis Courtney Scott and Derek Walcott are studied and taught primarily as poets rather than playwrights; in studies of African literature, Ama Ata Aidoo and Ngugi wa Thiong'o's plays are relatively less well-known (*The Trial of Dedan Kimathi* is an exception) than their fiction; and from South Asia, Mahasweta Devi's drama has received scant critical attention in contrast to her fiction. In a study published the same year as Crow and Banfield's account, Helen Gilbert and Joanne Tompkins note the inattention to drama in postcolonial criticism, and observe that since "dramatic and performance theories, particularly those developed in conjunction with Brechtian, feminist, and cultural studies criticism, have much to offer post-colonial debates about language, interpellation, subject-formation, representation, and forms of resistance, this marginalisation of drama suggests a considerable gap in post-colonial studies" (9). My analysis of national pedagogies envisaging model citizen-subjects and postcolonial dramatists' resistance to these pedagogies through their representation of women and sexual minorities is indebted to Gilbert and Tompkins's theorization of postcolonial drama. Their attention to the three main areas of postcolonial performance—dramatic language, both vocal

14   Feminist Visions and Queer Futures in Postcolonial Drama

and visual, as expressed through the performing body; the arrangement of theatrical space and time; and the manipulation of narrative and performative conventions of drama—has directly influenced the readings of performances and playscripts offered in the chapters. A key feature of Gilbert and Tompkins's study is their multivalent theoretical framework marked by equal reliance on work done separately in the fields of performance and postcolonial studies. Analyzing performance elements such as ritual and folklore, bodily movements, theatre spaces, sounds, and silences, they offer an interpretative methodology for cross-cultural analysis. Yet their primary focus on these elements precludes a detailed analysis of the plays themselves. My research into circumstances of production of the plays and their possible impact on spectatorial communities extends the scope of Gilbert and Tompkins's study.

Gilbert's anthology of postcolonial drama, published in 2001, supplements the theoretical focus of the book she coauthored with Tompkins. The anthology brings together important playscripts and provides a more recent overview of the field. Its introduction indicates that the lack of availability of primary texts, whether scripted or visual, while undertaking research in drama, is the most serious problem facing scholars working in the field. Hence the collection does not include many plays due to "lack of space, copyright difficulties, limited access to texts preservable in publishable forms, or the simple failure of communication technologies" (2). Taking up the challenge of Gilbert and Tompkins's suggestion that postcolonial drama is an archive waiting to be systemized, I studied playwrights and theatre groups whose work is recognized as significant but does not possess a secure place in the canon of postcolonial drama.

To do justice to the complexity of references in the plays I had to devise an eclectic methodology reliant on textual analysis, performance records in private collections, manuscripts of unpublished plays, magazines with limited circulation in special collections, documentaries, interviews, and personal recordings of performances made available by some of the dramatists and theatre groups. Collecting this material was always an exciting and rewarding endeavor, but sometimes also a frustrating experience since many of these documents are yet to be systematically archived and were obtained largely through personal contacts. One of the hardest aspects of my research was the discovery that performance records are not considered valuable enough for preservation. Jamaica remains a poignant case in point of this neglect since records of Dennis Scott's innovative use of drama for pedagogical purposes as well as his own playscripts carelessly stored in a cupboard at the Jamaica School of Drama were damaged during Hurricane Gilbert in 1988 (Ford Smith, "Performing Nation"). In 2004, the building housing Sistren Theatre Collective in Kingston burnt to the ground destroying a valuable collection of materials. Some of this material is in the safekeeping of individuals, awaiting cataloguing and an institutional repository.

Another challenge encountered was deciding on the degree of emphasis on the multiple versions of some of the plays. In the case of the Nigerian dramatist Tess Onwueme's play *Tell It to Women*, the Jamaican playwright Dennis Scott's *Dog*, and Sistren's *Bellywoman Bangarang*, the original versions are less easily available, although more radical in form and content, than the revised plays. The Indian playwright Mahesh Dattani's revision of *Seven Steps around the Fire* from a radio play to one meant for the proscenium stage, and his use of the central character Uma Rao in two other plays, marks significant departures from the original. Since these versions often involve substantial authorial or directorial revisions, and sometimes a complete change of the medium and audience they were originally intended for, it was often difficult choosing which version to discuss. Often the choice was contingent on the availability of the works since some exist only in manuscript form and there is hardly any video documentation of these performances. The larger and for the most part unanswered question raised by the neglect and non-availability of performance records is the role of cultural activities and their documentation in postcolonial nations. Drama as a cultural form in these nations draws on a legacy of performance theories that has addressed this issue in different ways.

AESTHETICS, POLITICS, AND THE APPARATUS IN POSTCOLONIAL DRAMA

Following Gilbert and Tompkins's emphasis on performance theory as essential to an examination of postcolonial drama, the ideas of Bertolt Brecht, Augusto Boal, and Jerzy Grotowski—whose theories and practice significantly impact South Asian, African, and Caribbean drama—have contributed to the argument of the book. Since some of these ideas are almost at opposing ends of the spectrum of materialist and aesthetic principles, an examination of key concepts such as "epic drama," "forum," and "poverty" in theatre is necessary to avoid a simplistic assessment of the nature and extent of their impact. Further, I deploy these concepts with an awareness of their different constituencies of influence: Brechtian principles have been used by dramatists working in first- and third-world locations with varying emphases; Boal's methods of theatre, therapy, and activism have impacted upon practitioners differently in Euro-America than in South Asia and Latin America; the sphere of Grotowski's aesthetic converts is primarily Western. Finally, an attention to aesthetic, temporal, and geographical spheres of influence is essential to chart a genealogy of performance that considers the applicability of these ideas to postcolonial dramaturgy and criticism. An explication of this work focuses on three related domains of inquiry: the relationship between aesthetics and politics; the dominant theatrical 'apparatus' and attempts to make meaningful dramaturgy in opposition to it; and a theorization of the female body in performance.[4]

The relationship between aesthetics and politics implicates the target audience and is contingent on the material resources required for cultural work. This emerges as a particularly postcolonial concern when cultural work, especially if allied to social activism, is either censored or dismissed as irrelevant, unless it is geared towards the consolidation of a specific version of national citizenry. Under these circumstances the choice of the form and content of drama is dictated as much by material constraints as by ideology. Ideologically, postcolonial dramatists subscribe to the dual emphasis of Brechtian Epic dramaturgy: inviting decisions from the bourgeois and proletarian audience the drama is aimed at; and fulfilling "paedagogic" ends by teaching "a quite definite practical attitude directed towards changing the world" (57). Brecht believed that the modern Epic theatre "demands not only a certain technological level but powerful movement in society which is interested to see vital questions freely aired with a view to their solutions, and can defend this interest against every contrary trend" (76). The drama I discuss has politicized the postcolonial stage through "vital questions" regarding women's work, reproductive and sexual choices, and the nature and incidence of social violence.

However, many of these performances do not fit Brecht's paradigmatic "technological level," if this is narrowly interpreted as a valuation of skilled stagecraft. There is a fundamental contradiction in Brecht's ideas about these paradigms. On the one hand he mentions the poverty or simplicity of small working class theatres constrained by lack of funds by clarifying that the simplicity of an acting technique that does not rely on extravagant emotions constitutes its 'poverty'. On the other hand he declares that once "it can overcome poverty the small working class theatre stands some chance of overcoming the simplicity which is the hallmark poverty gives to its performances" (148–49). This contradiction can be traced to Brecht's belief in the street scene as a model for Epic theatre. In Brecht's view the street scene is propagandist while Epic theatre possesses infinitely more value as art; the form mediating between the street scene and Epic theatre is "street theatre," described as "a primitive . . . but meaningful phenomenon with a clear social function that dominates all its elements" (126). By presenting political demands such as equal wages for men and women or justice to rape victims, in a form different from dominant theatrical appurtenances, street theatre and its variants have emerged as an extremely effective means of furthering feminist and working class agendas. Street theatre's denigration on artistic grounds by a staunch materialist like Brecht can be revaluated through drama that retains the notion of "poverty" in a different sense than the connotations of artistic simplicity implied by Brecht.

Grotowski is, of course, the most famous exponent of "a poor theatre" where performance is "an act of transgression" and theatre becomes "a place of provocation." Grotowski's Poor theatre is one without costumes and sets, music, or lighting effects, with the actor as its only essential element. This has also been called "an ascetic theatre" since no material success accrues to the actor. Although there is no financial stability for the actor who chooses to be associated with Poor theatre, there is an inherent satisfaction in the work itself. Grotowski's quasi-mystical listing of the attributes of poverty in theatre and the holiness of the actors working in it is in contrast to the actual conditions of poverty faced by many postcolonial theatre practitioners. Although sparse allocation of resources is common to theatre workers in most nations, there is a difference between the poverty willingly embraced by Grotowski and the actors with whom he experiments, and groups like Sistren Theatre Collective from Jamaica, Jana Natya Manch or People's Theatre Front from India, or the Kakaun Sela Kompany in Nigeria. For these groups, scarcity of resources reflects national economic conditions which justifies the state's denial of funding to cultural workers, and is often one of the grounds for dismissing their work. These groups also speak from, of, and to the material inequities faced by workers, women, and other underprivileged members of society, in contrast to Grotowski's aesthetics of poverty, that he describes in an interview titled "The Theatre's New Testament" as an exploration of the "national" through quasi-spiritual introspection or a "sincere and absolute search into our historical ego" (52). Despite these differences, the idea of a theatre independent of the material paraphernalia of traditional dramaturgy remains an important one for practitioners. Not merely a metaphorical but a literal evocation of poverty is an important concern in any account of postcolonial drama.

Among the most useful responses to poverty or material constraints theatre workers encounter in third-world locations is Boal's "Joker system," first outlined in his account of the Arena Theatre of Sao Paulo. Of the theatre theorists and practitioners in the genealogy of postcolonial performance, Boal's is the most candid statement regarding financial exigencies:

> Drastic limitation of the purchasing power of the public brought about a reduction in the consumption of superfluous products, the theater among them. Each situation must be faced squarely in its own sphere, not according to optimistic perspectives, and the facts are these: the theater lacks a consumers' market, it lacks human resources, it lacks official support for any campaign aimed at popularization, and official restrictions are overabundant (taxes and regulations). (*Oppressed* 179)

The "Joker" function not only counters Brecht's charge of artistic simplicity in poor working class theatres, it also outlines concretely how to achieve cost-effective simplicity in staging. Boal takes into consideration the economics of staging by specifying that only one costume is allowed for each social role such as the army, the church, proletariat, and aristocracy. If there is more than one character playing the same role then the same costume can be used by many actors simultaneously. With the exception of love scenes, which Boal indicates must be performed by members of the opposite sex, actors and actresses can perform masculine and feminine roles regardless of sex (*Oppressed* 183).[5] This is in contrast to Grotowski's productions, that metaphorized as well as literalized poverty by composing organic masks of the actor's facial muscles, stage props made of waste materials, and tattered costumes. The economy of staging is better explained by Boal than Grotowski, who is eloquent on evocations of poverty but not on its political rationale.

Although there are significant differences between Brecht, Boal, and Grotowski in their views on the relationship between aesthetics and politics, all three denounce the commercialism of the theatre of their times. Brecht's Epic dramaturgy was in part a reaction against the dominant theatrical "apparatus" in Germany and Western Europe. John Willett observes that Brecht's switch to pedagogics must be seen in the light of the political and economic crisis in Germany in 1929. In this period when revolutionary change seemed "not only desirable but imminent," Brecht wrote his most "communist" works (33). Speaking against the apparatus comprising the opera, the stage, and the press, Brecht observes that art that reinforces the status quo and does not threaten change in any form is "art as merchandise," or "culinary art" satisfying the general taste for spectacle and entertainment. His suggestions for theatre to achieve a social function include sacrificing illusion and encouraging free discussion so that the spectator casts a vote in favor of change rather than being content with a good theatrical experience (34–39).

Unlike Brecht, Grotowski's statements against commercial theatre refer primarily to the actor's training and performance. Contrasting the "holy actor" with the "courtesan actor," he says that the former fulfills the spectators' spiritual needs while the latter concentrates on satisfying cultural needs. This "prostitution" of the actor, that he also calls "publictropism," includes the caveat that the actor must not act *for* the audience but in "confrontation" with the spectators ("Actor's Technique" 213–14). Even if one ignores the obvious sexism of Grotowski's formulations, it is hard to overlook that his theatrical experimentations have been available to a select few, primarily male actors, trained under him. During the successive phases of his theatrical work he has withdrawn from audiences into the esoteric realm of theatre research with a chosen set of disciple-actors. This "peripheralization" of the spectator's role has been defended by Lisa Wolford and critiqued by Eric Bentley. It has increasingly become an indefensible position regarding the possible impact of his work. Addressing the charge of elitism in his work, largely closed to the general public, except invited audiences, Grotowski's statement that direct audience participation has become a new "myth" in theatre is at the opposing end of postcolonial practitioners' acknowledgment of Brecht's and Boal's techniques in ensuring audience participation towards public discussion and debate.

Boal's methodology of making socially relevant theatre has included a stepwise articulation of the spectator's transformation into the actor, a move that counters the soporific and cathartic effect of conventional theatre. If Brecht wanted to raise the spectator's critical consciousness through alienation, Boal's preferred method of presenting theatre as a "rehearsal for revolution" that "stimulates the practice of the act in reality" is to invite the spectator to intervene directly in the dramatic action and change it by his or her actual presence on the stage. The Joker provides an on-stage model for intervention and is thus the "contemporary and neighbor" of the spectator (*Oppressed* 142, 174). Boal's Forum theatre techniques, in which the spectator's role is described as "spect-acting," have revolutionized the stage and invigorated community drama in many parts of the world as much as Brecht's ideas. They are variously conceptualized by Eugene van Erven as the Asian theatre of liberation, Alistair Campbell's British theatre in education, and African Theatre for Development by Ross Kidd, Frances Harding, and Oga Steve Abah.

This methodology resonates with the concerns of feminist and socialist theatre groups exploring discriminatory social policies and legislation in postcolonial locations. In India, the street theatre group of Sachetana, a feminist organization based in Calcutta, and the Pandies student theatre group in New Delhi use similar dramatic techniques, with varying degrees of success, to expose discriminatory laws and social practices impacting on women. From the Caribbean, the Jamaican group Sistren Theatre Collective applied Boal's techniques to talk about teenage pregnancy, urban destitution, and women's employment in a privatized economy. African Theatre for Development groups in Nigeria, Zimbabwe, and Ghana have worked with women's and human rights forums to create awareness about female genital mutilation, dispel popular myths about AIDS, and advocate education of girls and women.

Boal's conceptualization of "legislative theatre" extends his ideas and arises from his experience of being elected as *vereador* (legislator) in Rio de Janeiro, Brazil. Boal outlines the aims of legislative theatre: "As the function of *vereadors* is to create laws and to ensure the proper enactment of those that already exist, the people's participation in this process could be achieved by means of theatre: transitive democracy." While citizens creating the show achieve the democratization of theatre, this process is furthered by their interventions during the part of the show designated "Forum" (*Legislative* 15, 66). Boal's conception of 'theatrical citizenship' can be counterpoised with Alexander and Mohanty's anchoring of feminist thinking in "the centrality of collective practice in transformations of the self and reenvisioning organizational democracy" (xxxvi). As collective practices that may lead to self-transformation and critical thinking, the genealogy of performance charted earlier also needs to be examined from the perspective of female or feminized citizens as spectators, actors, and spect-actors.

Feminist performance theorists have critiqued Brecht, Grotowski, and Boal for their incomplete assessment of the gendered and sexed body in performance. Speaking of the potentially facilitating connections between

Brechtian and feminist theory, Elin Diamond proposes an intertextual reading to arrive at a "gestic feminist criticism." Drawing upon Judith Butler's explication of performativity, Diamond envisages performance as a site where gender can be alienated by foregrounding "those moments in a playtext when social attitudes about gender and sexuality conceal or disrupt patriarchal ideology." In this way she amends Brecht's "blindness regarding sexuality and gender." She also redefines "apparatus" as involving "psychic and ideological relationships among text, stage, and audience" (45, 52–58). Privileging the female spectator's perspective on the events being staged, Diamond's retheorization of Brecht's principles focuses on the body of the female actor.

The following paragraphs present feminist revisions of Brecht's, Grotowski's, and Boal's ideas indicating the impact as well as questioning of their ideas in postcolonial contexts. My first example is from Nigeria. Tess Onwueme, a Nigerian diasporic playwright, subtitles her work *Tell It to Women* "An Epic Drama for Women," invoking Brecht's theories as formal and ideological intertexts. Structured in "movements" rather than acts and scenes, this play is an account of social conditions in postcolonial Nigeria where the upper and middle classes initiate fraudulent development programs in the name of grassroots women. It describes events in the 1990s when the military government's schemes such as the Better Life for Rural Women program invited international attention and foreign funding but did little to help rural women. The obvious references to frauds perpetrated by Nigerian dictators under the pretext of bettering people's lives, and the dramatic strategies involving social gests such as ritual offerings, community gatherings, music, masks, and incantations, are intended as alienation techniques. One of the many social gests in the play indicating the gulf between urban and rural women occurs in the stage directions to Movement Three:

> Sherifat and Yemoja together perform the traditional ritual honoring the Earth Goddess and Onokwu/ Yemoja, Goddess of the Sea, for whom the women are devotees and priestesses. Because they are in the city, away from the village where the traditional ritual items are readily available, they improvise with water and garden eggs in place of palm wine and Kolanut. Yemoja drums while Sherifat recites the incantation to which Yemoja responds. (95)

The city-based bureaucrat Daisy's comment on the ceremony: "Go on, drum! Drum, Voodoo Princess!" indicates the playwright's attentiveness to a Western audience's possible interpretation of this gest. Daisy's response alienates the ritual and prevents the audience from exoticizing either the ceremony or the women who enact it. Onwueme thus uses Brechtian principles in her dramaturgy to demonstrate the complex interplay of gender, class, and political power in the indigenous/Western, rural/urban, community/individual divide in postcolonial Nigeria.

As in the case of Brecht, commentators have observed that Grotowski's conception of the actor and the spectator in his para-theatrical experiments is not only elitist but also predominantly masculine and that the female body is largely absent in his theories. In one of the most strident postcolonial critiques of Grotowski's experiments in *Theatre and the World,* Rustom Bharucha feigns perplexity at Grotowski's motivations for coming to India to research Theatre of Sources: "But why did you need to go to a small town like Khardah in West Bengal and work with a group of actors on finding their 'sources'? What could you teach them about their selves that they didn't already know?" (50). Bharucha's analysis is applicable to Grotowski's techniques for training actors and to his almost completely androcentric productions. The most telling symptom of what Richard Schechner calls "structural sexism" is that although there have been a few strong women performers among those Grotowski has trained, the principals have always been men, leaving little scope for women as "inheritors" ("Exoduction" 482–85).

Postcolonial dramatists influenced by Grotowski inherit this masculinist bias. In her examination of the Jamaican dramatist Dennis Scott's work, Honor Ford-Smith observes that Scott was influenced by Grotowski's "poor" theatre to develop an aesthetic that "stressed a language of drama based on actor body and ritual." He "borrowed, transformed, adapted [. . .] and spliced it together with local codes to develop a mode of physical performance and knowledge production which emphasized actor body and ensemble imagery taken from popular religion and various carnival traditions." However, women remain subordinate in this borrowing since Scott's "performance strategies privilege men in ways which depend on the domestication of women" (Ford-Smith, "Performing" 14, 241). This privileging of the male body in Jamaican performance was implicitly contested by Sistren, an exemplary instance of the application, revision, and modification of Boal's Theatre of the Oppressed techniques.

Since Sistren's plays are about the lives of grassroots women, the performances reference women as actors and spectators. The group members were teenage mothers working in blue-collar jobs; their experiences were, in many ways, representative of urban Jamaican women. Sistren's innovative dramaturgy based on life experiences relied on an episodic structure comprising the group members' memories, children's games, and rituals. Presenting gender as ideology, the group sought to denaturalize the female body in its sexed and gendered roles. Some dramatic techniques necessitated by the all-female cast such as cross-dressing for male roles led to the group being labeled "sodomites" and "lesbians." Using the Brazilian literacy activist Paulo Friere's techniques of consciousness-raising as "conscientization" in the improvisational, workshop mode, Sistren interacted with rural communities in Jamaica to establish a network of women-centered theatre and activist groups across the island. Later this work had to be abandoned due to lack of funding. In many ways Sistren epitomized a "poor" theatre struggling to survive in a situation where cultural activism was and continues to be neglected in favor of developmental concerns. Long before Boal outlined his structure of legislative theatre with a network of partners structured as "nuclei" and "links," deriving from Paolo Friere's conceptualization of "culture circles" in Brazilian literacy campaigns, Sistren had already established connections with communities outside their urban base in Kingston. The financial difficulties in legislative theatre and physical dangers faced by the nuclei of groups that Boal mentions were lived realities for Sistren; this continues to be a major problem faced by postcolonial theatre and drama workers.

Engaging with urgent questions about citizenship and its entitlements, postcolonial dramatists have used, challenged, altered, and reconceptualized some of the most influential theories of performance. The struggles and successes of these dramatists and groups are similar to those of the women's movements, although the former are thought to occupy the cultural and the latter the social terrain of postcolonial geographies. While we must be cautious in drawing either neat parallels or distinctions between social and cultural movements, the interfaces between the two need to be examined to arrive at an assessment of political versus apolitical dramatic acts. Articulated through the intersection of the women's movement and postcolonial dramaturgy, the concern central to this book is an interrogation of a predominantly masculine and heteronormative conceptualization of citizenship responsible for a model of development that dismisses identity-based social activism and denies the material exigencies of cultural work allied with these activist efforts.

Postcolonial dramaturgy is informed by an emphasis on the politics of recognition and redistribution that is, as mentioned early on in the introduction, the legacy of a feminist activism originating from the same locations as the drama discussed. Feminists have argued for implementation of laws to protect citizens against forms of social discrimination based on gender and sometimes sexual orientation, and the need for a fair estimate and compensation of women's waged and unwaged labor. These efforts have acquired urgency with the deleterious effects of globalization and structural adjustment policies in developing nations in Africa, the Caribbean, and South Asia. The degree of success of these efforts remains to be seen. In the meantime, the onus of responsibility for disenfranchised citizens falls on local communities and the non-biological familial ties they may form with some members of these communities.

The expectation that the primary structure of feeling in the intersection of drama and feminism would be one of optimistic struggle is unfulfilled; in fact, many of the texts and performances analyzed focus on coming to terms with loss. The centrality of ritualized personal or political mourning in the following chapters is dictated as much by the 'action' of the play—some of them depict rituals such as the Nine-Night ceremony or the public keening of the *rudalis* (ritual mourners); others contain indirect but equally evocative expressions of public grief and outrage at the sickness, passing away, or murder of postcolonial ideals of social justice in neocolonial times—as by the anguish one observes in accounts of many decades of feminist efforts that have yielded less than expected returns. They also reflect grief, although not despair, at the distance between feminist ideals and the very real material, social, and geographical conditions confronting these ideals. This drama underscores that mourning can be an enabling condition for activism, since part of coming to terms with grief is the impetus to continue doing the work that is personally essential and politically meaningful. Charting a journey from hope to analysis, from grief to resistance, these chapters could have been arranged in several ways. The map eventually chosen is as follows:

Part I discusses how Jamaican dramatists' representation of communities of working classes and destitute women in the 1970s and 1980s presents ways of national belonging and citizenship that may, following David Evans, be called "sexual citizenship." This part introduces the possibility of sexuality as a vector in discussions of citizenship in the face of virulently misogynist and homophobic responses to dramatic representations of the social and sexual underclass in Jamaica.

Chapter 1 focuses on two plays by Dennis Scott, acclaimed dancer, poet, and Director of the Jamaica School of Drama from 1977 to 1982. Scott's dramatic career roughly coincides with Jamaica's experiment with democratic socialism under the People's National Party leader Michael Manley. Drawing attention to colonial history in Scott's plays *An Echo in the Bone* (1974) at the beginning of democratic socialism and social chaos in *Dog* (1978) during one of the worst periods of political violence witnessed in postcolonial Jamaica, the chapter first articulates the idea of normative citizenship propagated by the Jamaican state. It then discusses representations of community and kinship offered in the two plays with reference to the normative citizen as an Afro-Caribbean man engaged in productive labor. The chapter concludes by positing that Scott's dramaturgy, influenced by Brecht's and Grotowski's theories, exemplifies institutionalized cultural action contending with state ideologies in its conceptualization of citizenship.

Chapter 2 is about Sistren Theatre Collective, a grassroots women's group that arose out of the Jamaican national cultural policies detailed in Chapter 1. Under the direction of Honor Ford-Smith, Staff Tutor at the Jamaica School of Drama, a group of working class women wrote, produced, and performed plays on the private dimensions of women's experiences including teenage pregnancy, rape, and domestic abuse. Sistren's feminist program of drama for social justice is based on and supplements Augusto Boal's ideas about a people's theatre. The chapter claims that the group's work initiated a discussion of female sexuality in the public sphere to present material and sexual security as equally important aspects of 'postcolonial sexual citizenship' by emphasizing social support networks among destitute women. The chapter concludes by indicating the felicitous temporal conjunction of Sistren's work with the Gay

Freedom Movement's (GFM) efforts to forge a community in Jamaica in the 1970s. These efforts laid the ground for the 2001 campaign against discriminatory legislation and in support of effective citizenship for sexual minorities by the Jamaica Forum for Lesbians, All-Sexuals and Gays (J-FLAG).

Part II continues the discussion on feminist dramaturgy initiated through Sistren and furthers the analysis of postcolonial drama, kinship, and citizenship by looking at the trajectory of a street theatre group that has sporadically collaborated with the women's movement in India. It also examines the plays of a feminist and a gay dramatist who are giving voice to quasi-kin communities of transsexuals and female mourners, subaltern groups whose existence is relatively marginal to the postcolonial state's implicit endorsement of the middle or upper caste heterosexual male as a legitimate citizen.

Chapter 3 is about popular theatre and consciousness-raising in India by Jana Natya Manch's (People's Theatre Forum) focus on sexualized violence against women through street plays. These plays were written and performed in solidarity with the Indian women's movement's campaigns against rape and sexual exploitation of children. Jana Natya Manch's or Janam's (the acronym is the Hindi word for "birth") program of taking theatre to the doorsteps of the people can be seen as modification of Bertolt Brecht's vision of a theatre for the working classes to include the involvement of women and men workers as audiences. Since its formation in the 1970s Janam has maintained its primary focus on the working classes but also directed attention to the family and immediate kin relations as sites of gendered violence. These representations are marked by the awareness that gender issues cannot be subsumed or divorced from material inequities. Like Sistren, Janam is a case study in the mutually facilitating relationship between the women's movement and efforts for a socially relevant theatre. The central idea explored in this chapter is how the interaction between Janam and the women's movement in India has held the state accountable for an insufficient attention to women's rights and how the group's recent work allows for a possibility of extending gender justice to other marginalized groups such as gay men and lesbian women.

Chapter 4 discusses two plays, one by Dattani, a gay male playwright writing in English, and another by Ganguli, a woman dramatist writing in a local language, Hindi. Dattani writes about *hijras,* transsexual or transgendered men; Ganguli's focus is on *rudalis,* or female mourners. I examine these plays with reference to the women's movement in India, that has successfully interrogated caste as a gendered structure doubly oppressing women as citizens. However, the movement has been less than willing to discuss sexual orientation as an equally significant factor in second-class citizenship. Dattani's and Ganguli's depiction of the intersection of caste, sexuality, and non-biological forms of kinship anticipates the Indian women's movement's relatively recent and reluctant acceptance of sexual orientation as an important axis of oppression in the struggle to obtain gender justice. The chapter claims that the multiple colonization of this caste- and sexually marked subject by the postcolonial nation-state and by global vocabularies of identity affiliations ('gay', 'lesbian', 'bisexual', and 'queer') can be countered by a materially grounded exploration of 'queer subalternity' that acknowledges non-Western sexualities as influenced by but distinct from Western understandings of sexual identity.

Part III directs attention to the generation of Nigerian playwrights after Wole Soyinka who represent women as agents of revolutionary transformation as well as participants in a compromised postcolonialism. In the absence of explicit discussions of feminist and queer consciousness in Nigerian drama, it models strategies of reading to indicate how Nigerian, and by extension postcolonial drama, can be used to open a conversation on feminist and queer issues by drawing on local activism and indigenous understandings of gender, community, and kinship that illustrate queer subalternity.

Chapter 5 contends that Osofisan's Marxist dramaturgy, perfected through his work with university drama groups, can also be used to read the gender ideology of the Nigerian state. Osofisan's Brechtian play *Morountodun,* based on a peasant uprising, was first performed in the late 1970s during the time of Nigeria's second transition to democracy. Like Dennis Scott's drama, it was influenced by and commented on attempts at amendments in gendered structures of power in Nigeria. The issue of political representation for women that motivated both state-supported and autonomous women's groups in Nigeria during the late 1970s and early 1980s is the analytical lens in my close reading of Osofisan's play. I outline and critique recent theories of citizenship, democracy, and resistance in Africa by Mahmood Mamdani and Achille Mdembe to propose that the revolutionary kinship and the community of the exploited in Osofisan's play mirrors the national community Nigeria sought to engender during this period: both are characterized by an exclusion of women's contribution to postcolonial democracy.

Chapter 6 discusses how the work of the Nigerian diasporic playwright Tess Onwueme can be placed on the continuum of Nigerian cultural activism marked, on the one hand, by a critique of postcolonial governmentality and, on the other, by active support of the programs initiated by the state. Onwueme's focus on women's resistance to the developmental programs imposed by leaders and bureaucrats in Nigeria in her play *Tell It to Women* (1992/1997) can be seen in conjunction with the efforts of Theatre for Development (TfD) practitioners. Onwueme exposes the fraudulent claims of postcolonial Nigerian governance with respect to development; in contrast, TfD practitioners work in close conjunction with the government's development plans. Juxtaposing these differing cultural ideologies, I address the following questions: How is women's sexuality overdetermined by the imposition of developmental programs enlisting the aid of cultural activists? Can theatre and drama be useful in initiating a dialogue on sexualities in Africa? Is it possible for women-centric traditions within local communities to yield a model of postcolonial development that embraces alternative sexualities? The chapter answers these questions by suggesting that despite presenting sexual identity politics as separatist and irrelevant to the communitarian ethos of Nigerian society, *Tell It to Women* initiates a long-overdue conversation on alternative sexualities in Nigeria.

Finally, the Epilogue examines how the imagined models of citizenship analyzed in the preceding chapters reflect women's movements nurtured in educational institutions in India, Jamaica, and Nigeria. Since schools of drama, colleges, and universities are important loci of analysis in this study, I conclude by proposing a multidisciplinary pedagogical approach required to counter hegemonic gender ideologies. This initiative can be based in universities, such as the University of Delhi, India, the University of West Indies at Mona, Jamaica, and Ahmadu Bello University, Nigeria, that are already sites of feminist activism. In conclusion, the book claims drama as a form of public pedagogy that can bring about changes in social perceptions, provision of justice, and social and self-acceptance of non-normative life choices.

Part I
Jamaica

Part 1

Jamaica

1 Making Citizens
Community, Kinship, and the National Imaginary in Dennis Scott's *An Echo in the Bone* (1974) and *Dog* (1978)

> His disciplines are towards economy and austerity—a stripping away of whatever will obscure the sinews of the imaginative exercise. This alone is complex, as our lives are, where experience is prismatic and ironic, and where time, space, action and character are not sequential but relative.
>
> The Play asks a question about the experience of violence and attempts not to explain its constituents, but to recreate the complex organism. We may puncture it at any point in time and space, place or race. The same tissues pulse, the same blood spurts, and the same heart must be healed.
>
> (Caroll Dawes)

Written as an introduction to the University of West Indies' production of Dennis Scott's play *An Echo in the Bone* (1974), Dawes's description attests to the relevance of his drama to contexts and moments other than those of the production. Scott's reputation as a playwright has been overshadowed by his own fame as a poet and by dramatists such as Derek Walcott who share his focus on colonial history and its postcolonial legacy. Scott's career as poet, dramatist, and arts administrator in Jamaica in the 1970s is part of a pre-globalization narrative that may seem irrelevant in the face of Jamaica's current policies of a liberal, privatized economy, making it a willing although severely disadvantaged partner in the global economy. This career, however, inspired a generation of Caribbean theatre and drama workers, and Scott's legacy continues in the experimental and socially conscious work of the Jamaican playwrights Pat Cumper and Pauline Forrest-Watson, and groups such as Sistren Theatre Collective and Jamaica Youth Theatre. As Director of the Jamaica School of Drama from 1977 to 1982, Scott's key contribution was initiating theatre for development programs in Jamaican prisons, hospitals for the mentally ill, youth clubs, and sugar cooperatives. He wrote in an unpublished paper titled "Theatre in Development" that the kind of theatre he envisaged gave "people a chance to define, choose, and extend themselves" as both participants and spectators (6). Scott's belief in local communities as the locus of historical and political consciousness coincided with Jamaica's experiment with democratic socialist governance introduced by the People's National Party leader Michael Manley. Defined as sustainable development within broadly socialist ideologies, democratic socialism as the state policy was abandoned in the late 1970s under international pressure to privatize the economy. Analyzing two plays by Dennis Scott, this chapter outlines multiple connotations of community and kinship towards an understanding of citizenship during this crucial period in Jamaica.

In the absence of performance records, the direct influences on Scott's dramaturgy and on Caribbean performance history during this period can only be estimated.[1] From the available records we know that Scott's drama was influenced by the national cultural policy and intercultural performance theories.[2] Rex Nettleford's account of the role of the arts in Jamaica in the 1970s, Bertolt Brecht's ideas on theatre as pedagogics, and Jerzy Grotowski's concepts of performance and spectatorship are the basis of my interlocution of Scott's plays. These enable a dialogue on the possible impact of the plays on audiences as 'spectatorial communities' participating in definitions of postcolonial citizenship. The audiences for Scott's plays, which were and continue to be performed mainly in university settings, were, of course, different from the audiences of his community drama experiments in rural and urban locations. Through his encouragement of community drama Scott attempted to create a theatre for the masses, but his own plays were for a more specialized audience that were potentially the agents in creating such a theatre.

Focusing on the representation of colonial history in Scott's play *An Echo in the Bone* (1974) at the beginning of democratic socialism and the social chaos depicted in *Dog* (1978) during one of the worst periods of political violence witnessed in postcolonial Jamaica, I outline the contours of normative citizenship propagated by the cultural policies of the Jamaican state. Next, I discuss representations of community offered in the two plays with reference to the normative citizen as an Afro-Caribbean man engaged in productive labor, and speculate on how these representations may have impacted specific audiences as spectatorial communities. I conclude by positing that Scott's dramaturgy offers a limited but significant demystification of normative citizenship by introducing community and kinship as ideas central to an understanding of Afro-Caribbean history and contemporary Jamaican politics.

SPECTATORIAL COMMUNITIES AND KINSHIP

Scott's representation of history and politics illustrates how cultural work contends with state ideologies in the creation of a 'national imaginary'. This can be defined as a horizon of expectations for citizens of Jamaica as a nation including a monoracial (African) heritage, participation in a stable family unit, and a traditional assignment of gender roles. Within this imaginary men are expected to contribute to the national and domestic economies as the primary breadwinners, while women participate in these economies in both productive and reproductive capacities, evident in the government's encouragement of women as wage earners under the democratic socialist experiment. Surprisingly for a playwright so closely attuned to state policies, Scott's plays were not primarily meant for the audiences who were the focus of his community drama and theatre in development programs. The performance venues of the plays can help conceptualize the specifics of audience interpellation in the national imaginary envisaged microcosmically as a spectatorial community. *An Echo in the Bone* was performed as a commemoration play at the University of the West Indies (UWI), Mona, showcased as Jamaica's entry into the Caribbean Festival of Arts (CARIFESTA), and at the Lagos Festival of Black Arts in the 1970s. The revivals of *Echo* in the 1980s include a much acclaimed production by Talawa, a black theatre company based in London. *Dog* was written when Scott was director of the Jamaican School of Drama, and was first performed by the Caribbean Theatre Workshop at the UWI, Mona in 1978; subsequent performances include those in Trinidad and in London as part of the Black Theatre Season. Clearly, these plays showcased Jamaica for international audiences. However, since they have been revived most often at the UWI, an examination of this performance venue is crucial to understanding the creation of spectatorial communities.[3]

Formed under the aegis of the British government to fulfill the educational needs of its colonies in the West Indies, the UWI can be seen as embodying what David Scott (no relation to Dennis Scott) has perceptively identified in *Refashioning Futures* as the "crisis" of the postcolonial state. This crisis involves "a decline of the hegemony of the middle class nationalist-modern" whose project was "to integrate progressively the social and cultural formations that composed the plurality of Jamaica around a single conception of the national good and a single portrait of the national citizen-subject." This is an optimistic view of "hegemonic dissolution" that considers the "increasing moral, social, and economic autonomy of the popular classes." The sites for the propagation of the nationalist modern are elite dominated and include "university lecturers, psychologists, journalists, radio talk-show hosts, politicians"; those of the popular modern arise from performative locations such as dancehall and reggae and constitute a "subaltern cultural-politics" (David Scott 191–93, 214). An analysis of UWI's role in the developmental and cultural agenda of the Jamaican state indicates a somewhat different picture of the crisis in postcolonial Jamaica than that presented by David Scott. I am suggesting that a modification of these pertinent ideas can account for the different realms of the 'national' and the 'popular' in Jamaica: theatre and drama categorized as national culture inhabit institutional and community settings often with explicitly pedagogical aims; dancehall, within the popular domain, often relies on commercial or mass appeal in settings devoted almost exclusively to entertainment with no explicitly pedagogical aim.

The pedagogical dimensions of national culture during the 1970s are outlined by Rex Nettleford in his interview with David Scott. Manley's "conscious cultural policy," according to Nettleford, was aimed at *"shaping a society"* (222, 231). In *Caribbean Cultural Identity* Nettleford mentions that UWI's Extra-Mural Department was the nodal point for culture put to developmental purposes; its Creative Arts Centre was the "bridge between the campus and the community through practice of the arts" (50). The UWI can thus be examined as a site for the consolidation of the state's cultural agenda, dependent, in large measure, upon eliminating distinctions between the national and the popular by using culture for development. To put it differently, under the democratic socialist ideology the university as one of the sites of the "nationalist modern" was urged to make connections with the "popular modern." It is against this background of the goals and aims of UWI and some of its constituent departments—outlined not by communities but by the dictates of the nationalist modern supposedly for the benefit of those very communities—that Prime Minister Manley's cultural program can be assessed.

In 1972 Manley appointed an Exploratory Committee on the Arts headed by Nettleford which reported that the responsibility for arts lies on the *"community"* rather than exclusively on the government. The government's role is to provide "constructive guidance" to cultural development "linked to economic and social development through the country's educational policy, adult education and youth community programs as well as direct assistance to *national cultural groups*" (*Caribbean Cultural* 90). Trevor Munroe has defined civil society in Jamaica as referring to both the "non-political voluntary associations occupying the space between the state and the market" and "the networks and relationships which may or may not crystallize into groups but which nevertheless connect individuals together in some non-coercive, reciprocally purposive manner." Munroe mentions the existence of many such groups in third-world contexts that sometimes develop into formal structures; he also emphasizes the role of voluntary efforts, aided by either the government or the private sector, in forming civic associations (78–79). The university is one such locus of networks and relationships that draws strength from "voluntary efforts," although it does not fit voluntarism neatly as a schema for civil society that is valorized (and sometimes necessitated) in locations with scarce resources such as the third world at large and Jamaica in particular. The university can thus be seen as a site of waged as well as voluntary labor that subsidizes state expenditure through its work with communities in civil society, including the important theatrical experiments in the 1970s mentioned at the beginning of this chapter. Scott's focus on drama for underprivileged local communities is in keeping with the national cultural pedagogy envisaged by Manley and Nettleford. However, in his own plays, that are the focus of this chapter, he offers a somewhat different view on community.

Caribbean theorizations of community have primarily been in the geographical terms urban, semiurban, or rural offered by Carl Stone; on the basis of affiliation with political parties as suggested by Gray; and more recently, as involving a "conception of difference" in which "conflict, dispute, argument, contestation—in short, agonism—are seen as constitutive rather than dispensable to a common life" according to David Scott ("Permanence" 298). Related to this idea of the community and the reiterated but largely amorphous state-defined program of the well-being of social groups as communities, but also opposed to its claims, are the demands of kinship or personal/familial well-being.[4] Kinship and community as represented in *Echo* and *Dog* can be read through Joseph Roach's formulation of the relationship between memory and performance as "surrogation." For Roach performance "stands in for an elusive entity that it is not, but must viably aspire both to embody and to replace" in the same way as relationships within the community aspire to the obligations of kinship relations (3). The close approximation of community and kinship in these plays is, in my view, a validation of non-biological associations that helps sustain people in times of social conflict and hardship. This is often the case in situations marked by unequal access to resources as well as income disparities exacerbated by the state's neglect of its poor and disenfranchised populations.

The social purposes of memory, mourning, and performance suggested by Roach serve as my points of departure for an examination of the forms of kinship and community explored in *Echo* and *Dog*. Roach has suggested that *Echo* "dramatizes the cultural politics of memory, particularly as they are realized through communications between the living and the dead" (34). Structured around ritual as a medium of social interaction, *Echo* is about impoverished Afro-Caribbean peasantry in the 1930s, who suffer under the control of wages, resources, and markets by the Creole landowners. Its central incident is the black farmer Crew's murder of a white landowner, Mr. Charles, when the latter refuses his request to divert water from his large landholding to Crew's small farm. Crew's disappearance (it is assumed he has drowned himself) is the topic of speculation and discussion in the rural community. The Nine-Night ritual arranged by Crew's widow Rachel in her husband's memory comprises the action of the play.[5] Rachel invites a few close friends to the ceremony, that is marked by ritual drumming, sharing of food, drink, ganja smoking, and recounting stories about the dead person. The incantatory, call-and-response nature of the ceremony builds a natural rhythm, one in which all members of the community participate:

> MADAM: Who is Dead?
> RACHEL: A man.
> P: What is his name?
> RACHEL: Crew.

DREAM: Where him come from?
RACHEL: Darkness.
SONSON: Where him gone to?
RACHEL: Darkness.
JACKO: What him life was like?
RACHEL: Sorrow.
STONE: What his life was?
RACHEL: Smoke.
BRIGIT: Who going remember him?
RACHEL: Friends.
STONE: Who going remember him?
RACHEL: Sons.
P: What him leave with us?
RACHEL: Smoke. (85)

The older folk of the village, Rachel, Mas P., Stone, Madam, and Rattler, understand the structural connections between the past and the present better than the young people such as Rachel's sons Jacko and Sonson, her daughter-in-law Brigit, Madam's granddaughter Lally, and Lally's admirer Dreamboat. Despite participating in the ritual, Brigit and Lally constantly question its value. The young people's skepticism, although it does not affect the bonds within the community, is in contrast to Madam's compassionate understanding of Rachel's desire for the mourning ceremony.[6]

The teleological sequence of the mourning ritual is disrupted by a series of historical and contemporary events: re-enactment of Afrocentric history depicting the middle passage, a slave auction, a slave owner's encounter with the maroons, and a Creole landlord's inhuman treatment of his servants. The non-naturalistic staging of these events not only reveals the shared history of those participating in the ritual but also sets the tone for relations within the rural community. Based on material and social transactions, the interactions between members of the rural community can be defined as a communal kinship. The material manifestations of this kinship are the transactions on "trust" in Madam's shop: "Trust, trust, all the time, how you think I can live when de whole village taking food out of my shop and not a penny coming back in?" (85). When Rachel cannot afford to purchase in cash she pays Madam in kind, in contrast to Dreamboat whose credit in the shop is unpaid until he is told that he must give back something once in a while. Ironically it is Dreamboat who reminds the gathering in Rachel's house of the class and racial dimensions of this subsistence economy:

> You grow a little corn and potatoes, and take it to the market, how much can you sell it for? The white ladies, all of them go into the town to buy their goods, nobody in the market to take the provisions off you hands except poor people like you, hungry the same way, poor the

same way. You laugh a little, drink a little, trust a little, eh Madam? Who is to say a man should hold his life to the straight path all week, year in, year out? That is the way the world is friend. (108)

Tangible connections in the community include a pooling of resources; less tangible are the spiritual connections facilitated by the ritual. Rattler's drumming is the aural accompaniment to the communal kinship enacted in the Nine-Night ceremony. Within the structure of the ritual and the play, the past that echoes in the bones offers a stronger sense of connection than the blood in the veins.

One of the ways in which this scene can be read is through Butler's signification of kinship as "social arrangements that organize the reproduction of material life, that can include the ritualization of birth and death, that provide bonds of intimate alliance both enduring and breakable, and that regulate sexuality through sanction and taboo." (*Antigone's Claim* 72). The phenomenon of surrogation as spirit possession in the ritual introduces the specter of incest that according to Butler marks a limitation of kinship. This spectral figuration haunts Scott's play: when Sonson is possessed by Crew's spirit during the Nine-Night ceremony he becomes both husband and son to Rachel. Spirit possession, central to the Nine-Night, is, as Renu Juneja argues in her essay on *Echo,* "the most appropriate choice in terms of the history Scott is making or remaking because it signals at the outset that this history is *possession* of the black people and very different from sanctioned colonial accounts" (99). This history also involved dispossession of biological kin, intuitively sensed by Sonson when he meets Mr. Charles. Although he has no knowledge of his mother's previous relationship with the landowner, he says: "[T]he minute his eye and mine make four my spirit turn against him. If he never say a word to me, I would know. Why is that, Ma?" ("*Echo*" 112). Since the spirit possessing him is that of Crew, who later murders Mr. Charles, Sonson's hostility to Mr. Charles arises, in retrospect, due to a perception of conjugal and material violation. When possessed by Crew's spirit, Sonson's relationship with this mother as son/husband "delineates lines of kinship that harbor incest as their ownmost [sic] possibility, establishing 'aberration' at the heart of the norm" (Butler 67). However, Scott's play lays this threatening figuration to rest by establishing a communal kinship culminating in a politics of love, with filial relations and heterosexuality as its key constitutive elements. The concluding stage direction of the play reads: "Sonson goes to Brigit. Stares at Jacko. Pushes her gently towards her husband. Jacko nods silently. Rachel holds Sonson holds . . . tenderly," indicating a paradoxical restoration of established "lines of kinship" even as the play holds out the possibility of non-biological, non-heterosexual forms of kinship extending into the community (137).

Despite the reinstatement of communal and familial harmony at the end of the play, Scott's representation of colonial rural life in *Echo* is not utopian. However, the poverty and destitution in Scott's *Dog* indicates a postcolonial dystopia that makes the community in *Echo* appear utopian by comparison. In an assessment of political commentary, music, films, and literature on Kingston, Nadi Edwards claims that its representation as dystopic makes it a "city of bare life, which to all intents and purposes becomes a camp, biopolitical paradigm of modernity" (3). Although Edwards does not mention *Dog*, which was written in the late 1970s when the People's National Party (PNP) and the Jamaica Labor Party (JLP) were engaged in widespread violence, the guerilla warfare between the underdogs and the upper classes in *Dog* can be seen as one of the test cases of Edwards's contention. One of the groups represented in the play are literally dogs "naked, except for scraps of materials which cover their genitals" (58).[7] A narrator serves as the eye of events unfolding in the "inner city," where the "First Citizen Volunteer Vigilantes" are engaged in nightly combat with packs of dogs to preserve their class privileges. When they discover that it is no longer possible to protect their privileges and property, the upper classes contemplate leaving the ravaged country, literally, to the dogs. Mummy, a homemaker, and Daddy, an insurance salesman by day and dog hunter by night, are the privileged citizens contemplating migration, while Dog, Bitch, and Father (a singer before he joined the pack) represent the exploited noncitizens. Mummy and Daddy's gardener and handyman, Finger, is precariously positioned between the two groups.

Although ritual does not structure this play explicitly as in *Echo*, the central incident titled "Rites of Passage" is Dog's quasi-ritualistic initiation into the pack. Despite her belief that her son is too young to join in the hunting, Bitch initiates him just before her death:

> DOG: (*slowly.*) Dis is away from me mother. Dis is away from me father. I. I. . . .
> BITCH: I take dis.
> DOG: I take dis. Call. I voice. I war. I walk. I peace. I.
>   (BITCH *waits.*)
>   I without you. I with you. In the pack, power. Ma. Is only you' fader you suppose to take it from.
> BITCH: Finish.
>   (*Pause.*)
> DOG: Call I one. Call I call.
>   (*Silence.*)
> BITCH: (*She moans.*) Now. De blood. Here. (It is a joke.) I have dat.
>   (*She takes a palmful of blood from her wound. Smears it on his mouth with a single gesture.*) Go on now. Come now, I.
>   (DOG *rises, turns his back on her formally, faces north, south, east, and west.*
>   *He turns again and hugs her tightly. It hurts.* BITCH *smiles a little.*)

That is right. Now you can die, proper.
(They go quickly. Painfully.) (67–68)

Bitch smears the blood from her wound on Dog's mouth to complete his baptism into the culture of violence demanded by the times, indicating that the brotherhood of the pack is sealed by an oath of allegiance and cannot be dissolved easily. When Father decides to renounce his membership in the pack later in the play, he faces threats against his life before he is grudgingly allowed to opt out in another ritualistic ceremony, "Manway," to pursue his vocation as a singer. Of the two communities that comprise the inner-city dystopia, the vigilante "first citizens," whose attacks on the dogs are a nightly occurrence, are shrouded in mystery, while the "brotherhood" of the dogs is vividly depicted in a quasi-ritualistic manner. Although ritual does not structure this play as explicitly as it does *Echo,* it provides Scott a way to represent community belonging in an urban setting.

If the bonds between the people in Crew and Rachel's village echo the shared history of slavery in the bones, those in Mummy, Daddy, Father, and Bitch's city are literally etched in blood. Yet a communal kinship sealed by ritual in this play is less the focus of Scott's attention than a reinterpretation of kinship. Violence and sexuality are inextricably connected in the kin relations in *Dog.* Scott's rendition of violence as a form of sexual consummation occurs in Daddy's orgasmic dream: "Mummy is resting. Daddy has touched her. *Unless* [sic]. Now he has gone to sleep. He dreams of killing dogs. There's juice on his leg, his belly. Satisfaction. Warm as blood" (97, emphasis added). A comparison with Scott's unpublished manuscript reveals the crucial word "Useless" which has been substituted with "Unless" in the printed version. Hence it would be correct to assume that Daddy's violent masculinity is presented as a form of sexual sublimation; it also makes him incapable of fulfilling Mummy's physical and emotional needs. Scott's representation of violence in *Dog* (and in *Echo*) implicates masculinity more than femininity, but does not absolve anybody, masculine or feminine, from their responsibility in supporting and promoting a culture of carnage: Mummy's fear of the dogs leads her to murder the already injured Bitch; her friend Madeline benevolently intends to have her lapdog Fifi put to sleep when she migrates to Toronto.

The bloody violence perpetrated by the "first citizens" is in contrast to Finger's solicitude for the dying Bitch and her injured son, Dog. Sensing Mummy's apprehension, he reassures her by offering to take care of them. He buries the dead Bitch in the garden and soothes her frightened son as if he were his own before giving him to Mummy. As in *Echo,* the specter of incest haunts Mummy's surrogate kinship with her adopted "son," who "starts to explore her face her body" but suddenly lurches away from her in fright to be comforted by Finger. Dressing Dog in clothes fetched by Finger, Mummy recounts this moment of filial recognition, but her reiteration of surrogate kinship underscores anxiety about this relation: "I'll be your mother now, your face was so smooth and I bent down to kiss you goodnight as if you were my son, really. You're my son, will you be my son? I will make you a soft house and keep you safe from the dogs and never go away if you'll be my son" (77). After Mummy and Daddy have migrated to Toronto, leaving Finger and Dog to fend for themselves, Finger's incorporation into the biological family comprising Dog and Father makes it an all-male family comprising a son and two fathers (including Finger). According to Ford-Smith this "queer male family" challenges "notions of nation that rest on images of the heterosexual nation" ("Performing" 239). *Dog* redraws norms governing biological kinship. This is, in a sense, the logical conclusion of the disruption represented by *Echo*'s focus on the "lines of kinship that harbor incest" as a possibility in the filial-conjugal relation between Rachel and Sonson that ultimately reinstate biology and heteronormativity as markers of kinship. These plays illustrate how Scott's extension of kin association through representations of communal and surrogate relations implicates history and politics. It remains to be seen whether the representation of colonial history and postcolonial politics in the plays successfully interpellates spectatorial communities in a state-validated notion of citizenship.

BRECHTIAN MUSE OF HISTORY

In *Echo* Scott dramatizes the period before constitutional independence by directing attention to the situation of the landowning Afro-Caribbean peasantry in the 1930s. The stage directions stating "All characters are black" indicate the centrality of Afro-Caribbean identity in this history (75).[8] The historical focus of the play closely fits the occasion of its performance, marking the silver jubilee of the UWI. Derek Walcott's historical pageant *Drums and Colours* (1958), written to commemorate the establishment of the West Indian Federation at the suggestion of the Extra-Mural Department of UWI, may be seen as a precedent for historical dramaturgy marking such occasions. Scott's play, commissioned to celebrate twenty-five years of the UWI, remembers the common history of the Federation envisaged by the governments of the Caribbean island nations in the late 1950s.

Staging *Echo* for a primarily university-based audience was a performative occurrence in more than the obvious sense of it being a performance. Homi Bhabha elaborates on the nation's people as existing in a "double time": the historical objects of a nationalist pedagogy, giving the pedagogical discourse an authority based in the past; and the subjects of a process of signification that must erase any prior or originary presence of the nation people to demonstrate the living principles of the people as contemporary. This split between the "continuist, accumulative temporality of the pedagogical" and the "repetitive, recursive strategy of the performative" can explain the possible impact of the play's performance (Bhabha

139–70). The audiences of *Echo* become a spectatorial community through a recognizable but repetitively 'alienated' history of economic and sexual exploitation under slavery and after its abolition. Although their interpellation into a pedagogy reinforces Afrocentrism, normative family structures, and strict division of gender roles,

Scott uses the Brechtian technique of transposition by setting the action of the play in the immediate and long historical past. Crew's murder of Mr. Charles and his subsequent disappearance after thirty years of hard and fruitless labor occur nine days before the ceremony organized by his wife, Rachel. Rachel's anguished response to Brigit's doubts about the necessity of the ritual wake calls for remembrance of things past: "Am I to forget him too! Is my man, I going satisfy his ghost with whatever respect I have to give him. You think you can wipe out thirty years of him together just so?" Mas P's long historical view of time and mourning, "Three hundred years crying into the white man's ground, to make the cane green, and nothing to show," and Rachel's response reveal that the Nine-Night ritual is also a racial mourning (79–80, 86). Unwilling to be possessed or committed for murdering the white landowner, Crew's son, Sonson, 'possessed' by Crew's spirit, equates thirty years of struggle and a final act of rebellion with three hundred years of slavery: "I not going to jail for this, you hear me! I suffer too long—three hundred years! Three hundred!" These indications of the passage of time are stated at the outset: "The action moves through the present, a ship moored off Africa in 1792, Madam's shop two days ago, an auctioneer's office in 1820, woods near an estate in 1833, Crew's house four years ago, a Great House in 1834, a field in 1937, and outside the Great House last week" (131, 75).

Historical and racial memories are refracted through the role of women in subsistence and reproductive economies. The scenes set in the eighteenth and nineteenth centuries interrupt the ritual to depict slave women as sexual and economic commodities; those set in the early part of the twentieth century indicate the continuity of this servitude and exploitation after Emancipation. Crew, the primary breadwinner in his family, toils unsuccessfully on a small plot of land, while his wife, Rachel, is subjected to the humiliating sexual advances of the white landowner. Madam and her granddaughter, Lally, form a family different from Crew and Rachel's, one that belies the myth of masculine economic prowess and female dependency, articulated by Crew when he forbids Rachel to work for Mr. Charles. Rachel's daughter-in-law, Brigit, is the central figure in this dialectic of Rachel's economic dependency and Madam's autonomy. She articulates the contradictions in the situation of women by justifying her choice of Jacko as a husband over Sonson: "Which one of them have more liking for the land? Jacko will settle down and raise him family, and you grandchildren will know where father is all the time?" Marriage with Jacko provides Brigit with reasonable protection against sexual exploitation and a chance at economic security. She tells Rachel: "I born poor, you hear me, and black and the only thing I have is my pride. That is what Jacko see, even if him is quiet and soft talking." Her dissent to sexual servitude is in expressly racial terms since she vehemently asserts her right to refuse the advances of "the owner of this estate." Like Crew's historicization of his experience as three hundred years of slavery, Brigit's outburst references the history of women's economic and sexual servitude: "Black people used to work for this land for nothing and they [white landowners] used to treat them like beast, they could amount [sic] them anytime. I not breeding for any man just for pleasure. I is not an animal. I is a human being" (114, 75, 115).

Brigit thus expresses the contradiction in women's lives in a productive and reproductive economy that continues to deny them material and sexual security while privileging their social roles as mothers and wives. Her pregnancy guarantees continuation of Crew's lineage at the conclusion of the play at the same time as Sonson's potentially suicidal possession by Crew's spirit is averted through his reintegration into the family circle.[9] Rachel believes that "[n]o matter what is past, you can't stop the blood from drumming, and you can't stop the heart from hoping. We have to hold on to one another. That is all we can do. That is what leave behind, after all the rest" (136). The focus on family as an essential unit for the reproduction of race and an incipient sense of nationhood evinced in the play echoes Manley's vision of the family, envisaged in specifically African terms, as the basic component of Jamaican society: "Society is, as every African knows, an extension of the family and therefore, for societies to be moral, they have to achieve in their extended context, the same instinctive moral sense of the worth of every member of the family" (38). Manley's focus on family and the moral worth of every person is first, a plea for the recognition of the idea of kinship in forging a national community and next, a repudiation of 'immoral' sexual relations under slavery that are a part of Jamaican history.

The visual emblem of these social relationships is the chain looping across the roof of the barn where Rachel holds the wake for her husband. The chain serves as an alienation device that reveals "the social gest" or "the mimetic and gestural expression of the social relationships prevailing between the people of a given period" (*Brecht on Theatre* 139). Signifying enslavement, enforced labor, and dehumanization, its rusty links are also a reminder of the biological and social connections between the slaves and their Afro-Caribbean descendants like Rachel and Crew. The rhythms played by mute drummer Rattler establish an aural connection to Africa. Yet another set of mimetic expressions conveying the social relationships are quotidian acts of sharing food, drink, and smoking together. Since the land is arid and opportunities for cultivation and employment are few, this sharing is reminiscent of the communal bonds that enabled the slaves to survive on meager resources. The rum poured to appease Crew's spirit, later consumed at the gathering, is a reminder of the triangular trade between Africa, Europe, and the Caribbean, reliant on slave labor for the cultivation of cane to produce sugar and rum for Europe. Mas P's illegal cultivation of the "weed" that he passes around at the wake earns him Stone's warning about being used by the "white man" who might any day betray him to the authorities. These aural, visual, and other sensory gests in the ritual are testaments to the historical and contemporary "unfreedom" of the Afro-Caribbean population. Stone's impassioned response, "Someday there is going to be blood. This land is used to it, and it is crying out for rain, for two thousand years that is what the cane grow with, and I fraid to see into the future. It looking too much like what gone before . . ." predicts an immanent revolution, the result of widespread social disaffection (110).

Since *Echo* is set in the 1930s it invites an examination of British colonial policies on Jamaica during that period; given its moment of performance in the 1970s it also invites an examination of the cultural agenda of the postcolonial Jamaican state. The play's lack of accommodation of racial and gender concerns, other than those related to "African patrimony," underscores the kind of citizen it aimed to pedagogically shape and govern. The relationship between the performing arts and the state outlined in the close fit between Manley's cultural and social programs and Scott's dramaturgy can be annotated by Brecht's ideas on theatre as "paedagogics" that may be used in the service of or in opposition to ideologies propagated by the state (65). Manley's government envisaged cultural growth as "an instrument of development policy" with institutions such as UWI as active agents of such a policy. A play such as *Echo* was the perfect vehicle for presenting an Afrocentric history focusing on plantation slavery and its aftermath studied by its student audiences during the period when pioneering work on Caribbean colonialism and slave history was produced by historians Lucille Mathurin Mair and Orlando Patterson, among others.

Scott's representation of the limited economic and sexual autonomy of women disrupts the declamatory pedagogical compact between race and gender that valorized Afrocentrism. Crew's murderous act, the male subaltern noncitizen's revenge for centuries of exploitation, is in the realm of what Ileana Rodriguez labels "ungovernability," or "a cultural behavior that does not conform or submit to the norms" ("Apprenticeship" 362). However, Rachel reinscribes these norms at the end of *Echo*: "The white man is right after all. Is only brute force can make us change our ways! Is only blood that people like us understand, is only revenge that satisfy us. And we is no better than beast in the field, that don't know nothing about love!" (133). A utopian moment in this politics of love that tips the balance against racial antagonism (Crew's murder of Mr. Charles) in favor of racial reconciliation occurs when Jacko dissuades Sonson (possessed by Crew's spirit) from suicide by stating that Mr. Charles has given him permission to pick breadfruit from the trees. This hopeful lie anticipates dissolution of racial and class privileges based on the "permission" of those holding the reins of power. The celebration at the end is for those Crew has "left behind," including his sons Jacko and Sonson and his pregnant daughter-in-law, who ensure continuation of the family. Thus despite a gesture towards social upheaval and sexual disruption in Crew's murder of Mr. Charles and Sonson's filial-conjugal relations with Rachel, the play ultimately reiterates social and sexual norms for its spectators at the UWI and elsewhere by bringing the ungovernability of Crew's actions within the realm of English Creole governance.

GROTOWSKIAN AESTHETICS AND SOCIAL UNGOVERNABILITY

Dog proposes two aspects of social ungovernability: class warfare, that indicates a failure of governance sidestepped by the utopian conclusion of *Echo;* and gender ambiguity, virtually a non-issue in *Echo*. The guerilla warfare between the citizens and the dogs in this play is, as I suggested previously, an extended metaphor for social conflict between the bourgeoisie and the lumpenproletariat. Performed in the late 1970s and early 1980s, when democratic socialism as a viable model of social development had lost out to the capitalist agenda of the Jamaica Labor Party, the play is also a statement on the consequences of a profit-driven model of development antithetical to community consciousness. There is no attempt in *Dog* to create an incipient sense of community among the audience that emerges as an important facet of Scott's presentation of Afro-Caribbean history to student, faculty, or other audiences of *Echo*. The influence of the Polish theatre director Grotowski's methods can help explain why *Dog*, revived much less frequently than *Echo,* has not enjoyed the same theatrical success either in the Caribbean or in other locations. Although Scott ensured that the major elements of *Dog* are transferable to "any place that has an 'inner city,'" for the sake of "convenience" he assumes it to be Kingston. The authorial expectation of the transferability of the performance has not been fulfilled to the degree expected, presumably because Grotowski's unsettling theatrical methodology—used by Scott to represent social collapse as interspecies conflict in *Dog*—is less amenable to the nurturance of an interpellated spectatorial community than the Brechtian aesthetics of *Echo*.[10]

The nakedness of the dogs, except for scraps of material covering their genitals, represents their subhuman status. Stripped of all possessions and social rights, they attempt to snatch back their tattered humanity by organizing into the brotherhood of the pack under their leader Scraps. At one level, their nakedness signifies social vulnerability, a technique used very effectively by Grotowski to different ends in his early productions. For instance, in *Akropolis* (1965) the actors wore costumes made of bags full of holes covering their nakedness, suggesting torn bodies and erasure of distinctive signs of sex, age, and social class. Another cardinal rule of Grotowski's stagecraft is the near total independence from costumes and props. The sets are reduced to objects "indispensable to the dramatic action" (Flaszen 75). Following this minimalist aesthetic, Scott specifies at the beginning of the play, "*Set, props, and costumes should be entirely transportable in the back of a van. Anything bulkier will constitute a director's mistake"* ("*Dog*" 58). As a teacher of drama, Scott was aware of the relevance of Grotowski's minimalist stage settings and precise actor-training techniques to the development of stagecraft in Caribbean nations struggling with limited funding for cultural activities.

The poverty of this theatre, not to be mistaken for artistic simplicity, is also evident in the limited number of actors. In *Echo*, the structure of the ritual, including spirit possession and historical events, was the rationale for each actor taking on several cross-class and cross-race roles as indicated in the stage directions; in *Dog* there is no apparent logic to the cross-class and cross-gender roles. Here is where Scott's manuscript version of the play is once again useful. In the manuscript Scott's notes specify that "Narrator, Schoolboy, Blind Man, Pack Leader, Landlord, and Madeline are to be performed by one actor. The roles of Bitch and Fifi may be performed by one actress" (*Dog* MS 1). Within this gamut of social roles performed by the same actor, there is, as Ludwig Flaszen says of Grotowski's *Akropolis,* "no character set apart from the others by his own individuality. There is only the *community, which is the image of the whole species in an extreme situation*" (73, emphasis added). The apparently random assignment of roles in the play can be attributed to Scott's representation of social classes as a "species in an extreme situation."

At the outset, Scott's presentation is symbolic rather than explanatory of this extreme situation. The city belongs to the well-fed, well-clothed "citizens," and the "stinking place," elsewhere spoken of as a "garbage dump," belongs to the hungry, naked dogs looked upon as social vermin. While the citizens aim to exterminate the dogs, the dogs are primarily marauders rather than killers, looting shops and houses for provisions. Bread, clothes, blood, and garbage are the structuring symbols of the play, giving it a "shivering unity." The "Rites of Passage" scene early in the play shows the naked, injured, starving Bitch and her son, Dog, looking for shelter after a violent ambush. There is a piece of poisoned bread on the road that Dog knocks out of his mother's hand when she attempts to eat it. When they reach the garbage can outside Mummy and Daddy's house, Mummy beats Bitch to death with the lid of the can. Much later in the play Scraps, the pack leader, reminds Father of the reasons for struggle in an attempt to dissuade him from quitting the pack: "You forgetting what them do we so long! You forgetting this stinking place that is all we have unless we take it from them!" Tired of the violence, Father in turn reminds Scraps of the original aims of the guerilla warfare: "We have to take what is ours, that's what you say to me that day in the yard when the smoke was a rope joining us together. And we start it together, to take some of what was ours, so that the singing could happen again" (73, 72).

The "singing" Father refers to is the reggae, ska, blues, and work song tunes in the play that are the dramatic devices essential to the creation of a spectatorial community. These songs are associated not with the citizens but with the dogs, or those located between the citizens and the dogs, "half and half," like Finger. Scott's larger point about a culture of violence destroying other aspects of culture, which may also be means of negotiation in socially conflictual situations, is made through the Bob Marley and Don Drummond tunes hummed by Father and Finger in the play. The point is reinforced when one recalls that gunmen of warring political factions, the Jamaican Labor Party and the People's National Party, approached Marley to perform at a concert marking a truce between them. The 'One Love' Concert took place on 22 April 1978. During the concert Marley persuaded Prime Minister Manley and the opposition leader Edward Seaga to join him on stage where they shook hands as a symbolic truce to end political violence.

Unlike the disadvantaged rural population in *Echo,* the urban social and sexual hierarchies in *Dog* defy neat categorizations. Besides the dogs and the citizens, there are other stratifications indicated by the blind man, the landlord, and the narrator, each suffering from varying degrees of economic and social vulnerability. In contrast to the Creole landowners and the Afro-Caribbean working class in *Echo,* two extremes of the socius, and the recognizable but distant history of the middle passage and plantation slavery, multiple levels of social distinctions and the uncertain outcome of the political conflict in *Dog* unsettle an interpellation into a spectatorial imagined community.

Racial and class antagonism defines ungovernability in *Echo;* carrying this idea over from his previous play, Scott presents the sexual as yet another realm of ungovernability in *Dog.* Like Mr. Charles's offer of a housekeeping job to Rachel in *Echo,* Finger's work for Mummy and Daddy provides him with a temporary refuge from the violence outside but involves sexual servitude: "Is a good work. Treat me good. I eat regular, and I sleep good. And de gyarden [sic] look good yes. I know. You t'ink I min' when you stand up in de house a watch me. No, ma'am, I don' min'. Is not a bad life. I don' min' living here. I don' batter batter up myself outside" (64). Mummy dictates the terms of her relationship with Finger, bartering sex for his silence on the circumstances of Dog's arrival in the house.

Economically, culturally, and sexually Finger straddles the world of the citizens and the dogs. Finger's sexuality is in direct contrast to Daddy's impotence, yet it is also enigmatic since he claims kinship with Dog as well as Mummy: "He's ours. Yours and mine." Exhorting Mummy to leave the "son" behind when she and Daddy migrate, he asserts a relationship with Dog: "I can keep him" (93). In the manuscript version of the play Finger's claim to kinship with Dog is explicitly in terms of species kinship: "Is the same thing, him and me. I know him. Half. Half" (*Dog* MS 33). The last two scenes of the play depict Finger's return to dwellings near the garbage heap that were once his home. He reaffirms his affinity with dogs by taking off his clothes and spilling his blood at the place in an ambiguous ritual of consecration, before making his way back to Mummy and Daddy's house in the city. Finger's in-betweenness is similar to Dog's, since after his mother's death he was adopted by Mummy. Dog's search for his mother's body in the backyard of the house, where he was adopted as a "son," inadvertently leads to a rediscovery of his biological parent, Father, and an unexpected anger against his surrogate parent, Finger. Father controls Dog's desire for avenging his mother's death by violence against Finger: "I na overstan' justice. I cyan' deal wid no justice. But every man deserve a chance to sing" (102). Eschewing blood and violence, the 'family' comprising Finger, Father, and Dog share bread and depart singing a song of hope. Clearly this queer male family is outside the realm of governability not only in terms of class but also in terms of a non-normative kinship that in its very possibility threatens the Afrocentric heterosexual national imaginary.

Early on in his career, in an interview with Eugenio Barba, Grotowski spoke of a national theatre "based on introspection and on the whole of our social super-ego which has been moulded in a particular national climate, thus becoming an integral part of it" (52). The national climate molding the social superego in the 1970s and 1980s Jamaica was, as I have argued in this chapter, based on a pedagogical view of cultural work aimed at shaping a national citizenry. Scott's plays were undeniably a product of this ideology. Yet, his disruption of the state-mandated pedagogical compact between race and class through the reconceptualization of community and family offered in *Dog* recognizes a kinship that is not based exclusively on heterosexual monogamy.

REFASHIONING THE NATIONAL IMAGINARY

This dialogue with Scott's plays may appear to suggest that Brechtian techniques were the only crucial elements in *Echo* or that Grotowski's influence was paramount in *Dog*. Such a demarcation of the multiple influences in Scott's work does injustice to his transformation of the ideas of Antonin Artaud, Brecht, Grotowski, and Africanist rituals and religious practices. Ford-Smith implicitly comments on these influences in *Echo* when she says that in this play Scott "translates the roughness of a rural nine night in a very poor community to a bare stage" by placing "the characters within the ritual itself" and using "the symbolic elements of the ritual (time-shift, role-shift, space-shift) to develop the intense minimalism of memory which tends to record images, feelings and textures rather than facts and chronologies of history" ("Performing" 210). The "minimalism of memory" Ford-Smith observes in *Echo* attests to Grotowskian elements of stage setting and design in the play, although the prominence of Brechtian elements facilitates an interpellation into normative citizenship. Similarly, Brechtian alienation elements in *Dog* include titles of the scenes that comment on the action, the narrator's presence as a choric figure directly addressing the audience, and a gestic use of music. These do not contradict the claim that Scott's adaptation of Grotowski's methods unsettles the spectatorial community.

I established that Brechtian aesthetics in *Echo* are more amenable to a shared conception of citizenship valorizing a monoracial Africanist heritage and heterosexuality at a particular historical moment in Jamaica than the Grotowskian elements in *Dog*. The history of plantation slavery in the former is more likely to draw people together than the unresolved social factionalism depicted in the latter, which is too close for the comfort level of the audiences. Another major difference between the two plays relates to the gender norms and family structures represented therein, that I have read as communal and surrogate kinship. While *Echo* conclusively enacts social and familial normativity through a politics of reconciliation and love, *Dog*'s inconclusiveness about social factionalism is counterpoised against a family Ford-Smith calls queer.

My purpose is not to recuperate Scott's drama for feminist or queer ends since the plays themselves resist such a reading. The somewhat tentative move away from normativity in Scott's drama does forward a querying, if not queering, of kinship and community. Accounting for the myriad cultural and performance influences on Scott's drama enables an assessment of various constituents of the Jamaican national imaginary in the 1970s and early 1980s: shared colonial history; postcolonial cultural, social, and political agendas; modes of community belonging including normative and extended kinship; and spectatorial investment in the performances. Exploring rural and urban destitution in *Echo* and *Dog* respectively, Scott extends the connotations of community and kinship as productive ways to recast the family, necessary for an understanding of Caribbean social realities. The existence of female-headed families as a norm rather than an aberration in the Caribbean, and attempts by gay men and lesbian women to form a community in the face of violent homophobia in the 1970s, when these plays were written and performed, are social realities adding resonance to important (although incomplete) revaluation of community, kinship, and citizenship offered by Scott.[11] The next chapter indicates the specific modes of such a revaluation by examining Sistren Theatre Collective's transformation of single women's life experiences to drama.

2 "We Shouldn't Shame to Talk"
Postcolonial Sexual Citizenship in Sistren Theatre Collective's *Bellywoman Bangarang* and *QPH*

> In this moment, theatre was discovered. The moment when Xua-Xua gave up trying to recover her baby and keep him all for herself, accepted that he was somebody else, and looked at herself, emptied of part of herself. At that moment she was at one and the same time, Actor and Spectator. She was Spect-Actor. In discovering theatre, the being became human. This is theatre—the art of looking at ourselves.
>
> (Augusto Boal, *Games* xxv)

> MARIE begins to deliver with the help of the MOTHERWOMAN who also removes the ropes MARIE was entangled in after the rape. She helps MARIE to stand, then teaches her to move. Together as one they move down the bridge into the central arena, where the other women have created a bath . . . They bathe MARIE and carry her down the ramp. . . . MOTHERWOMAN breathes into MARIE. She exits.
>
> (Sistren and Honor Ford-Smith, *Bellywoman* 60)

Brazilian theatre activist Augusto Boal's fable of Xua-Xua, "the pre-human woman who discovered theatre," connects the 'birth' of theatre to a post-parturition moment of split subjectivity. Boal's conceptualization of theatre as a humanizing process, an occasion to look beyond oneself at the moment of looking at oneself, can be juxtaposed with the figure of the "Motherwoman," a composite character formed of three interlocking figures, who "squats as if imitating a woman in labor" and "mimes the action of a midwife attending the birth," that provided an image of collective birthing and nurturing in the first version of Sistren's and Ford-Smith's play *Bellywoman Bangarang* (56).[1] The group's process of making theatre took motherhood as a point of departure, rather than the originating impulse it is in Boal's account of the birth of theatre. In 1977, when some women workers employed by the government decided to perform a play for Worker's Week celebrations, the state was forthcoming with assistance in the form of institutional support at the Jamaica School of Drama. Since the political climate of the time was supportive of progressive cultural activities, the success of their first production, *Downpression Get a Blow,* encouraged these workers to nurture their fledgling theatrical endeavors with the formation of Sistren Theatre Collective, a Jamaican grassroots theatre group that has become a model for politically committed postcolonial dramaturgy.

Given the emphasis on institutional structures under democratic socialism, it is unsurprising that Sistren received support from the Women and Development Unit at the University of West Indies (UWI) and the Jamaican School of Drama (JSD). As part of the Cultural Training Center, JSD, headed by Dennis Scott, was instrumental in providing a base to Sistren in the form of a rehearsal venue and training; Sistren's founding Artistic Director, Honor Ford-Smith, was a Staff Tutor at the School. The Women and Development Unit at UWI under Peggy Antrobus helped the group with some financial support at crucial moments in its growth. Later, with the introduction of economic liberalization policies under Edward Seaga's government, there was little institutional support available to the group.[2]

During the late 1970s and 1980s feminist cultural activism, academic work, and political work in Jamaica functioned in an uneasy alliance with state-supported pedagogy that reinforced traditional roles for women in domestic and reproductive capacities even while it acknowledged their crucial participation in formal and informal sectors of the economy. One of the controversial governmental schemes directed towards women's participation in the waged economy was the Special Employment Program. Of the ten thousand women who were given jobs as street cleaners under this scheme some, including members of Sistren, were later trained as teachers' aides.

Tracing Sistren's origins to the emphasis on female workers' participation in the democratic socialist script of national development, I argue that the group dramatized resistance to gender ideologies valorizing heterosexist domesticity and familialism. It thus waged a 'sexuality battle' that was different from the Gay Freedom Movement's focus on sexual identity in Jamaica during the 1970s—that I briefly mentioned in the previous chapter—but felicitously, although inadvertently, furthered recognition of sexual identity politics.

Sistren's translation of women's life experiences into politically interrogative drama enacts what David Evans identifies as a "discrepancy between *ideal and real families*, the one with simple, natural rights, the other propped up by a mass of civil, political and social sealing wax" and aims at representing "modern female sexual citizenship" (245, emphasis added). Continuing M. Jacqui Alexander's pioneering scholarship on citizenship, law, and sexuality in the Caribbean, Tracy Robinson's account of citizenship beyond the bill of rights in the Caribbean indicates how marriage and motherhood have served "as key sites where women prove they are good citizens or not" (246). Sistren's unique achievement was to subvert these morally inflected debates by making poor women the subjects of their own discourse on sexuality and citizenship. This chapter foregrounds Sistren's representation of the female body to propose that considering sexuality in relation to class and violence is essential for dismantling the binary

Illustration 2.1 Sistren founding members, Lorna Burrell and Bev "Didi" Elliot, stand to attention in a performance of *Domestick*. Brooms carried like arms become militant symbols of women's work in the production. Photo courtesy Sistren, Honor Ford-Smith, and *Fuse* magazine, http://www.fusemagazine.org.

characterizations of citizenship: productive versus unproductive, moral versus immoral, active versus welfare. An emphasis on the inextricable relationship between sexuality and survival and a concomitant denial of emphasis on the connection between sexuality and morality is essential to a conceptualization of 'postcolonial sexual citizenship'.

The group's reinterpretation of Paulo Friere's and Augusto Boal's techniques of a pedagogy and Theatre of the Oppressed supported this conceptualization. Sistren's drama can be seen as a supplement to Boal's methods of theatre, therapy, and activism that enables an assessment of feminist applications of Theatre of the Oppressed techniques. With the UN Development Decade for Women (1975–1985) providing the international stage for national policies of "women and/in development," Sistren's staging of sexuality and citizenship references Jamaican feminist social analyses and the Caribbean women's movement that help extend the conception of community and kinship discussed in the previous chapter. This chapter claims that Sistren's focus on the material construction of subaltern women's sexuality in the plays *Bellywoman Bangarang* (1978/1982) and *QPH* (1981) was in advance of the second-wave Caribbean women's movement's focus on legal reforms, new legislation, and placement of women's issues on the national agenda since it looked forward to a more recent politicization of sexuality.[3] In addition, Sistren's depiction of female relationality helps place the discussion of citizenship in dialogue with forms of kinship already existing in the Caribbean to arrive at what I call postcolonial sexual citizenship.

EXPERIENCE, RESEARCH, AND PERFORMANCE

The circumstances of Sistren's performances including not only the social and cultural policies of the PNP, Sistren's own research, but also *social science research* that influenced and led to those policies, have been briefly discussed in critical accounts by Robert Carr, Sharon Green, and Karina Smith. I was prompted to undertake detailed contextualization after talking to Honor Ford-Smith and Vivette Lewis, two of the founding members of the group, and on reading the interviews and life stories of many others. Sistren's sense of their work is that it was inextricably linked to the sociopolitical climate of the times mandated by national and regional conditions in Jamaica and the Caribbean.

Bellywoman Bangarang was Sistren's first full-length production for the stage. The two Jamaican English words in the title of this play connote the troubles of pregnancy. Many of the members, single parents in menial jobs, wanted to make a play about their lives as women, based on common experiences of domestic and sexual abuse as girls and teenage mothers. Ford-Smith's research into church rituals of testimony and confession, and members' recollections of popular rituals (children's games, proverbs, and riddles), provided the structure for this play. *QPH* is based on the lives of three women, Queenie, Pearlie, and Hopie, elderly inmates of Eventide, an almshouse in Kingston that was destroyed by a fire in 1981. While conceptualizing this play, the group moved from the immediacy of personal experience to interviews, discussions, and research into the lives of destitute elderly women in Jamaica. Director Hertencer Lindsay's research into African folk culture in Hanover, Jamaica, led to it being structured on *Ettu* and *Kumina* rituals.[4] Both productions followed the model provided by Dennis Scott and other dramatists in the Caribbean in their use of ritual as a framework for performance.

The occasions of Sistren's performances facilitate an understanding of the conditions that favored the emergence of a working class women's theatre group and the changes that later made it difficult for this work to be continued. *Bellywoman* was first performed in 1978 when Manley's PNP-led government was negotiating with the International Monetary Fund to bail the country out of a financial crisis fueled by rising oil prices in the international market. The playwright Rawle Gibbons directed a second version of the play in 1982. Gibbons made many changes to the original script and experimented with performance techniques. *QPH* was performed in 1980 when the PNP had already been voted out and the conservative JLP, firmly committed to a capitalist path of development, was in power. The play received widespread popular and critical acclaim despite the changed political and economic scenario.

The PNP's advocacy of women's issues in the early years of its governance (the period in which *Bellywoman* was conceptualized and performed) has been described by Gray as a "vulgar cultural gesture" related to the postcolonial state's trading of cultural forms of social power for nullified expressions of democratic citizenship ("Predation" 12). Such a view fails to give sufficient credit to the state for creating gender-inclusive governance by implementing policy decisions to remedy lacunae in Jamaican social legislation although, as indicated in the chapter on Dennis Scott, the national pedagogy postulated the normative citizen as heterosexual and male. Tracy Robinson has convincingly argued that legislative reform need not always translate into gender equality and citizenship as continuous with each other since women's rights are often considered secondary to civil and political rights (240). With this qualification, I juxtapose the two plays under discussion with research undertaken by the Institute of Social and Economic Research (ISER) at University of West Indies. ISER looked upon Sistren as an important organization while developing its database "for teaching, research and planning purposes and to develop guidelines for a cohesive social policy which recognizes the needs of women and draws on their skills and talents for program planning and execution" (letter to Ford-Smith). Some of the programs at ISER, discussed in the next section, specifically Erna Brodber's study of yards in Kingston and Gloria Cumper's account of the establishment of the Family Court in Jamaica, addressed concerns similar to those articulated by Sistren.

Sistren's movement from personal experience to research in their performances was also a move from individual to collective experiences including collaboration with professional sociologists and historians (Cobham and Ford-Smith). Some of the feminist inquiries that were translated into social policy in conjunction with Sistren's plays point to the interrelatedness of PNP's cultural focus on communities with its social policies regarding those communities. I also explain the influence of Latin American methodologies of pedagogy and performance on Sistren's work, with a special focus on the group's representation of women's interactions with the state. Ford-Smith mentioned in a personal interview that the pedagogic and dramatic techniques of Friere and Boal were used at a later stage in the group's work in community outreach. However, an examination of the letters and documents of the group from the late 1970s reveals many references to these ideas in the period under discussion in this chapter. Here I explicate the implicit and explicit influence of these ideas on Sistren's productions.

The opening stage direction of *Bellywoman* specifies a yard setting in a typical rural or urban community:

> The set suggests a yard, either in rural Jamaica or Kingston. Props, which will be needed during the course of the play, can be hung on a bamboo fence, which surrounds three sides of the stage. They consist of a bathpan, a grip and aprons on clothesline. Blocks, also made from bamboo, suggest furniture or walls. All other elements of the environment are created by the actors' bodies. On stage left and right there are two aprons. A bamboo bridge runs down the aisle of the theatre to a small raised platform in the center of the audience. (83)

The sparse stage reflects the sparseness of resources in the lives of the young girls whose experiences and memories structure the play. Additionally, the bamboo bridge marks a non proscenium setting where the audience is not separated from the actors, suggesting continuity between the actions on stage and the social environment. Foregrounding the "actors' bodies" in the creation of the stage environment serves the dual purpose of presenting acting as "work" involving bodily labor and the consequences of a violent, abusive, and exploitative environment on bodies as material entities. *QPH* demonstrates this even more vividly through the physical effort required of the actresses to move the coffins arranged to form a cross on the stage. A round disc above the coffins, symbolizing the moon and the cycle of womanhood, ensures that "a bird's eye view of the coffins and the disc gives the universal symbol for woman."

That this imagistic representation is concretely rendered as gendered labor is ensured by the stage direction to Act 1 Scene 1: "It is important that the women in the ritual bear the burden of moving these coffins and that no stage hands come onstage." The "Almshouse yard" in this play serves a similar purpose in the activities taking place in the harsh environment: "The Chorus, Queenie, Pearlie and Hopie become old people in the yard engaged in various activities. Along the length of the yard extends a fence" ("*QPH*" 158, 169). Although a fence protects the yard, demarcating it as a shelter for old and disabled people, the space is not safe from the violence in its

Illustration 2.2 Queenie, the Pukkumina mother, played by Bev "Didi" Elliot, addresses her flock in the collective creation of *QPH*, directed by Hertencer Lindsay. The actresses stand on coffins with a cutout of the moon as backdrop. Photo courtesy Sistren and Honor Ford-Smith.

immediate environs. The "Dreads," or the rough young boys in the neighborhood, stand on the other side of the fence to threaten the inmates. In *QPH* the fenced yard represents a porous border between two topographies: the violent social space outside the almshouse and the relatively (although not absolutely) safe but materially deprived existence within it.

There is a long tradition of Jamaican literary uses of the yard setting and critical analysis of the drama of yard life. Among others, Roger Mais and C. L. R. James have fictionalized yard life in their novels *Brother Man* and *Minty Alley*. Erna Brodber's study on the subject describes the yard as an instrument of transition from country to town and a major unit of community life in urban areas. Another common characteristic of yard communities identified by Brodber is an inherent mistrust of post-pubescent female sexuality along with parents' lack of openness about biological and sexual processes.

The consequent pattern of teenage pregnancy, familial rejection, lack of economic support from the male partner, and destitution is explored in both *Bellywoman* and *QPH*. The Chorus of masked women on stage articulate this pattern ritualistically, particularly since the events recounted in the plays are based on either the actresses' personal memories or patterns of collective memories identified in Sistren's research. The life stories enacted in these plays indicate that the social hypocrisy sanctioning sexuality only within conjugality, combined with lack of economic security for single mothers

54 *Feminist Visions and Queer Futures in Postcolonial Drama*

Illustration 2.3   Miss Freeman (Cerine Stephenson) and Goddy (Lillian Forster) spy on Yvonne and her boyfriend in this second production of *Bellywoman Bangarang*, directed by Rawle Gibbons in 1992. Photo courtesy Sistren and Honor Ford-Smith.

abandoned by their partners, was an urgent cross-class issue needing redress. One of the consequences of politicization of teenage pregnancy and female destitution during this period was the establishment of the Family Court in the Kingston and St. Andrew parishes in Jamaica. Gloria Cumper's monograph on this important institution comments on existing lacunae in the Maintenance and Bastardy (later Affiliation) Laws in Jamaica—particularly the fallacious morality distinguishing between children born in and out of wedlock—in court decisions regarding maintenance that "reinforc[e] the link between poverty and birth out of wedlock" (2). Cumper forecasts that the political will to remedy legal lacunae and offer social services "will depend

Illustration 2.4 Didi (Vivette Lewis) listens as her mother (Lorna Burrell) expresses concern over her pregnancy in *Bellywoman Bangarang*. Photo courtesy Sistren and Honor Ford-Smith.

on the priority accorded to claims . . . in the consideration of expenditure in the social welfare field" (62). The state is responsible for this 'action' since it is deemed the guarantor of social welfare of teenage mothers and elderly women, existing on the margins of society. Cumper's and Brodber's research identifies the social conditions typical to rural and urban working class communities with the aim of suggesting and securing changes in government policies, particularly regularization of living conditions and financial support for single mothers.

This belief in the efficacy of state interventionism and a commitment to women's empowerment is echoed in Sistren's focus on gendered and sexual oppression in postcolonial Jamaica. Sistren used many of Friere's techniques such as "conscientization" or dialogue as "continuing aspect of liberating action" while conceptualizing their plays (where the gap between literate and nonliterate members was mediated by dialogic interaction and improvisations) and in community outreach workshops. Boal's translation of Friere's ideas into theatre and his reinterpretation of rituals as structures of oppression are also relevant to an analysis of Sistren's plays.[5] For Boal the "social code" that "does not answer the needs and desires of the people to whom it is addressed" turns into a ritual that is the "vehicle for some form of oppression" (*Games* 184). The rhythmic chanting of "Bull inna di pen and him cyan come out! [Bull in the pen and he can't come out]" in *Bellywoman,* followed by a list of the "pens" imprisoning the girls' lives—"Punishment Pen," "Run-All-About-Pen," "Church Pen," and "School Pen"—indicates the oppressive social codes of housework, religion, and educational institutions governing their lives (107). The "shawling" that is part of the *Ettu* ceremony in *QPH* illustrates Sistren's use of ritual as a "form of approach" to Forum theatre, creating the conditions to ensure that it is "theatre first and foremost, and not solely forum" (Boal, *Games* 189). Sources of oppression are imagistically represented through articles of clothing used in shawling the three women. Hopie's aunt examines a "skirt" which she was to have sewn as domestic servant to the family. While talking about Pearlie's engagement, her mother rearranges a "chiffon scarf" around her neck that almost "chokes" her. Queenie, the Pocomania mother, wears an "elaborate headwrap" symbolizing her leadership of the church group. The red-colored wrap she is forced to wear instead of a white one earns the ire of the church members who feel that she is unrighteously trying to usurp leadership in the absence of a male preacher. These articles of clothing indicate the pens constricting the lives of women in an inherently patriarchal society that exerts the strictest possible control over women's sexual and economic autonomy.

An important aspect of the liberatory premise of the theatre of the oppressed, modified and later challenged by Sistren, is verbalization of oppression. In the words of one member of the group, "By talking my problems I find that others have the same and even worse ones [. . .] We shouldn't shame to talk because by talking we help not ourselves alone but also other women" (Jasmine Smith qtd. in Cobham and Ford-Smith). One of the most common concerns in Berenice Fisher's feminist evaluation of Boal's methodology is that the focus on verbalization and action leads to a neglect of political reflection that undermines the importance of research and documentation. In their move from experience and research to performance, Sistren did not neglect political reflection to focus exclusively on verbalization. The safe space for and encouragement of political reflection provided by the group enabled a successful transmutation of experience into performance: "Di group was a way to keep out of di area. Me was so glad fi di relief from di violence. Me used to stay out till all various hours"

(*Lionheart* 253). In addition, although scarcity of resources prevented complete documentation of their methodology, Sistren realized early on the importance of an archive, leading to the formation of a research component. While ritual and testimony provided the explicit framework to the plays, Freirian and Boalian techniques, with adequate consideration for political reflection and research, structure the translation of experience into performances of active female citizenship.

Sistren's dramaturgy thus exists on a continuum with the work of Freire and Boal in Latin America, itself influenced by Bertolt Brecht's conceptualization of the function of theatre and Frantz Fanon's views on the role of culture in anticolonial resistance. Recent analyses have directed attention to the relevance of Fanonian ideas to postcolonial cultural conditions in Jamaica. David Scott reads Fanon through Foucault's theories to "keep alive a productive tension between, on the one hand, a politics that aims to find a ground for consensus, and on the other, an ethics that is suspicious of any normative foreclosing of the assertion of difference" (*Refashioning* 201). Although Scott's argument does not take this direction, the productive tension between consensus and difference is especially relevant for feminist cultural activism if racial, class, educational, and sexual differences are not to be subsumed under a paradigm of feminist sisterhood. Since its inception Sistren's members were aware of and sensitive to these differences. They attempted to minimize these by workshops in verbal, mnemonic, and physical exercises, improvisational techniques, collective dramaturgy based on shared life experiences, and consensual decision making in the groups' internal organization.

WELFARE CITIZENSHIP IN ADJUSTED DEVELOPMENT

Ford-Smith has used the rubrics funding and democracy—as processes internal to the organizational structure of the group and as external factors impacting on its functioning, particularly the social contexts of the performances as events—to analyze Sistren's struggle for survival in the changed political scenario in Jamaica. *Bellywoman* and *QPH* indicate that a functional democracy does not necessarily guarantee its citizens basic rights. This may be either due to lack of funds for welfare services or because the emphasis on welfare differs according to the ideological and economic proclivities of the government in power. If freedom of expression is another one of the cornerstones of democracy, then this too is compromised in certain conditions, as happened with Sistren in 1981 when the filming of *QPH* was terminated by the JLP government's perception of its subversive intent. Jacqui Alexander's identification of heteropatriarchy as the "organizing episteme" of a "homosocial, homophobic, and in a real sense, a morally bankrupt state to position itself as a patriarchal savior to women, to citizens, to the economy, and to the nation" is useful in examining the early phases of the PNP's social welfare policies in relation to women, their curtailment due to the economic crisis, and their subsequent abandonment by the JLP government ("Erotic" 99). As a woman-centered organization in a region where the label feminist is associated with a first-world movement and often carries negative connotations, Sistren's position was rendered precarious once the democratic socialist conditions under which it had emerged changed. Sistren's articulation of gendered and sexual citizenship was thus most necessary at a time when it was also extremely difficult and dangerous for a women's group to stage such opinions.

The two institutions indicating a breakdown of social services are the provision of health care in *Bellywoman* and services for the aged, disabled, and poor in *QPH*. The discrepancy between ideal and actual rights guaranteeing equality to women in theory but not in practice is noted in the plays. Such piecemeal equality is critiqued by one of the nurses in *Bellywoman*: "They like to think we have men to support us. That way they pay us less." The motif of the nurses' strike, introduced in the second production of the play, indicates the situation of overworked employees in the health care system leading to conditions such as these: "Last night a mother held out her dead child to me. She'd been waiting six hours for attention" (85). *QPH* indicates a similar withdrawal of medical services to the poor and their reliance on non-biological structures. Queenie remarks that she cannot afford "sulphur bitters" from the drugstore for her "sugar" problem but that a friend helps her with herbal cures for her ailments. Despite the pattern of failed familial and institutional support sketched previously, the women refute victimhood by forming alternative support networks. The four women in the labor ward in *Bellywoman* help Marie deliver her child since the nurses are on strike for better wages and working conditions; the old women in *QPH* lend a helping hand to each other, in some measure compensating for the lack of facilities. These women make do with their slender resources without blaming the caretakers or their surroundings.

Thus the plays reveal a dualistic conception of the state as an entity that both withdraws support to the most vulnerable members of society yet is also the repository of demands made by these semicitizens, not merely as welfare but as their just entitlements. Although their unwaged status in the economy and their 'immoral' sexuality severely disadvantages them, the women claim citizenship and refuse to be characterized as recipients of charity.

The women are not represented as a homogenous group of the oppressed since they belong to different class strata, although they now face common problems such as lack of familial protection, abuse, and neglect: Yvonne and Marie in *Bellywoman* are middle class girls with some education; of the women in the almshouse depicted in *QPH*, Pearlie is light skinned and belongs to a prominent family. Yet neither class nor education proved to be safeguards against sexual abuse and familial ostracism. Like Sistren's collection of life stories in *Lionheart Gal* where "patriarchal dominance by men in the household often seals the severance of the social pact within the home itself," the plays direct attention to internalization and imposition of patriarchal sexual codes (Carr 227). These norms dictate that 'unproductive' sexuality severs the social pact at home, leading to a similar breakdown in the public sphere, especially through increased threat of sexual violence and lack of social services.

In both the social and theatrical arena, working class citizens' demands are presented as a process of interaction and negotiation between the state and various sections of the population such that there is a renewal of the social contract in the public sphere which will, hopefully, impact gender and sexual relations in the private sphere. Zillan Eisenstein has observed that internationally mandated "antigovernment imaginaries" often distort "possibilities available for creating democratic publics by assuming that all government, not just bad government, is the problem" and that such imaginaries ignore the history of success of "government largesse" (25). In the scene concluding *Bellywoman*, when the nurses on strike inform the women in the hospital about their talks with the government, they express a hope in government largesse as a right that needs to be earned through dialogue: "We got a few points sorted out but we have plenty more to fight for. It will be a long struggle before we have a decent health service." Didi responds by affirming the women's "support" for their struggle (131). Such interaction and negotiation is also evinced in Queenie's "witness" before the Investigative Commission inquiring into the causes of the almshouse fire in *QPH*. Her moving speech before a jury that concludes the play offers concrete suggestions for improving conditions of habitation for the inmates and a desire for reinstatement into the social fabric as productive citizens rather than as dependents: "We old but we active and waan occupation" (176).[6]

The pedagogic and dramatic techniques used by Sistren are based on a paradox identified by Michael Taussig and Richard Schechner in an interview with Boal. Schechner observes that although "opposition has always been the meat of political theatre," it has "worked only when the government sponsored it" (18). It is useful to remember this when examining Sistren's impact on Jamaican and Caribbean audiences and the struggles faced by the group once the political climate in Jamaica changed. The ritualistic dramatic techniques in *Bellywoman* have been analyzed as "an image of the cycle of failed nurturance which is played out from state to institution to individual and back to state" (Cobham 240). This analysis foregrounding "failed nurturance" uses as a point of contrast the image of collective nurturing epitomized in "Motherwoman," a composite character formed of three interlocking figures, who imitates a woman in labor and a midwife delivering a child in the first version of *Bellywoman* (Sistren and Ford-Smith 56). Familial ostracism of young girls and neglect of elderly women is matched by an institutional breakdown in the provision of medical care and hospitable living conditions that is compounded by cutbacks in social spending. Such a withdrawal of state largesse needs to be recovered through dialogue. The recent history of the democratic socialist government in Jamaica—although based on heterosexist familial ideology and notions of gendered state benevolence—provided Sistren with a model for imagining an alternative to the rhetoric of privatization while representing the disempowerment of Jamaica's most vulnerable citizens: teenage mothers and old women.

SLACKNESS, SODOMITES, AND MAN-ROYALS

An immediate consequence of such large-scale disempowerment was the constant threat of physical and sexual violence exacerbated by Sistren's existence as an exclusively women's group and its representations of non-biological kinship on stage. Sistren's testimonies "Veteran by Veteran," "Foxy and the Macca Place War," and "Eva's Diary" in *Lionheart Gal* attest to women's precarious existence in the period of bitter political rivalry in Jamaica in the 1970s when armed gangs of partisans terrorized supporters of other political persuasions. Women were easy targets in this game of political power. Sistren's personal correspondence during this period mentions several incidents of potential and actual violence against members occurring outside the sphere of performance in the perverse theatricality of politicized social spaces. Although their plays were extremely popular with Jamaican and Caribbean audiences in authorized spheres of performance such as theatres or local community gatherings, the group did experience moments of conflict with some audiences. For instance, among the audience who came to the 1982 performance of *Bellywoman* in Montego Bay, many were expecting to see a "sex farce" as advertised by the local organizer. The audience's unmet expectation of titillating sexuality on stage originated, in some measure, from the hypersexualized and misogynist representation of women in dancehall.

These expectations can be analyzed through Carolyn Cooper's opposition between "culture" and "slackness" that offers a way to understand differences between elite and popular citizenship in Jamaica. Slackness is Jamaican for sexually loose behavior, as described in a conversation between Didi and Jasmine in *Bellywoman:* "Di man pon top a di woman [...] A slackness" (100). Cooper's genealogy of Caribbean performance—Louise Bennett, Sistren, Bob Marley, and Michael Thelwell—can be read in conjunction with her commentary about hierarchies of slackness in dancehall DJ lyrics. While these hierarchies primarily denigrated gay men, they were also implicit in the charges leveled against Sistren and translated into speculations about the group members' sexual orientations, for, as Cooper writes, "heterosexuality, however indulgent its excesses, is infinitely superior to its homosexual variant. Heterosexuality is culture and class; homosexuality is slackness and ass" (*Noises* 148). Sistren's theatrical contribution to the "body" of Jamaican culture and society indicates that not all heterosexuality is "culture and class" since there are further hierarchies of slackness categorizing adult/teenage, marital/nonmarital, voluntary/commercial sexed bodies in a hostile environment.

Dramatizing popular cultural opinion in the tradition of Louise Bennett's performance poetry, which foregrounds the common woman as an enlightened, politically aware citizen critical of state apparati, Sistren's plays enact how sexual abuse of and physical violence against women are often justified by accusations of slackness. These accusations, leveled at victims of sexual violence, follow a predictable pattern of abuse: "Dutty gal / Old whore / Yuh did like it / Leggo gal / Ole pasart / A weh yuh used to" (*Bellywoman* 116). The burden of proof falls upon the victim rather than the perpetrator of sexual violence, and evidence of slackness is reason enough for rejection by family and guardians: in *Bellywoman* Goddy turns her ward, Yvonne, out of the house even though she has been raped by a boy in the neighborhood; in *QPH* Pearlie's sexual relations with the gardener lead to a similar fate. On the streets Pearlie is subject to harassment and innuendoes about her voracious sexuality. This verbal and physical violence is dramatically counterpoised against the female support systems in the plays also concretized through feminist cultural and political collectivity in Sistren. Such solidarity was suspect and subject to another connotation of slackness as unnatural sexual behavior when the group members were called "man-royals" and "sodomites." The proof of these accusations was thought to be self-evident in Sistren's depiction of the female body in its biological, sexual, and gendered socialization, performance techniques including cross-dressing by the actresses playing male roles, and supportiveness among the group.

Some scenes from the two plays under discussion frame this body within homosocial environments such as the labor room in a hospital or the female ward of the almshouse. These spaces question the state's relationship to its citizens but also favor non-biological, non-generational articulations of kinship. When Yvonne, Gloria, and Didi help birth Marie's baby in *Bellywoman,* they include female members of the audience in the birthing process. Didi expresses solidarity as collective female responsibility: "A di four a we in yah. All a we a go through di same pain. Suppose she was yuh? Yuh would a waan help too." This female supportiveness contrasts with a graphic image of violence described in one of the previous scenes when Marie is raped by a neighbor: "Two men appear with stockinged faces behind Marie. [. . .] They lift her till she hangs on the beams overhead. They stretch her legs apart, one on each of their shoulders. The Boxer aims his blows between her legs, the speed and rhythm increasing. After the climax, there is silence. Marie falls to the floor." The ritualized life-threatening violence of collective masculinity in this imagistic rendering of rape is juxtaposed against the ritualized birthing experience in the last scene of the play: "Breathe, Marie. All a we here. We not leaving yuh. [Marie squats. All breathe together and perform birth dance.]" (128, 116, 129).

In *QPH* sexual violence and harassment takes the form of arson threatening the lives and meager possessions of the already dispossessed women. The penultimate scene set in the female dormitory can be juxtaposed with the descriptions of random criminal acts by groups of idle young men: verbal and physical harassment of women; burning tenement areas or public buildings such as the almshouse. In this scene, as in the birthing ritual in *Bellywoman,* the rituals of female friendship counter the oppressive rituals that circumscribe the women in "pens." Breaking the circle of oppression involves counter-rituals of women's help, advice, and concern for each other including gestures of physical intimacy such sharing each other's beds and plaiting hair. Although connoting no more than female supportiveness, these can be interpreted as signs of a 'deviant' sexuality.[7]

Examining the significance of these counter-rituals through Theatre of the Oppressed (TO) methodology one encounters an impasse. In his recent works Boal has discussed the function of ritual in relation to bodily regimens but, as Philip Auslander observes, he has not "theorized the performing body in any continuous or systematic way" (124). Unlike his clear delineation of the role and function of ritual in TO acting and spect-acting (action by the spectators in a forum) techniques, Boal's conceptualization of the body in or out of performance can be gleaned only from the exercises and games for actors and nonactors.

One of these excercises involved an eighteen-year-old Swedish girl who "showed as a representation of oppression a woman lying on her back, legs apart, with a man on top of her [slackness], in the most conventional love-making position." When the spect-actors were asked to suggest an "Ideal Image," Boal reports that a man from the audience "approached and reversed the positions: the woman on top, the man underneath." A young woman from the audience made a counterimage of a "man and woman sitting facing each other, their legs intertwined" as a "representation of two human beings, of two 'subjects', two free people, making love" (*Games* 3). Auslander interprets this exercise as revealing "how ideology (in this case the ideology of male dominance) is expressed at the most basic material level through everyday, habitual routines and regimens of the body" and "how non-hegemonic ideologies might be expressed through bodily counter-routines exploring physical alternatives to the oppressive regimen" (129). This interpretation needs to be supplemented by an awareness that while the lovemaking 'ritual' is here depicted in its oppressive dimensions of male control, Sistren's testimonies identify threat of sexual and economic violence as forces in maintaining that control. The group's expression of "bodily counter-routines exploring physical alternatives to the oppressive regimen" is material rather than merely sexual. The materiality of these physical alternatives is important when social violence makes survival a basic issue, as is evident from the women's caregiving rituals—sharing food, medicines, and clothes—in the two plays. Finally, without reifying traditional notions of motherhood and womanhood, the "Ideal Image" suggested by Sistren is one of collective nurturance and responsibility rather than the sexual egalitarianism proposed in the TO representation.

Boal comes closer to a material theorization of the body in his description of another subject treated through Forum theatre techniques in Sweden where "young people . . . depicted unproductive, contemplative old people, awaiting death, soliciting help to cross the road, holding up the traffic etc." The suggested ideal image was of the young folk helping the old people and acting as nurses to them in "scenes in which the old people were just as unproductive and useless as before." Boal's suggestion of an "Image of the Possible Transition" led to "a change in the attitude since the young people started to show old people engaged in activities which were productive or creative, or at least not merely contemplative; for example, looking after children, reading a book, painting a picture, teaching etc" (*Games* 5). At the end of *QPH*, Queenie's speech paints a picture of this possible transition by arguing for old people as productive and creative members of society rather than a burden: "Mek space fi we plant and do lickle cultivating. We old but we active and waan occupation" (176).

An all-female cultural, economic, and emotional environment, Sistren was perceived as a threat to male-dominated institutions such as the clientelistic systems of patronage operating in public spaces in legal and extralegal forms.[8] Expressing demands for unqualified citizenship rights for supposedly unproductive members of society, specifically teenage mothers and elderly women, earned the group a reputation of being radical in the conservative political climate of the 1980s. Early on in the decade Sistren was told to leave the Jamaica School of Drama as it was felt that the group had outgrown the resources offered by this institution. The funding crisis faced by the group at this juncture was directly related to the fact that cultural work was not recognized as 'productive' and did not fit into national and international paradigms of 'development'. Ironically, Sistren became susceptible to the very same criteria about the morality of public spending (this time on cultural development that yielded intangible, unquantifiable returns) that it was dramatizing in relation to disenfranchised women.

Boal has mentioned at least two problems associated with TO techniques in economically and socially unstable locations: scarcity of resources that makes it difficult to justify expenditure on consciousness-raising educational and cultural programs with no obvious material gains, even where the will for expending state resources for such programs is present; and the potential violence faced by cultural workers in hostile environments (*Legislative*). As mentioned previously, the socially conflictual situation in Jamaica had a direct impact on Sistren, leading to the increased threat of violence and censorship in the politically charged climate of the 1980s.

Sistren was perceived as "pro-woman" and hence "anti-man," leading to "all the negative stereotyping attached to such a label in the Jamaican context" (Cobham and Ford-Smith viii). Among the factors which led to the group being charged with encouraging homosexuality were an uninhibited discussion and exploration of each other's bodies by adolescent girls curious about their sexuality in the plays, the almost complete absence of positive images of men in the households and the social landscape detailed, and the male roles played by some actresses. In *Bellywoman* Didi's experiences of a tough life with her mother, who did not receive any support from her husband, embitter her against heterosexist domesticity. A similar situation is described in *QPH* when Queenie rejects Sister James's suggestion to take up with another man and save a little something for herself once the Bishop abandons her. Her response that she "nuh want to depend pon no man again," and her encouragement to other inmates of the almshouse to be financially independent by starting some small business for themselves signals a possible rupture in the all too common and oft-repeated pattern of financial distress leading to unwanted sexual relations (*QPH* 168, 175).

Homosexuality was never represented or discussed in any of Sistren's productions, although there is some reference to alternative sexual preferences in the group's published narration of their life experiences.[9] The lesbian women in the group chose not to be out in the performances. Ford-Smith mentioned in an interview that the group steered clear of representing alternative sexuality owing to intense homophobia in Jamaica. Her clarification of Sistren's different focus in the "sexuality battles" is understandable, but I believe that the group's concentrated attentiveness to female sexuality did pave the way for feminist-oriented mobilization in Jamaica and the Caribbean that concerns itself with the provision of legal rights and full citizen status for sexual minorities. Although the plays offer a timely critique of heterosexual conjugality as the preferred mode of sexual and social organization and kinship, it seems overly optimistic of Cooper to propose that Jamaican society is "slowly moving in the direction of giving visible cultural space to homosexuality" (*Sound Clash* 177). I suggest, more cautiously than Cooper, that Sistren's critique of the fallacious morality associated with heterosexual conjugality led to staging of alternative forms of kinship that have always been a part of Caribbean society, but had not till then been presented as viable social arrangements of choice from a feminist perspective.

FURTHERING CARIBBEAN FEMINISM

In a lecture on the International Women's Decade (1975–1985) Jamaican feminist historian Lucille Mathurin Mair reviews the successes and failures of national and international policies meant to integrate women into developmental processes by stating that "bread-and-butter concerns" were at the heart of women's political mobilization in this decade, which saw women "propelled by moral outrage on the public stage" (9–10).[10] Sistren's public staging of this moral outrage challenged the economic morality of supposedly welfarist democracies such as Jamaica on the wider international stage of the global public sphere. *Bellywoman* and *QPH* are cultural acts questioning the quality of democracy in Jamaica by presenting an alternative to the state-sponsored ideology of male citizen employed in the formal economy as the primary agent of national development. Sistren's dramatization of economically, socially, and emotionally supportive networks of subaltern women outside the framework of heterosexual monogamous (re)productive womanhood, written out of scripts of national development as welfare recipients, forces an acknowledgment that "good citizenship" often acts as the site of recolonization when connected to women's and men's proper gender roles as procreating, heterosexual, married citizens (Spurlin, "Broadening" 195). Sistren itself emerged as one such female support network in the national, regional, and global public sphere—initially outside institutional structures, but soon acquiring an organization in which conceptions of democracy and funding were as essential as in the structures external to it—engaged in critical dialogue with the Jamaican state to provide economic and sexual security to girls and women. Its performances used techniques of a pedagogy and theatre of the oppressed to politicize subaltern women to a better understanding of their position as citizens in the processes of democracy and development impacting on their public and private lives.

Any definition of sexual citizenship involves considering women's sexual disempowerment as a consequence of their socio-economic vulnerability in postcolonial democracies. *Bellywoman* and *QPH* comment on the quality of democracy in postcolonial Jamaica by presenting class, gender, and sexuality as linked axes. Drawing on various levels of social analysis that encompassed economic, political, legislative, and cultural resources, Sistren's accessible performances were conceptualized on the premise that "women's bodies have been ideologically dismembered within different discourses." In Jacqui Alexander's resonant phrase, the group recognized that "the work of decolonization consists as well in the decolonization of the body" ("Erotic" 374). The women's movement in the Caribbean set about this work of decolonization through an evaluation of the place of women in programs of national development. This involved reconceptualizing legal provisions on the status of women and children in marital and extramarital alliances, redefining notions of women's work in the private and public domains, and granting adequate recognition to extended female kin and nonkin support networks, but not a consideration of non-heterosexual familial arrangements (Cumper; Ellis; Senior). Such work continues to be necessary despite the progress made since Sistren performed in the 1970s and 1980s. Although it would be anachronistic to point to lack of discussion of homosexuality in the women's movement in the Caribbean given the virulent homophobia, the forms of kinship expressed in Sistren's performances can be seen as important moves to emphasize the connection between sexuality and survival.

66 *Feminist Visions and Queer Futures in Postcolonial Drama*

Two examples illustrate the forms this work has taken. The first is an organization called Jamaica Freedom for Lesbians, Gays and All-Sexuals (JFLAG), which continues the efforts of the Gay Freedom Movement that emerged around the same time as Sistren in the late 1970s. In 2001, JFLAG made a representation before the special parliamentary committee appointed to review the Charter of Rights in Jamaica to argue for "the same rights and protections under law, which have already been afforded the majority of Jamaican society" by pointing out that such inclusion "will only enhance the right of self-determination and self-expression for all citizens in this plural society" ("Parliamentary Submission"). Although this forceful plea does not appear to have had much effect toward the inclusion of an anti-discrimination clause on sexual orientation in the proposed charter, activists remain hopeful of the possibility.

The second example indicates the fluctuating fortunes and impact of Sistren in Jamaica. In 2004 the building on Kensington Crescent, Kingston, which housed Sistren, burnt to the ground, destroying the space and the materials within, a case of 'art imitating life imitating art' when one recalls the fire and the death of a hundred inmates in the Eventide Almshouse which was the impetus for *QPH*. Not only did the fire destroy the Sistren archive, it also made the group temporarily homeless thereby severely curtailing the scope of its already diminished activities following the migration and death of many of the original members. Sistren was down but definitely not out. In January 2009 Sistren performed a play demanding legalization of abortion before the Jamaican parliament, indicating its continued relevance and strong voice. Like JFLAG's presentation, it is hope that sustained Sistren's performance since the bill legalizing abortion has not yet been passed into law.

My account of the political consciousness that Sistren sought to inculcate has been framed by a critique of the Jamaican state's preservation of the heterosexual family as essential to its programs of gender justice to the exclusion of alternative forms of biological and non-biological kinship existing in Jamaican society. Looking forward, or "moving on," to use the title of a documentary on Sistren, the recent mobilization of sexualities in Jamaica can also be seen as an extension of Sistren's transformation of public spaces by a politicization of sexuality that was consistently labeled deviant. Since the privatized Jamaican state has divested itself of the responsibility of economic and material well-being for all by investing its energies in cultural, moral, and social consolidation through exclusion of economic and sexual deviancy, a project like Sistren's is as urgent today as it was nearly thirty-two years ago when the group was formed.

Part II
India

3 A People's Theatre from Delhi in Alliance with the Women's Movement

> The other day I met my audience.
> In a dusty street
> He gripped a pneumatic drill in his fists.
> For a second
> He looked up. Rapidly I set up my theatre
> Between the houses.
> He looked expectant.
>
> (Bertolt Brecht, "My Audience" 147)

When Jana Natya Manch (Janam) began performing in 1973, the women's movement in India was beginning to direct its focus on domestic and social violence, the state's apathy, and often its active collaboration in such violence. Janam's program of taking theatre to the doorsteps of the people adapts and modifies Brecht's vision of a theatre for the working classes in the Indian context. Extending the examination of Dennis Scott's adaptations of Brecht and Grotowski that postulate the heterosexual, male worker as the model Jamaican citizen-audience, this chapter directs attention to citizen-audiences of Indian drama directly influenced by Brecht's vision. Although Brecht created powerful women characters like Mother and Mother Courage in his plays to indicate the important role of women in class-based struggles, he predicates the male worker holding a "pneumatic drill in his fists" as the representative audience for street theatre. Emphasizing women's rights as citizens, the chapter seeks to revise Brecht's emphasis on a gender-neutral (hence implicitly male) spectatorship by examining the documented and possible impact of Janam's performances on multiple audiences, especially women from varying class backgrounds, including workers, activists, and students.

Janam's performances arose out of a vacuum in left-oriented cultural work following the demise of the Indian People's Theatre Association (IPTA) in the late 1950s. Safdar Hashmi, then a student at Delhi University, and a few of his friends decided to revive the IPTA under the name People's Theatre Front (the acronym Janam means "birth" in Hindi). Since its formation in the 1970s the group has maintained its primary focus on working classes but also directed attention to gendered and sexual discrimination with an awareness that these cannot be subsumed under a class politics even as they cannot be divorced from it. One of the key premises of Janam's cultural program is that women's struggle for equal rights is part of the larger struggle for workers' rights. The group's engagement with the women's movement's response to sexual violence from the 1970s to recent times can be charted from its first women-centered performance of *Aurat* (*Woman*) to later productions such as *Police Charitram* (*Characterizing Police*) and *Aartanaad* (*Echoing Wail*).[1] My attention to these particular plays is dictated by the mutually facilitating relationship between the women's movement and the efforts for a socially relevant theatre as revealed in the work of the Sistren Theatre Collective from Jamaica. Like Sistren, Janam's focus on community and kinship is an essential aspect of its transformative vision. Continuing the discussion from Part I, this chapter also examines how the interaction between the women's movement and socially oriented drama in India has impacted upon the state by holding it accountable for violation of women's rights and the response it has elicited in the form of legal measures and academic institutionalization of women's issues.

STREET THEATRE IN POSTCOLONIAL TIMES

Janam's plays are among the earliest experiments in postcolonial street theatre influenced by and influencing other groups with a similar ideological focus. Eugene van Erven's extensive research and documentation of Asian theatre reveals certain features of activist theatre that he calls the "theatre of liberation." Noting the decline of political theatre in the West, Van Erven contends that the Asian theatre of liberation can "invigorate the increasingly depoliticized Western theatre" (233). Listing characteristics of this kind of work, Van Erven observes that political repression often serves as a catalyst for the theatre of liberation. Its main agents of development are middle class, city-based artists, many of whom, although certainly not all, are left-oriented, and conceive of themselves as "generating an alternative, people controlled culture through small scale media to provide a healthy democratic counterweight to the often manipulative, doctrinaire, and mind-narrowing culture disseminated by the official and commercial media in their countries" (229). Van Erven mentions in particular the Philippines Educational Theatre Association (PETA) network as a model worthy of emulation for the development of political consciousness among postcolonial theatre practitioners. PETA's early experiments were in proscenium theatre, before repression under Philippines' president Ferdinand Marcos in the 1970s politicized it into a vehicle of resistance against the state's economic and cultural policies.

One notices a similar trajectory in Janam's development from an amateur theatre group, initially performing for the proscenium stage, later galvanized into a forum for left-oriented street performances in the post-Emergency period, although the group continued to perform for the stage as well.[2] Early on in Janam's career Safdar recognized that theatre faced intense competition from cheap, mass-produced entertainment disseminated through television and film, and that these could be powerful media for influencing opinion. His scriptwriting for television and affiliation with women filmmakers marked an astute recognition of the power of other forms of public communication besides theatre.[3]

In 1988 Safdar visited Pakistan for a conference of theatre workers in Lahore. The Karachi branch of his extended family was also involved in political theatre in the country. Pakistani theatre groups have adapted many of Janam's plays since political repression and control of mass media have ensured that, as in the Philippines, artists there look upon theatre as a viable medium of protest. In democratic India, Safdar's life and career stands as a testament to attempts at silencing progressive cultural action through violent repression. While performing with his group for workers in Sahibabad in 1989, Safdar was brutally murdered by hired thugs at the behest of a local election candidate tacitly supported by the party controlling the government. Janam has survived the tragic death of its talented founding member. It continues to perform political theatre in Delhi and outside it under the guidance of a core group of dedicated theatre workers. Of the plays discussed in this chapter, Safdar wrote *Aurat* and *Police Charitram* primarily as topical pieces, although these have subsequently outlived their topicality because the exercise of state power in public life has intensified over the past two decades in the country's rapid march towards globalization.

While street theatre often originates from political repression, it is by no means adequate to see it merely as a response to these conditions. In Asia, the work of PETA, Janam, and Pakistani theatre groups such as Ajoka and Lok Rehas demonstrates that street theatre has continued relevance as a mode of protest and awareness even when political conditions are no longer repressive. A special issue of the journal *Theatre and Drama Review* entitled "Social Theatre" discusses contemporary performance in Asia as influenced by Boal's use of theatre for popular education, consciousness-raising, and social action. Social theatre, according to the contributors, includes, but is not confined to, working class, feminist-oriented, and university-affiliated theatre groups working in urban metropolitan locations in India, Bangladesh, Pakistan, and other parts of South Asia. Although this nomenclature does not directly mention street theatre experiments, this is in fact the major form of social theatre in the Indian subcontinent today. Safdar and Janam's contribution to the development of this form cannot be underestimated. To cite only a few instances, student theatre groups such as Pandies' Theatre under Sanjay Kumar of Delhi University, or the Kirori Mal College Players at the same university follow many of the theatrical techniques popularized by Janam's performances to advance theatre as a political platform with varying degrees of success.[4]

This influence is not limited to metropolitan locations, for Janam has organized street theatre festivals that have brought together groups from various parts of India. The commemoration of Safdar's death anniversary through performance has become an annual feature of the theatrical scene in India. Janam has preserved Safdar's legacy of street theatre transcending cultural and geographical boundaries such as those between metropolitan and mofussil locations, Hindi and other South Asian languages, India and Pakistan, among others.

Janam has produced plays on concerns directly affecting the lives of common people such as the steep increase in public transport fares, bureaucratic corruption, globalization, and structural adjustment policies; on the commercialization and privatization of education; on socially conflictual situations arising out of communal riots and retrenchment of workers; and in solidarity with strikes called by the Center of Indian Trade Unions (CITU) and the Delhi University Teachers' Association (DUTA) for better wages and work conditions. These performances are checks and balances necessary to the functioning of a democratic society and cannot be analyzed simply as a cultural response to political repression. In an interview with Eugene van Erven shortly before his death, Safdar emphasized the value of cultural work in the process of democratization: "[S]hort story writers, poets, song squads, they all do important work in that spiritual field of the movement" (79).

The reference to the "spiritual field of the movement" from a committed Marxist like Safdar appears discordant only when we forget that literature and art can work towards the creation of an ethical sensibility about human life and labor, its value, worth, and meaning through what Rajeswari Sunder Rajan has called "literary affect." Sunder Rajan defines this affect by mentioning the underestimation of literature and art in extending our sympathies through representations of human suffering towards social transformation. A concrete instance is the significant decline in the rate of female infanticide in areas in Tamil Nadu where street theatre was employed as a means of "conscientization" (201–2).[5] Without valorizing the function of art or overestimating its importance, it needs to be underlined that the affective impact of such work as Janam's or Sistren's in Jamaica cannot be measured in quantitative terms, although the sheer numbers these groups have reached over the years since their inception is substantial.

This chapter focuses on Janam's interactions with audiences and the state by reading a representative selection of plays foregrounding women's concerns. These performances connect the group's dramatization of violence against women (beginning with the 1978 production of *Aurat*) to the autonomous feminist movement's activism against rape in India. While Janam's left-oriented cultural agenda differs from that of the autonomous feminist movement in India—which diagnosed structural factors responsible for violence against women and suggested legislative change as a partial remedy—the common ground of creating citizen-audiences aware of their rights connects them in mutually invigorating ways. In the process the analysis also foregrounds Janam's class-based conception of community in its early plays and its modification in recent performances.

AURAT AND ITS AFTERLIFE

The earliest of Janam's plays to deal with women's issues, *Aurat* is one of the most successful and, till recently, the most frequently revived of its productions. It was first performed in 1978 on the occasion of the Conference of Northern Indian Working Women. The conjunction of class and gender concerns in the play reflects the second-wave feminist movement's focus on social violence affecting women of all classes during the 1970s. Gail Omvedt's significant body of writings on socialist consciousness in women's mobilization makes the obvious but often-missed point about the differing agendas prioritized by rural and urban women, where the latter often speak of "oppression" and "resistance" in terms un-understandable to the former, whose hard lives reflect the reality of that oppression and the innovative culture of resistance they have developed. Omvedt's account of new social movements and the socialist tradition in India includes an assessment of the intersection between feminist and leftist ideologies which leads her to conclude that left organizers did not easily accept "nonclass" issues affecting women's lives (78). This is an important caveat to heed when examining left-oriented cultural work, particularly since Janam's unofficial but sustained links with the Communist Party of India (Marxist) provided the occasion for the performance of *Aurat*.

Janam's steady awareness of nonclass issues marks its development as a cultural forum with a coalitional rather than a single-issue cultural and political program. *Aurat* primarily dramatizes women's lives within the broad framework of class relations; it also succeeds in highlighting other seemingly nonclass sites of oppression, specifically the family and the state. My analysis of the play is based on interviews with Moloyashree (Mala) Hashmi and a film on Safdar that focuses on his life through Janam's productions of *Machine* and *Aurat*.

Aurat was cowritten and directed by Safdar and Rakesh Saxena with inputs from other members of the group. Various features of the play including the opening scene containing a poem by the Iranian revolutionary poet Marziah Oskoi, its division into vignettes depicting a woman's life from childhood to old age, and performance strategies such as one actress taking on all the female roles, were all decided upon by Safdar during the process of conceptualization (Mala Hashmi Interview 2004). Practical considerations determined the decision to have one woman play all the female roles since Mala was the only actress in the group at the time. Subsequently the play has been performed with the roles being split for two or even three actresses, yet Mala feels that the impact is greater when one woman appears before the audience in different roles. Along with this there is also a balancing out of other roles, presenting a multi- rather than unidimensional view of the characters: the father is a tyrant at home but a browbeaten worker in the factory; the actors playing the husband and the father-in-law enact facets of social violence in the interchangeable roles of ruffians and workers. What emerges is a multiplicity of social representations by the same actors at different times and locations in the play, initially dictated by the paucity of actors in the group, but soon evolving into a characteristic feature of Janam's performances.

Aurat begins with a poem that places the woman in the social roles determining her life: a mother, sister, daughter, and a "good" wife. Six male actors and the female actress recite the poem to present a generalized picture of a working woman as the victim of sexualized violence who analyzes her subjugation:

> I too am a worker
> I too am a farmer
> My body is a picture in pain
> The fire of hatred burns me
> And you shamelessly declare
> That my hunger is imaginary
> That my nakedness is a dream.
> A woman whose importance
> Cannot be described by any word
> In your obscene language (85).[6]

The actress playing the female roles emerges from the circle of male actors surrounding her; the encirclement visually conveys her circumscribed existence; her stepping out of it is an act of defiance (see 3.1 below). She steps out of the circle to directly address the audience at various moments in the play.

Two of the five vignettes comprising the play convey gender-based educational and employment disparities drawing support from socially sanctioned

Illustration 3.1 Moloyashree Hashmi amid the circle of actors in a performance of *Aurat* in Delhi in 1995. Photograph by Jana Natya Manch, Delhi, India.

patriarchy. These scenes may appear anachronistic to contemporary audiences since feminist activism has won significant victories in the twenty-five years since the play was first performed. The audience's consciousness of possible anachronisms is addressed in the play: "These days we are not treated as badly, but even so, we are still considered a burden, hence my marriage was arranged. The ceremony is today. The boy earns two thousand five hundred rupees per month in the mill where my brother works" (86). The next two scenes depict her stepping outside the family in the public sphere, as a student seeking admission to college, and as a graduate seeking employment. Sexual violence is a constant subtext in all the scenes. From childhood to adulthood

Illustration 3.2 The woman worker holds up a red flag in Janam's 1981 performance of *Aurat* for a working class audience in Haryana just outside Delhi. Photograph by Jana Natya Manch, Delhi, India.

she faces sexual harassment, particularly from those in positions of authority such as the police and her employers. The vignette concluding the play is of the woman as an exploited factory worker whose politicization into a union supporter—a change from her initial reluctance to join the union—marks a transformed consciousness. The last scene, where she holds aloft a red flag after the police have felled the male workers, is reminiscent of Brecht's play *Mother,* in which a united front against exploitation invokes the woman as a revolutionary (see 3.2).

Janam's message of capitalist and patriarchal responsibility for gendered inequality has remained relevant over the years. The group continued to perform *Aurat* regularly for various audiences till 1995 with minor alterations to the central character, the woman, who Mala feels was somewhat naïve in the earlier productions. In subsequent performances she has been made more canny and wise in the ways of the world (Mala Hashmi Interview 2004).

The play has been also performed in translation in India, Pakistan, Bangladesh, and Sri Lanka. Fawzia Afzal Khan describes Tehrik-e-Niswan's presentation of *Aurat* as *Aurat ki Kahani* (*A Woman's Story*) on the occasion of International Women's Day in 1997 in Pakistan as directing attention to "the triple constraints—religion, patriarchy, and capitalism [. . .] working hand in glove to crush the female protagonist of the play." In Pakistan the added element is religious oppression, represented in the play "by the radically symbolic gesture of the protagonist throwing off her *dupatta*—the chador like long scarf most Pakistani women are enjoined by Islamic ideology to drape over their heads and/or bosoms as a gesture of female modesty and purity" (Afzal-Khan, "Unholy" 75). Afzal-Khan notes responses to this production in the predominantly Christian Dastagir Colony in Karachi—with an audience including women of all ages, some girls, and several young men—as identification with the events depicted. Such identification, that Mala calls "a point of relation," is one of the most common responses to the play.

Janam has performed *Aurat* for college audiences in Delhi and elicited a stunned silence. It has also been presented at factories and nonmetropolitan locations before an audience of several hundred people, leading to two kinds of reactions (see cover image). The first and most common one is of open appreciation when men and women tell Mala that the play reminds them of their daughters' situation and that she is very brave to raise such issues in public. The other kind of response is a complete denial and lack of acknowledgment that the gendered discrimination depicted in the play takes place in the audience's homes.

Aurat highlighted concerns that were to become central to Janam's representation of women's lives such as the threat of sexual violence faced by girls and women on a daily basis, the indifferent and often instigatory role of the police in these circumstances, the family's concern with the preservation of women's chastity as linked to its "honor" and standing in society, and the hapless plight of an initially reluctant but eventually politicized woman worker. Community in this play assumes a specific class dimension in tune with the Marxist credo "Workers of the world, unite!" Feminists in India and other countries in South Asia have ensured the play's afterlife by a strategic use of the script in their campaigns to emphasize various nonclass conceptions of community that disrupt the workers' solidarity presented by Janam as incipient community consciousness.

STREET THEATRE MEETS FEMINIST ACTIVISM

Janam's earliest foray into women's issues in *Aurat* mentioned rather than emphasized the rampant misuse of state power, particularly the police. When the group collaborated with feminists in Delhi to produce a play on the anti-rape agitation, its immediate context was the issue of "custodial rape" or rape of women in police custody that had galvanized women's groups since the Mathura case in 1972.[7] This collaboration between feminist and cultural activists resulted in the play *Police Charitram* (*Characterizing Police*). Janam had joined a group of fifteen different women's and student's organizations to protest against rape and sexual harassment of women through this performance, inviting an analysis of Safdar's statement that "although JANAM didn't agree with the Joint Action Committee's treatment of rape as an isolated phenomenon, it did use its agit-prop street theatre to mobilize public opinion to join the women's day rally on 8th March" (*Right* 19).

The following account of the Mathura case, a landmark in Indian feminist legal history, is derived from analyses offered by Flavia Agnes and Vibhuti Patel.[8] The picture that emerges from Agnes's and Patel's collation and analysis of data on the incidence of rape in India is a dark one. Often the custodians of public safety become the perpetrators of violence by rampantly misusing the authority vested in them. Some common causes of what has come to be called custodial rape are: for satisfying prurient desires by those in positions of authority in the police, army, forest departments, and welfare and medical institutions; a method of repression and warning to women against participation in social and political protest movements; and a mode of torture for men and women in custody for political or criminal reasons.[9] While girls and women from lower castes and classes are particularly susceptible to sexual assault from authorities, women (and indeed, men and children) from other classes and castes are by no means safe from this form of violence.[10]

The infamous case in which Mathura, a sixteen-year-old tribal girl, was raped by two policemen when she was brought to the police station by her brother on the charge of elopement, falls into the first category of the causes just listed. Constable Ganpat raped Mathura in the compound of the police station, a drunk Constable Tukaram looked on, while her relatives waited outside. Ganpat came out to inform Mathura's relatives that she had already left the police station. When Mathura came out of the police station she told her family that the policemen had raped her. The incensed relatives, who had already attracted a crowd threatening to beat up the policemen and burn down the police station, were persuaded to disperse. The police also managed to influence the medical examination that took place some twenty hours later. When the case came up for hearing, the Sessions Court judgment stated that Mathura was "habituated to sexual intercourse," there was "no satisfactory evidence to prove that Mathura was below 16 years of age [and hence a minor]," and that she was "a shocking liar whose testimony is riddled with falsehood and improbabilities" leading to the conclusion that she had not been raped although sexual intercourse had taken place. The Bombay High Court reversed this acquittal and convicted the two constables under Sections 354 (indecent assault) and 376 (rape) of the Indian Penal Code. The High Court judge stated that the Sessions Court had erred in not appreciating the difference between "consent" and "passive will" since "mere passive or helpless surrender induced by threats or fear cannot be equated with desire or will" (Agnes, "Anti-Rape" 104–5).

The immediate motivation for the anti-rape agitation in various parts of India was the Supreme Court's reversal of the High Court judgment in 1978. The convicted constables were acquitted because the Supreme Court refused to believe that Mathura was so overpowered that she could not make an attempt to resist sexual advances. Her allegation of rape was held to be a lie since she had not raised any alarm, leading the court to posit that sexual intercourse but no rape had occurred. A year after the judgment, four legal activists—Upendra Baxi, Lotika Sarkar, Vasudha Dhagamwar, and Raghunath Kelkar—wrote a public letter to the Chief Justice of India stating that the judgment "snuffs out all aspirations for the protection of human rights of millions of Mathuras" and demanded a reopening of the case. The letter was circulated to progressive individuals, women's organizations, and civil liberty groups around the country, eliciting a tremendous response in the form of a countrywide agitation on 8 March 1980 (Agnes, "Anti-Rape" 106–11). In the interim period many other instances of custodial rape and fabricated evidence such as the Rameeza Bee case in Hyderabad (1978) and the Maya Tyagi case in Bhagpat (1980) had come to light, making sexual violence the rallying point for the autonomous women's movement in India.

Janam's street play was part of this agitational response planned by Delhi-based feminists to frame rape within a broader matrix of violation of citizens' and workers' rights. The following account of the incidents comprising the structure of the play indicates how Janam accomplishes this goal. In the circular acting area a city dweller, the prototypical citizen, is eating. Suddenly three thugs leap towards him. One gags him and snatches the plate from his hand, yet another takes his wallet, and the third stabs him. As the man falls, and the thugs are running away, three policemen leap into the acting area. Uttering platitudes such as "The duty of the police is to ensure law and order, protect the life and property of the city dwellers. Everything, everything, everything must be according to the rule of the law," they accept bribes from the thugs and let them off scot-free. As the actors carry away the body, another set of actors representing the Seth (capitalist) and four workers enter the central arena. The workers get to work on the orders of the Seth, slowly increasing their pace, punctuated by his orders to work faster.

One of the workers stops and declares that they're "men, not machines"; the other replies that they cannot work anymore, earning the abuse of the owner, "Bastards, how dare you argue with me? Get out!" While the workers are protesting against the unjust dismissal, the police enter and declaim on their duty to preserve law and order. Like the thugs in the previous scene, the Seth bribes the police, who shoot at the workers. Only after these two scenes have established a scenario of rampant lawlessness, systemic corruption, and capitalist exploitation does the performance address the central question of how these structures impact on women.

The next tableau is of a girl walking briskly on the road followed by a group of three thugs. Sensing danger she begins to run pursued by the thugs. She puts her hands on her ears, screams, and collapses on the ground. As the thugs encircle her (she is no longer visible to the audience) and start breathing heavily, the girl screams in terror. After a moment of silence the thugs get up, brush off their clothes, while the girl is senseless on the ground. While the girl is wailing the policemen arrive, repeating the sequence of actions in the first two scenes.

The policemen state: "Eve teasing is a crime under the law. Those found guilty will be subjected to the harshest sentence. Please help the police in this endeavor." Before the audience has recovered from the shock of this imagistic rendering of rape, euphemistically described as "eve teasing" by the police, the offenders bribe the police so that their official pronouncement changes to deliberate misinformation: "Yesterday night in a disreputable

Illustration 3.3 The girl slowly rises up after being raped by thugs in Janam's performance of *Police Charitram* at a Delhi University College. Photograph by Jana Natya Manch, Delhi, India.

80   *Feminist Visions and Queer Futures in Postcolonial Drama*

part of the city, a young girl was found unconscious on the roadside. It is suspected that her honor was violated. The girl has been admitted to the hospital. Investigations are under way." As the police take away the girl, a female vendor who earns her living by exchanging old clothes for utensils occupies the acting space. Circling the area while peddling her goods, she finds herself surrounded by the police. They fire a barrage of questions to establish her identity, her dwelling, and her business in the area before pouncing on her as they did on the girl in the previous vignette. After molesting her they reiterate the duties of the police by emphasizing how "these jobs fall under the jurisdiction of the police. None should interfere in these matters. Citizens should not take the law into their own hands" (*"Police Charitram"* 91).

In the final sequence of events, as the girl is led into the courtroom by a doctor, the capitalist appears as a judge, and the policemen follow. The woman vendor silently witnesses the proceedings where the judge exhorts the girl to "truthfully" narrate the encounter. Such a mode of cross-questioning is intimidating since the police threateningly repeat everything the judge asks the victim. The onus of proving the crime rests on the victim rather than the accused, although the doctor confirms that the girl's "honor" was violated. This case is dismissed due to lack of proof because the police declare that the girl was found alone in an unconscious state. Two dissenting voices in this scene are those of the citizen and the vendor. The former's plea that the judge should instruct the police to find evidence

Illustration 3.4   A street vendor is surrounded by the police in Janam's performance of *Police Charitram* at a Delhi University College. Photograph by Jana Natya Manch, Delhi, India.

is ignored, for, according to the judge, this is not the way things are done in India. After everybody leaves the courtroom, the vendor rises to question the meaning of citizenship in the nation: "What kind of a system is this, what kind of law and order? / What kind of justice, what kind of society, what kind of nation?" ("*Police Charitram*" 92).

By presenting public perception of sexual violation as loss of 'respectability' and 'honor', this play, like *Aurat,* foregrounds one of the key concerns feminists sought to politicize in the 1980s. Because rape continued to be seen as an attack on a woman's chastity and hence linked to the family's honor and standing in the neighborhood and the community, activists argued that the discussion obscured the nexus between patriarchal gender ideologies, norms of respectability, economic vulnerability, and abuse of authority evinced in the Mathura rape trial and in other incidents that were subsequently brought to light. Another important consideration, as pointed out by Amiya Rad, Sudesh Vaid, and Monica Juneja, is the "environment of fear of sexual assault in which women grow up right from childhood" (93). Despite an attempt to present a holistic account of the conditions that lead to sexual violence, in this play Janam focuses on it primarily as a law-and-order problem experienced by all women, including those of the lower class. However, *Police Charitram* does a fine job of enacting the "victim-baiting" which inevitably accompanies any report of rape, provided the case is registered by the police and manages to reach the court. Reiteration of the word "proof" no less than eight times in the last vignette indicates the most frequent reason for the rapist's acquittal is lack of evidence against the accused.

One of the ways in which the gains and losses of the women's movement have been assessed is through the legal consequences of the anti-rape campaign. Most activists agree that there were few effective gains since the amendment to the existing rape laws proposed by female members of parliament in 1980, that was finally passed as the Criminal Law (Amendment) Bill 1983, was retrogressive in its propositions. Among the key suggestions made by women's groups were: all state officials interacting with a rape victim should be women, the trial should be held behind closed doors (in camera), there should be stringent punishments for rapists to act as deterrence, and the victim's previous sexual history should not be admissible as evidence during the trial. The last proviso was particularly important for the police often used fabricated evidence of prostitution or sexual immorality by producing witnesses to destroy the (most often female) victim's credibility (Agnes, "Anti-Rape" 114–15). There is an indirect reference to this in *Police Charitram* when the police declare, "[A] young girl was found unconscious in a *disreputable* section of the city" (90, emphasis added). Not only did the lawmakers ignore this suggestion while drafting the bill; rather its final provisos strengthened the state at the expense of the victim's rights by making publicity about a rape trial a nonbailable offence, later amended to a bailable crime.

Among others, Agnes and Patel have commented that feminists retrospectively recognized many of these demands as politically naïve. For instance, the insistence on closed-door, in camera trials backfired because publicity of rape trials had in fact made rape one of the most recognizable forms of sexual violence against women and helped create a nationwide campaign against it. In the context of the national awareness campaign headed by women's groups, Safdar's remark that although Janam did not agree with the Joint Action Committee's view of rape as a single-issue phenomenon, it helped create "public awareness" about it, needs to be examined. Like the women activists, Janam played a role in conscientizing people about the incidence of sexual violence by revealing the discrepancy between the proclaimed and the actual functioning of the state through its characterization of police.[11] Perhaps it is also not coincidental that the Hindi equivalent of the word rape is never once used in *Police Charitram* and that the victim frames her violation in traditional terms as loss of honor since the vocabulary for it was derived largely from legal and juridical processes. The poem by Bertolt Brecht concluding *Police Charitram* presents a stark contrast between the bleakness of the present scenario and the bright future when "the system will change" (51).

Since the play's focus is engagement with state apparati, the idea of community is more amorphous than in *Aurat* where community was envisaged in class-specific ways. Mathura had become a rallying point for feminist activism in India calling for legal change marked by the recognition that legislation wasn't enough. Janam's politicization of rape would be carried a step further, not only in stylistic terms but also in its altered focus on community efforts to seek justice in cases of sexual violence, almost fifteen years later in *Aartanaad*.

COMMUNITY, KINSHIP, AND THE STATE

The years between *Police Charitram* and *Aartanaad* were marked by Safdar's death at the hands of hired hooligans in 1989. This inspired artists to direct attention to the state's culpability in suppressing forms of social drama perceived as subversive. This period was also characterized by nationwide campaigns to further publicize violence against women and to enact effective protective and punitive legislation. Growing incidence and reports of child rape led to a revival of the campaign based on lessons learned from the past. The long process of women's organizing and the piecemeal legislative gains were accompanied by an awareness that "any attempt to revive the campaign has to evolve ways of supporting individual victims and creating a climate where there is less social stigma, and rape is viewed as a criminal offence rather than as an offence against our chastity and morality" (Agnes, "Anti-Rape" 149). The state's response to the decade and a half of women's activism against violence—marked by the formation of independent organizations such as Forum Against Oppression of Women in Bombay, Sachetana in Calcutta, and Saheli in Delhi—was to institute the National Commission of Women (NCW) in 1992. Continuing the preceding discussion of Janam's performance of *Police Charitram* that drew upon autonomous feminist legal activism on rape, this section reads *Aartanaad* in the light of NCW's 1992 report on child sexual abuse and its 1997 seminar on child rape. It concludes with an account of recent legislation to bring rapists to book and provide speedy justice to victims.

Janam's use of improvisation to develop their plays as relevant to *Aartanaad* is discussed in detail by Sudhanva Deshpande in "Sculpting a Play," which mentions that the group started rehearsals with two "proto-scripts" that were used as "take-off points" to build scenes (104). Contrary to Jacob Srampickal's assertion, "Delhi's Janam does not even have a director," and that it follows the method of "democratic discussions during practice sessions" to arrive at the "final shape of the play," this is not the most common method followed by the group (127). According to Mala, although there are some difficulties in implementing this process of creation, the director provides a shape to the collective ideas (Interview 2004). While *Aartanaad* is one of the plays constructed collectively, it also carries the unmistakable stamp of Sudhanva Deshpande and Brijesh Sharma, whose directorial and poetic inputs give it the structure it finally acquired.

An emphasis on the private dimensions of the trauma of sexual abuse through a greater focus on the family and the neighborhood rather than the ostensible organs of security and justice, the police, makes this play less propagandist than Janam's previous productions. During the conceptualization process, Janam members had attended citizens' forum meetings where lawyers, teachers, and medical professionals attempted to arrive at a definition of rape. A three-month-long process of improvisation led to members' questions relating to sex education and poetry expressing a child's curiosity about these matters. The actors were responsible for creating the characters and scenes, such as the one in which the family talks about the abused child and the parents go to the police station to file a complaint. Sudhanva carved the structure out of all the material obtained through improvisations; Brijesh's poems were actually written before the play was conceptualized except one poem which originated as improvised dialogue, which he later converted into free-flowing prose (Mala Hashmi Interview 2004).

Based on this preparatory work to devise the form and content of the play, a collective decision was taken not to sensationalize the child as a victim of sexual assault but to direct attention as to what "we, as citizens" can do. Thus the raped child, although she is the subject of her family's, friends', neighbors', and the police's conversation, is never present on stage. The plot revolves on the after-effects of the rape of ten-year-old Preeti by her tutor Pawan Kumar, a resident of the same neighborhood. The play begins with the recitation of a poem by two women while the actors move into the acting area with colorful masks, scarves, and other props (see image 3.5). While a woman is reciting the poem, the removal of a veil-like scarf that she throws upwards imagistically indicates the child's violation.

The poem itself is based on tales told to children by elders in the family. Fantasy and terror in these tales are often a child's first introduction to the dangers she faces in real life:

84 *Feminist Visions and Queer Futures in Postcolonial Drama*

> Granny, granny, tell me a story
> Tell me about the dark man
> Tell me about the tree ghost
> Tell me about the man with the sack
> Who puts children in his sack and carries them away
> Tell me about the two-horned monster
> Who carried away the little princess.
> But most of all, tell me about the princess,
> What happened to her?
> Granny, I'm afraid
> I've blocked my ears, shut my eyes
> I'm so afraid I cannot speak, not even a word,
> But granny, don't stop your tale (93).

Ironically, the police constable provides the audience details about the events imagistically depicted in the play. He recounts the scenario narrated to him by Preeti's parents, who came to file a report in the police station. The constable's insulting mannerisms and accusations are leveled against the victim's parents. When told that Preeti was sent to the school one hour in advance of the regular time for her special tuition, he responds: "If you send the child one hour early then this is what will happen." He insists that the victim be brought in for interrogation. When Preeti's mother mentions that her daughter is at home, cut and bruised all over, the constable experiences a moment of fear-induced rather than compassionate self-reflection: "I thought to myself after all the girl is only 10 years old. And I too have

Illustration 3.5 Janam actors enter the central area wearing masks and scarves in the opening scene of *Aartanaad*. Photograph by Jana Natya Manch, Delhi, India.

children. And then if the officer had arrived he would have pounced upon me for not writing the report, that is why I picked up the pen, wrote out the report, and went home" (94). The policeman is not being aggressive but uncharacteristically considerate. However, his brutalization is part of the desensitization so that despite his best efforts to be fatherly to the little girl, the systemic callousness ingrained in him is revealed in his account.

Mala clarified that the policeman's dialogues were structured out of a stream-of-consciousness scenario given to the actor who was playing the role. Towards the end of the play there is another long monologue in which the policeman reports on his visit to ascertain the facts, and comments on the incident and on the frequency of incidents involving disappearance of children in the city:[12]

> Today the officer asked: "Who will go for the investigation?" I said: "I will go, sir." I went to Puranchand's house and asked his daughter: "Look child, tell me if he undid your skirt—she didn't say anything. Okay, tell me where exactly did he touch you?" Again she didn't say

Illustration 3.6 One of the narrators throws her *chunni* (scarf) to indicate the rape of the child, who never appears on stage in *Aartanaad*. Photograph by Jana Natya Manch, Delhi, India.

anything. I said: "Look child, I am like your father. Tell me, did he kiss you as well?" Still, she did not speak. Now, what can I do if she doesn't speak? When I go to the police station, the officer will ask: "Tell me Deendayal what did the girl say?" I will reply that the girl did not say anything. Then the officer will say: "Rascal, you don't know how to ask questions." Now you tell me, I have been serving the Delhi Police for 18 years, and I don't know how to ask questions? But the one thing I can say with conviction is no son of a gun can force that girl to answer. (102)

These two monologues addressed to the audience reflect the police's callous methods of functioning and underline the social and psychological impact of the incident. They also illustrate that twenty years of women's activism has not affected the way rape cases are handled by the authorities. Although Janam's focus in this play is less on the state than on the family and the neighborhood community, the functioning of law enforcement agencies in these direct addresses to the audience effectively illustrates the consequences of such violence on the victim and her family.

Janam's contextualization of the incident within the matrix of the family and the neighborhood as an extended family in *Aartanaad* relies on evoking sexual violence through dialogue rather than visual representation, as was also the case in *Police Charitram*. Social circumstances are presented in much greater detail in *Aartanaad* in contrast to the exclusive attention on the act of violence in *Police Charitram* or a generalized overview of the exploitation of women in *Aurat*. *Aartanaad* presents the abused child's mother as a pillar of strength as she attempts to restore normalcy. She concentrates on the need for legal action and a normal life for the child by encouraging childhood rituals, games, and storytelling, against the opinion of the family and the neighbors that Preeti has lost these rights since she has brought "shame" and "dishonor" on her family. Social perception that provocative clothes, immodest behavior, or even coeducational schools for boys and girls, are responsible for incidents of sexual assault are hard to erase, despite the parents' attempts to logically disprove these arguments.

Of the myriad ways in which notions of sexuality, violence, and shame are propagated in India, films and popular media are the most significant. A particular scene in the play depicts children talking about a movie they have seen. The complex interplay of violence and sentimentality dished out in popular culture is evident from the title of the film that Sanju and Tony discuss. Recounting the plot of the film *Flowing Tears, Flashing Knives*, they describe the scene in which the hero's sister is raped by the villain, an incident that leads to the hero's transformation into the stereotypical angry young man in Hindi films made for mass audiences. Sanju hesitates from using the word "rape" before the younger children and repeats the phrase, "then 'that' happens," twice before being forced to explain himself:

CHUNNU: Sanju, tell us what happens.
SANJU: Shush! A dirty thing happens.

CHUNNU: No, tell me, tell me!
GABDU: If you don't shut up I'll slap you!
CHUNNU: No, tell me, tell me, tell me!
SANJU: Hey, she is raped.
TONY: She loses her respect, understood?
CHUNNU: It cannot be rape.
SANJU: Hey, why can't it be that?
CHUNNU: It cannot be rape. It can never be rape.
TONY: Why can't it be that?
CHUNNU: Because only little girls are raped. Day before yesterday wasn't Preeti raped?
(*He sits down crying. Sanju and Tony run away. Gabdu takes Chunnu away. Charu and her brother remain.*)
CHARU: Shall I ask you something, brother? What is this rape?
BROTHER: It's a very dirty thing. Go home now. (*Both leave*) (98)

The children's understanding of sexual violence is influenced not only by films but also by their friends' and neighbors' perceptions. Satyaprakash, a neighbor, hums a song he has composed about the incident. He also constructs the narrative in a filmic idiom comprising an extramarital affair, treachery, and betrayal perpetrated by Preeti's mother on the hapless 'victim' Pawan Kumar, who has been suspended from his job. At least two concerned neighbors take him to task for indulging in rumor-mongering and advocate strict punishment for the rapist. Mr. Mohanlal suggests violent tactics such as having the offender flogged in public and socially ostracized for his crime. Yet another of his vigilante schemes includes collective pressure on the molester's employers to suspend him from work as well as on the police who have thus far refused to take action regarding the case: "Why won't they act when the people form the neighboring community will gather and tell them: 'Look rascals if you don't take action regarding this case we will break your bones and set fire to the police station'" (100). These tactics are similar to those proposed by the community in the Mathura rape case. However, such public outpourings of wrath cannot be seriously considered effective or permanent solutions to the problem of violence against women and children.

When sexual violence is a pervasive rather than an incidental occurrence, as indicated by the story of a missing girl-child woven into the plot of *Aartanaad,* other measures are required to handle the problem at a systemic level. Like Preeti, who is always spoken of by her family, friends, and neighbors, the other missing girl never appears on stage. This, according to Mala, enables the spectators to relate the experience to children known to them in real life rather than empathize with the child depicted on stage as the immediate victim of a sexual crime (Interview 2004, 2009). The direction in the playscript reads: "*Aggarwal arrives. He mimes holding the hand of a little girl. This establishes the presence of the girl. He narrates a story to her*" (101). Satyaprakash, the rumor-mongering neighbor, warns Aggarwal against helping a girl found alone in the marketplace: "Mr. Aggarwal have you also started giving tuitions. . . . That Pawan Kumar was also tutoring Preeti. Some narrate a story, some tutor. Go on, narrate the story. Your name will also be mentioned on Page 3 of the newspaper. Go on, narrate the story" (101). Fear of being perceived as a potential rapist inhibits Mr. Aggarwal from helping the lost girl, later discovered to be Gangu's sister. The lost child metaphorically evokes the loss of childhood and innocence of the abused children. At the conclusion of the play all the characters collectively question the audience: "Can you hear the scream? This is not the cry of the distressed or the call of the innocent, it is the cry of a childhood lost in the wilderness. There is darkness all around. There is no ray of light here. In this darkness we perform about the darkness because we believe this cry will echo in your consciousness and a bright ray of hope will awaken" (103).

As suggested in the play, the most effective solution is the community, here presented as neighbors, collectively taking action to bring the offenders to book through legal means. Such a view of the community is in keeping with prevailing understandings of grassroots efforts to combat the effects of social violence. An attempt to rethink these ideas is made in Bharucha's *In the Name of the Secular* where the public sphere is presented as offering "unformulated, inchoate, processual spaces between the narrative of capital and community" that illuminate the "fragmented state of citizenship in India today." Bharucha acknowledges Safdar Hashmi's contribution in allowing for "unifying possibilities of cultural mobilization through class." He also mentions formation of *mohalla* (neighborhood) committees in Bombay that are playing a role in "fostering long-term collaboration between local communities and the police" to prevent the possibility of sectarian violence (99, 84). Preeti's mother too understands the value of community interaction with state authorities that will force them to take prompt action: "We will not take back the report. Along with that we will ask the *panchayat* [group of five elders in the community] to pressurize the police into taking action so that the case is resolved soon" (109). The community is seen in a combative rather than collaborative relationship with state authorities, illustrating both the fragmented state of citizenship in India as well as a somewhat paradoxical realization that both community and the state need to be partners in securing justice.

This position is also concurrent with the two aspects of the women's movement for securing gender justice: first, the autonomous feminist movement's initial belief in new and improved legislation as a solution to the pervasiveness of sexual violence against women and children, before it arrived at the conclusion that the community may be more operative in providing redress and support to the victim; and second, state-sponsored bodies', such as the National Commission of Women's (NCW), sustained emphasis on legal solutions. In its 1992 report on child sexual abuse NCW suggested extending these legal solutions by proposing the enactment of a "special law" since "children are subjected to secondary victimization by investigative agencies which ask them to recall minute details of sexual acts and experiences" (*Velvet Blouse* 25). While this report primarily focused on child prostitution, an NCW seminar on child rape held five years later reinforces its belief in legislation as the most effective safeguard against the crime, a belief held by autonomous feminists over fifteen years ago and subsequently abandoned in the aftermath of the adverse Supreme Court decision in the Mathura rape trial and the ineffectiveness of the Criminal Law (Amendment) Bill passed in 1983.

Considering the medico-legal, psychological, and rehabilitation aspects of abuse, the Commission recommended state efforts at changing the "social perception of rape" in coordination with nongovernmental organizations. Janam's collaboration with the People's Forum Against Child Sexual Abuse that resulted in *Aartanaad* is part of these extra-state efforts to change the definition of sexual violence by drawing on the lessons learned from the campaign for improved legislation. Talking about the play in an interview, Mala rhetorically asked, "*Aakhir besti kiski hui hai?* After all, *izzat* can't be in the hymen? [Who is the one insulted here? After all, respectability and honor can't be in the hymen?] Why is rape always linked to *izzat* [honor]? Is it not violence?" (2004) This is in tune with the uses of street theatre for articulating a feminist understanding of sexual violence such as V. Padma's clarification between protest and resistance specifying that the latter involves "contesting the crime of rape as well as resisting the morality based on rape" ("Re-presenting" 219). Besides focusing on legislative improvements, the NCW took its cue from such activist efforts aimed at changing the social perception of rape. Janam's position on child sexual abuse is closer to the autonomous feminist movement's disillusionment with (although not complete abandonment of) the state machinery, and its reliance on the community to transform the understanding of sexual violence.

The very recent controversy over the reopening of the Ruchika Girhotra case in which a fourteen-year-old girl from Panchkula was "molested" by Inspector General Rathore of the Indian Public Service in 1990, expelled by her school authorities under pressure from the officer, and eventually committed suicide three years later, has brought to the fore the contested issue of state versus community once again. Although the judgment made early in 2010 sanctioning Rathore to six months in prison and a fine of ten thousand rupees (two hundred dollars) in consideration of his age has been a blow to women's rights groups and to the victim's family, one of the aftereffects of the reopening of this case has been a reassessment of the Criminal Procedure Court (Amendment) Act 2008. This not only ensures protection to rape victims but also provides for completing trials for sexual offences within two months. Whether these changes are likely to restore victims' and their families' belief in the limping legal system or serve as another means of bypassing justice by ensuring speedy decisions largely in favor of perpetrators like Rathore remains to be seen.

THE AUDIENCE IS THE MESSAGE

Since Janam's position indicates disillusionment with the state machinery and arrives at conclusions similar to the lessons learned by feminist organizing of the 1970s and 1980s and, more recently, in the first decade of the new century, the question remains: Why is there so little belief in the state's intentions to provide sexual security to women and children during a period when the establishment of a national body (NCW) may lead one to believe that these intentions are unquestionable? Perhaps an answer can be found in the process of systematic co-optation of feminist activism by an institutionalization of issues affecting women. This co-optation was successful in the legal arena with the enactment of laws that enhanced the power of the state rather than empowering victims of sexual assault or those seeking justice for them. The emergence of specially funded women's studies programs in the 1970s and 1980s in various universities all over the country is yet another instance of this since here too the course modules and reading material, some of which have been used in this chapter, lean towards documenting the legal advances made in recent years.[13] In this scenario both women's groups and cultural activists allying with these groups' campaigns need to serve as citizens' forums against a complete dilution of the radical aims of feminist and workers' politics.

Janam's primary audience is the working classes, yet it has considerable influence on student audiences of all classes. Originating with Safdar's affiliation with the Student Federation of India when he was a student at Delhi University, over the years many of Janam's members have been students or teachers associated with the university. Although the group cannot accept all invitations to conduct workshops that it regularly receives from educational institutions, its sustained and strong links with the university have, according to Mala, a twofold educational impact: it purposefully connects to institutions to spread awareness about working classes and women and provides a rudimentary political education to students. Mala feels that while many young people are eager to join the group, circumstances constraining women students include the timings of the rehearsals, which are mostly held late in the evenings. Janam's potential female actresses are thus prevented from assuming an active role as performers by the very same threat of sexual violence enacted in the plays discussed (Mala Hashmi Interview 2004).

Sexual violence remains a pervasive concern and a topic of debate for feminist groups in India. One recent development is a call to de-link child abuse from general laws attempting to prevent violence against women, particularly since the existing provisions contain lacunae in the definition of both a "child" and "rape." There is also a consensus on retaining the word "rape" and not substituting it by euphemisms such as "molestation" and "eve teasing" that may detract from the gravity of the offence. The importance of an appropriate vocabulary for categorization is indicated in the difference between *Police Charitram* and *Aatranaad;* in the latter the word rape is used and problematized in the context of child abuse through children's understanding of it. Following up on a writ petition filed by Sakshi, a Delhi-based NGO, in the Supreme Court, asking for the definition of the expression "sexual intercourse" contained in Section 375 of the Indian Penal Code, three organizations—Sakshi, Interventions for Support, Healing, and Awareness (IFSHA), and All India Democratic Women's

Association (AIDWA)[14]—drafted the Criminal Law Amendment Bill 2000 that expands the definition of 'consent' and 'custodial', and asks for sexual assault laws to be made gender neutral (Saheli 15). A national-level meeting of feminist groups to discuss the proposed bill was almost unanimous in agreeing that the provision of gender neutrality in the bill would further empower the state at the expense of the women, gays, lesbians, and other sexual minorities. In this way sexual violence came to be linked to concerns of sexual identity, although in the absence of legal recognition of sexual minorities, groups representing their interests are "extremely cautious of any purported interest in the curbing of violence" (Saheli 18–19). Feminist lawyer Flavia Agnes observes that the assumption behind advocating a gender-neutral rape law is that "by rewriting a sexual crime located in a phallocentric culture, the social norms and values of a predominantly heterosexual society will automatically change" ("Law, Ideology" 844). Such a position indicates a cautious reliance on the state and a realistic perspective on proposed legislative changes.

Janam's plays thus raise the vexed and contentious issue of reliance on the state for providing legal redress to citizens. A brief note on Janam's relations with state apparati concludes my focus on the group's collaboration with the women's movement and its coalitional agenda encompassing gender and class in the provision of rights and justice. Sudhanva Deshpande observes that Safdar's complete distrust of funding agencies and state apparati helped in maintaining the radical cultural activist aspect of the group. Deshpande's article and van Erven's interview with Safdar indicate that one of the reasons why Safdar and his comrades left the Indian People's Theatre Association to form Janam was due to pressure to align with the Congress, then the political party in power ("Sahmat" 1587; van Erven 152). However, even while being cautious against possible co-optation, Janam has retained a focus on the state in its cultural activism.

A similar trajectory is apparent in the women's movement in India, which has taken the state to task by holding it responsible for protecting and ensuring the quality of women's and children's lives. These trajectories—meeting at different points in Janam's career and resulting in powerful performances—are indicative of what Bharucha has called "transitions between movements": an overview of the situation of girls and women in *Aurat* led to a performance in solidarity, although not complete agreement, with women's groups coming together for the anti-rape agitation in *Police Charitram;* the struggle was revived as the campaign against child sexual abuse many years later and elicited a timely response from Janam in *Aatranaad*. The controversy over the long trial and speedy judgment in the Ruchika case as this book was in the final stages of completion are salutary reminders of the continued necessity of these efforts. Street theatre and the women's rights movement have subsequently added new concerns to their agenda, the antiglobalization agitation and recognition of sexual minorities being just two among these. The next chapter furthers this exploration by looking at modern Indian dramatists' response to some of these concerns.

4 Queering the Subaltern
Postcolonial Performativity in Mahesh Dattani's *Seven Steps around the Fire* and Mahasweta Devi and Usha Ganguli's *Rudali*

> Theatre is neither a text nor a commodity. It is an activity that needs to be in ceaseless contact with the realities of the world and the inner necessities of our lives. If theatre changes the world, nothing could be better, but let us also admit that this has not happened so far.
>
> (Rustom Bharucha, *Theatre and the World* 10)

Writing on the politics of cultural practice in India, Bharucha argues that a public discourse on sexuality is slowly emerging in the country. *Bandit Queen* (1994) and *Fire* (1998), two landmark films that contributed to this discourse, led to a contentious debate on the representation of religion, caste, and alternative sexuality in post-independence India. In contrast, there has been little discussion about the prolific Indian dramatic scene where caste, gender, and sexuality had been pervasive concerns much before these films politicized the discussion of sexuality. One possible reason for this could be that drama, despite its direct address to the audience, is a relatively marginal cultural form as compared to film or fiction. Among the proliferation of dramatic traditions in India, proscenium theatre productions in Indian languages and in English occupy a privileged role.[1] They are staged almost exclusively in urban locations, the very centers of state power, and are often taken as representative of Indian drama at large, owing to national and international performance opportunities available to dramatists writing in English.

This chapter examines two proscenium productions, *Seven Steps around the Fire* written in English and *Rudali* written in Hindi, to reveal how drama has spoken out on stigmatized gendered and sexual labor and contributed to the emergent discourse on sexuality in India. If these plays are seen as cultural strategizing to demand adequate recognition of gendered and sexual labor, specifically homosexual and heterosexual prostitution, they anticipate recent feminist engagements with caste and alternative sexualities. The multiple foci on caste and gender in Indian feminist thought furthers an understanding of a reliance on and belief in the state's ability to provide citizen status to those sections of the population who have been denied their rights due to sexual orientation, location in the caste hierarchies in the Indian social fabric, or an intersection of both, as is the case with ritualistic performers, the *hijras* (transsexual or transgendered men) and the *rudalis* depicted in the plays discussed. This chapter reiterates necessity for critical vigilance about the institutionalized exploitation marking forms of labor depicted in the plays when examining the status of these communities as citizens of postcolonial India.[2]

Mahesh Dattani, a Bangalore-based professional playwright, writes in English for a primarily urban Indian and an international audience. Mahasweta Devi, an activist for the economic, political, and social rights of tribal and *dalit* (lower-caste) populations, writes in Bengali for a largely local audience, although her writings have been translated into English and many other Indian languages. In 1992, Usha Ganguli, a Calcutta-based playwright, adapted Devi's story into a play in Hindi. Dattani's, Devi's and Ganguli's commitment to present unrecognized and stigmatized forms of domesticity, sexuality, and productivity characterizes their work. They present alternative domestic and sexual arrangements reliant on ritualistic gendered and sexual labor including heterosexual and homosexual prostitution, performances by *hijras* on occasions such as the birth of a child or a wedding in the family, and by *rudalis* (professional mourners) at funerals of upper-caste landowning and money-lending families.[3]

Discussing women, law, and citizenship in postcolonial India, Rajeswari Sunder Rajan proposes that second-wave feminism in India has interrogated the liberal premises of the postcolonial Indian state while working in close collaboration with it. This proposition is central to my focus on Indian feminists' belief in the discourse of rights that has been crucial for the politicization of gender and sexuality in the country. Fundamental rights are daily violated in the Indian state's dealings with sexually marked groups (gay men, lesbians, bisexuals, and transsexuals) and lower caste men and women who may define themselves as a community. Reading the cause-and-effect relationship between these communities' extra-legal, economic, and sexually disadvantaged status in *Seven Steps around the Fire* and *Rudali*, I briefly outline the subaltern categories that have been central to Indian feminist analysis and activism in keeping with Spivak's assessment that "subalternity is where social lines of mobility, being elsewhere, do not permit the formation of a recognisable basis of action" ("Scattered" 476). Next, I analyze these plays to indicate how these works complicate the subaltern categories that are the basis of third-wave feminist politics, specifically its sustained emphasis on caste as the basis of women's oppression and its reluctant attention to non-heteronormative sexuality, that helps explain this inattention to communities marked by both their caste and extralegal sexuality. Applying Judith Butler's ideas I suggest 'postcolonial performativity' as an interpretative rubric with an awareness of the problems of an easy co-relation of Euro-American theorization of sexual identities to a postcolonial context. My claim is that the representation of sexual alterity by Indian dramatists has resignified gendered and sexual identities in ways that anticipate and contribute to the burgeoning but as yet tentative feminist discourse on legal and economic security for multiple sexualities in India.

POSTCOLONIAL PERFORMATIVITY

One of the earliest applications of performativity to gender studies discusses the philosophical and theatrical senses of the word "acts" to posit gender as an act "which has been rehearsed, much as a script survives the particular actors who make use of it, but requires individual actors in order to be actualized and reproduced as reality once again." Continuing with the theatrical metaphor, the critic adds, "[J]ust as the play requires both text and interpretation, so the gendered body acts its part in a culturally restricted corporeal space and enacts interpretations within the confines of already existing directives" (Butler, "Performative" 276). Looking at the resignification of gender and sexual identities (through feminist activism and nascent queer politics) in India helps determine the applicability of Butler's idea to the Indian context. The denaturalization of gender as revealed in a proliferation of identities beyond the sex/gender binaries underscores Butler's exploration of performativity at the level of the assignment and interpellation of gender roles. However, to be effective, gender roles must be continually repeated. The necessity of repetition also leads to a possibility of repetition in ways different from the regulatory imposition of gender categories as masculine and feminine positing cross-gender sexual desire (where gender corresponds to biological sex) as normative by policing non-normative sexuality. The following analysis underscores aspects of performativity pertinent to the assertion of identities beyond "already existing subaltern positions," that is, in advance of social categories validated by and comprehensible to state apparati and social movements such as the Indian women's movement.

Butler's discussion of identity at multiple levels—the subject and its gender identity, the homogeneous identity presumed to be essential for women's movements or feminist politics, and the flexibly heterogeneous identity imperative for a radical resignification of feminist and queer politics as sites of democratic contest—enables us to think of postcolonial performativity in relation to subalternity. In postcolonial India, subaltern is most often understood as corresponding to the overly generalized categories 'women', 'lower castes', and recently 'lower-caste women', but often ignored and misunderstood if marked by shifting gender affiliations and alternative sexual preferences. At the most obvious level, postcolonial performativity destabilizes some of these categories by recognizing the claims for recognition and redistribution made on behalf of transgendered and transsexual citizen-subjects like *hijras* (often compared to transvestites or drag queens, despite a mismatch between Western labels and the self-presentation of the *hijras*), women like Sanichari in *Rudali* who perform gender for their livelihood, and those whose sexual preferences do not correspond to their presumed gender. Second, this formulation allows us to analyze the class and caste differences intersecting the presumed homogeneous identity of the Indian women's movement.

Finally, the concept is useful in allowing us to see how these intersections hold out the possibility of a resignification of feminist politics in India to include alternative sexualities within its organizational ambit. Some of these intersectional identities are illustrated in two recent accounts—Richa Nagar's ethnographic narrative of *dalit* same-sex domesticity and Ruth Vanita's cultural commentary on the filmic representation of a *hijra's* familial bonds—that implicitly reference postcolonial performativity.[4]

Amanda Swarr and Richa Nagar interrogate 'lesbian' struggles for identity and survival in India and South Africa by reading development theory for its exclusions of lesbian struggles in poor countries of the South at the same time as they take to task lesbian theorists' exclusive focus on sexuality to the exclusion of the social and material context in the formation of identities. Arguing for "intersectionality" between the two approaches, they state that this "necessitates that we reconceptualize difference as constituted and (re)configured in relation to place specific struggles over rights, resources, social practices, and relationships—including sexual and emotional intimacies—that people enter into with or without labels" (496). Global vocabularies of identity affiliations are not overtly present in Nagar's narration of the life stories of Geeta, a *dalit* (lower caste), and Manju, an *adivasi* (tribal) from Chitrakoot. Despite the almost instantaneous attraction and the obviously sexual relationship between them, neither Geeta nor Manju identify as "lesbian." As I have argued elsewhere, these labels have limited applicability as descriptors of same-sex relations in India.[5]

Ruth Vanita's discussion of male-male love in Hindi cinema through the concept of "dosti" (friendship) and the figure of the *hijra* also indicates the limits of Western identity categories, such as gay, lesbian, or queer, to describe South Asian sexualities. Vanita traces multiple facets of identity while discussing Pooja Bhatt's film *Tamanna* (1997), based on the life story of a *hijra* named Tikoo whose primary identification is as a devout Muslim and father of an adopted child. In pointing out how Tikoo's "body language and camp mannerisms" (besides his profession as hairdresser and makeup artist to film stars) are "suggestive of the self-presentation of urban gay men in India today," Vanita suggests that the film avoids direct discussion of homosexuality but "allows slippage between the *hijra* persona and that of a gay man" ("*Dosti*" 154). Rather than look at this slippage as an avoidance of a discussion of homosexuality, it can be seen as a necessary referencing of gay identities in relation to indigenous sexualities, where neither the global nor the indigenous is valorized as a more authentic form of existence, and both are recognized as part of everyday life in India.

Multiple affiliations of caste, class, religion, gender, sexuality, and nonbiological kinship in these essays indicate that there is an urgent need for reexamining the exclusions and margins of postcolonial identity categories through gender theory. An examination of these exclusions towards an inclusive notion of postcolonial performativity is mandated by the Indian feminist project of democratic futures. This performativity would involve feminist coalitions with sexually marginalized groups and recognition of non-biological conceptions of kinship. The second-wave women's movement in India has, according to Sharmila Rege, underlined the sexual as political primarily in terms of issues of "violence, conjugality, reproduction, and to a limited extent sexual orientation." Rege proposes an understanding of the caste and class basis of patriarchy that includes controls over labor and sexuality since in its absence "the political edge of sexual politics is lost" (493). Devi's, Ganguli's, and Dattani's conceptualization of the nation-state foregrounds the political edge of their representation of sexuality. Theirs is a politics of indictment that holds the state accountable for failing to protect the social, economic, and legal rights of minorities marked by their caste, gender, and sexuality. As argued in this chapter, recognizing these rights is one of the most crucial tasks for a performative resignification of feminist politics in India.

THE INVISIBLE STATE

Mahasweta Devi's story *Rudali* and Usha Ganguli's play based on this story are about Sanichari, a low caste woman forced to eke out a meager living as a ritual mourner. Her companionship with another woman, Bikhni, late in life and their work together as *rudalis* or professional mourners helps them survive. Their initiative in organizing prostitutes into *rudalis* underlines the correlation between sexual and economic oppression in rural India. The homoerotic familial arrangement worked out by Sanichari and Bikhni (present more in the dramatization than the story) and the possibility of a coalition of the oppressed dramatizes a non-biological conceptualization of family and kinship. The view of community presented in the story and play is not only class specific but also marked by the gendered and sexual labor of the *rudalis* and the prostitutes. This, it should be evident, is somewhat different from Jana Natya Manch's representation of working class community in its early plays and neighborhood communities in its later work.

Devi has analyzed multiple facets of tribal and low caste existence in relation to the state in almost all her work. The sexual consequences of destitution on women are the cornerstone of her critique of the nation-state in her celebrated short story "Douloti."[6] Juxtaposing this story with *Rudali* enables a clear perception of the state as an invisible but ever-present actor in Devi's account of Sanichari's and Bikhni's lives. In "Douloti," Devi illustrates the institutionalization of sexual exploitation through upper caste hegemony in the village and the nation by marking feudalism's transmutation into governmental bureaucracy and its monopolization of material and sexual resources; in *Rudali* there is no such transmutation since the mechanism of exploitation remains largely feudal. That the state is a missing but powerful actor in this performance of power is evident from the representation and categorization of work in the story and the play.

Ganguli's translation of Devi's story into the idiom of drama and theatre also involves a translation of its emphasis. Devi implicitly cautions against attaching too much importance to the fact that the play was translated and adapted by a woman director since Devi claims to have written the story as an example of people's confrontation with the "system" to look at the "class, not the gender problem" (qtd. in Katyal 16). Therefore it is unsurprising that there are more references to the "system" in the story than in the play. The story begins in an unspecified colonial time and chronicles three generations to show that postcolonial governance has not improved the precarious social and economic situation of the low caste *dushads* and *ganjus*. Sanichari indicts the colonial and postcolonial system that looks upon the lower castes as "criminals" to be imprisoned at the behest of the landowners, as "bodies" to be medically protected against diseases, or as "corpses" to be disposed of during an epidemic.

Just as the colonial state provided intermittent medical attention to the poor in makeshift hospitals during epidemics, the modern Indian state provides inadequate services and employment in its developmental projects such as building railways and roads. The state's presence in the story is subsumed within the feudal governance of the village economy, thus marking it as a feudal heteropatriarchy, one that is actively involved in disenfranchising lower castes and outcastes. Significantly, while the deleterious influence of national developmental forces is mentioned only in passing, the microcosmic unit of governance, the *panchayat,* emerges as the primary source of exploitation in Devi's story.[7] As an upper caste male body extracting compulsory labor from the villagers, the *panchayat* in this village does not guarantee any compensatory returns. Sanichari performs "her obligatory share of repair work on the panchayat meeting ground" but informs Bikhni that the water at the *panchayati* well is "bitter" ("Rudali" 87, 66). Sanichari's and Bikhni's 'choice' to become professional mourners is a metaphorical lamentation at the bitterness of the well of scarcity (and loneliness) in their lives.

Like the intermittent opportunities for labor offered by the state, this too is an uncertain occupation reliant on the chance deaths of people who extract labor from caste marked bodies. Devi's story scrutinizes the mutually advantageous relations between the upper caste landowners and the state continuing from colonial times. The landowner Gambhir Singh's accountant tells the "illiterate woman" Sanichari that this nexus is a natural state of affairs. Decreed by the gods themselves, it has been sustained through successive postcolonial governments, and is likely to persist indefinitely. Devi's class analysis arraigns the mode of surplus extraction legitimized by the nation-state microcosmically reflected in the village economy. High caste families raised their prestige by spending lavishly on the death ceremonies of a family member. Although there is a concomitant rise in the "status" of the *rudalis* performing at these ceremonies, the "price for these ceremonies was paid by the dushads, dhobis, ganjus and kols from the hides of whom the overlords extracted the sums they had overspent." In these circumstances, Sanichari's neighbor Dulan's suggestion that since the coal miners have a union, Sanichari and Bikhni can also "form a union of rudalis and randis [prostitutes]," with her as "pishiden [president]," is an ironic commentary on the efficacy of these organizations in safeguarding workers' rights. Sanichari's horror at Dulan's suggestion reiterates her ingrained caste consciousness. According to her the market prostitutes are "a separate caste," a perception of 'otherness' that is similar to her reaction on learning of a landlord who kept a "Mussalman [Muslim]" woman as a whore. Bikhni's response to Dulan indicates that she has understood the connections between subaltern groups he is trying to make better than Sanichari. Promising to get the market prostitutes, she declares: "It's the women who are ruined by the malik-mahajans who turn into whores" (Devi, "Rudali" 80). This exchange indicates that exploitation can be countered by collectivity, but also that any such collectivity is intersected by the fault lines of caste and religion.

Ganguli's play begins with Sanichari working on a *chakki*, a hand mill for grinding grain into flour, symbolizing her livelihood. The endless circle of hardship indicated by the grinding wheel of the *chakki*, marking the circle of events in her life and her companionless existence in her old age, are the twin foci of the play. Ganguli's emphasis is evident from the first scene in which three generations of women in Sanichari's household are united in their "hunger." Sanichari's invalid mother-in-law Somri cries out with unsatisfied hunger that the endless cycle of work cannot satisfy, while her daughter-in-law Parbatia craves food, luxuries, and sexual satisfaction. Ganguli's focus on Sanichari's familial arrangements is in contrast to Devi's emphasis on her relationships with the rural community. Given the individualization of the central figure in the play, the brunt of class analysis—that is also a critique of caste based hegemony in the nation-state—is lost in the plays' plot as is the historicity of this hegemony from colonial to postcolonial times.

Although the state is less visible in Ganguli's adaptation than it is in Devi's story, one of the characters in the play briefly mentions its alliance with the upper castes: "These people have the power of money—the law, the police, the government, are all firmly in their grasp." The state appears to be a benign power, for Bikhni plans to go to the "government office" to obtain fertilizer for the vegetable garden she wants to cultivate, yet its hallmark is corruption, since "everyone from the Prime Minister to the lowest untouchable takes cuts" (Ganguli 128). In this feudal heteropatriarchal economy the poor are left to fend for themselves, and bodily labor (menial or sexual) is their only means of sustenance.

Performing physical, sexual, and ritualistic labor, these caste-marked bodies are caught in a vicious cycle of hunger, debt, and destitution. Devi's emphasis on class precludes a hierarchy of respectable versus stigmatized work. In Ganguli's rendition one notices that the feminist agenda faces the paradox of bodily labor classed according to degrees of respectability. Introducing Sanichari and Bikhni to the landlord's house as *rudalis,* Dulan's bargaining point is that they are "decent women." Sanichari's trip to the red-light area to rope in the prostitutes as *rudalis* is based on the assumption that mourning for money is preferable to working as a whore. She asks the prostitutes whether their work brings them any "self-respect." The grading of honorable versus dishonorable work is complete when she tells them, "Look, this is work, you hear me? Work. Better work than yours" (Ganguli 150). Where Devi had emphasized caste and religion as fault lines in the collectivity of female labor, Ganguli prioritizes respectability as the cornerstone of Sanichari's characterization of work. It is clear from Sanichari's comparisons that this respectability is inextricably linked to productivity. Since prostitution is 'unproductive' sex work, the dignity accorded to other laboring classes is denied to the prostitutes.

The insidious yet invisible presence of the nation-state in Devi's story and Ganguli's play frames their representation of gendered and sexual labor. Patriarchal authority exercised by the upper caste landlord, moneylender, and the priest legitimizes the services provided by *rudalis,* while the prostitutes' labor is stigmatized as immoral. In the light of Sunder Rajan's delineation of three chief areas in the prostitution debates—female sexuality in prostitution, the agency of the prostitute, and prostitution as work—another valuation of this labor than the one presented in the story and the play can be offered. Without discounting the exploitative conditions that lead to primarily, although not exclusively, female prostitution, Sanichari's daughter-in-law Parbatia's rejection of her impoverished circumstances for life as a prostitute evokes the contested terrain of "agency" that Spivak avers is a call for "the putting aside of difference" ("Scattered" 480). In Devi's story Parbatia's "hunger" is described as "greater" than Sanichari's or her son Budhua's (60). Ganguli's dramatic representation follows the same trajectory. The major difference is that where the story elides the circumstances of Parbatia's departure, in the play she is depicted as hungering for both sex and material possessions and leaving the house with all of Sanichari's savings. Both the story and the play depict her as a misfit in the harsh, poverty-ridden domesticity laboriously sustained by Sanichari.

The conclusion of the play—unlike that of the story where a market prostitute Gulbadan leeringly winks at Madho Singh but remains a part of the *rudalis*—reaffirms Sanichari's view of prostitution as driven by hunger for sex and money. Ganguli's stage direction describes Sanichari looking at Gulbadan and Madho Singh leaving the funeral together: "Sanichari looks at them, and then down at the edibles left lying about" (154). Sanichari's gaze at the duo and then at the food reiterates her view of prostitution as deriving from a voracious appetite rather than a means of sustenance as the dominant one in the play, despite there being indications to the contrary in Devi's story. This reasserts rather than puts aside differences between various kinds of subaltern labor practices.

Ganguli's representation of sex as appetite rather than work is objectionable not because her emphasis on gender undermines the presumed collective class consciousness that is central for Devi, but because the accent on sexuality as a voracious appetite leads to a naturalization of sex as need, whether masculine or feminine. Given the circumstances detailed in the story and the play, positing the prostitutes' sexuality outside patriarchal domesticity as agency is as untenable as is Sanichari's implied characterization of it as unproductive and hence less respectable work, since it sustains the women who are engaged in it. Any agency then is circumstantial, as reiterated by Gulbadan's story in the play. Is her decision to leave her "father's" house to become a prostitute rather than a mistress to his nephew a 'choice'? The market prostitutes' sexuality is also in contrast to the almost completely desexualized intimacy between Sanichari and Bikhni. This domesticity is a comment on the devouring class- and caste-marked heterosexuality that is conveniently justified as a male (and female) need for sex. Conceptualizing sex as work rather than need entails recognizing the conditions that lead to prostitution and its function in the informal economy of cities, towns, and villages, as revealed in the *hijras'* sexual encounters. Such a view has the added advantage of distinguishing sex work from recreational sex and sexuality as affective intimacy.

THE PERVASIVE STATE

The politicization of sexuality by Dattani, a gay playwright who directs attention to *hijras* as a marginal community incompletely defined by the axes of caste, class, and sexuality, shifts the scene from a rural to an urban location. In contrast to the relative invisibility of the state in Sanichari's life, its pervasiveness marks Dattani's play largely through the presence of the police, and to a lesser extent through the university as a research institution. If class is central to Devi's project as a writer, and women's concerns are foremost in Ganguli's dramaturgy, an exploration of Indian sexualities best characterizes Dattani's oeuvre. Dattani is the first playwright to extend the connotations of secularism beyond its cultural and religious significations to recognize the multiple sexualities comprising India's diversity. His provocative statement in a dialogue with Lakshmi Subramanyam that "men and women are the biggest stereotypes in the whole world" can be connected to the exploration of masculinity and femininity beyond these stereotypes in his plays (131). The *hijras* defy normative constructions by embodying gender performativity. Their exaggerated feminine mannerisms, modes of dress, and stigmatization owing to their mixed gender attributes, comment on acceptable modes of gendered and sexual conduct in Indian society. Most of the available research on *hijras* focuses on their role as ritualistic performers on auspicious occasions, and discusses, almost as an embarrassed aside, that many earn their living as prostitutes. Over the past few years *hijras'* sexuality, kinship patterns, and community formation have been compared and contrasted with other sexually marked communities such as *kotis,* effeminate men who take submissive roles during sexual acts, and *pantis,* biological men who play a dominant role in homosexual relationships (Reddy 15)

The title of Dattani's radio play cites the Hindu marriage ceremony involving the bride's and the groom's seven ritualistic circumambulations around the fire to the priest's holy incantations. Its plot revolves around the missing photograph of a marriage between a *hijra,* Kamla, and a politician's (a minister) son, Subbu. The possibility of a redefinition of the heterosexual family held out by this marriage is foreclosed when Subbu's father, fearing social ostracism at his son's homosexual liaison, arranges to have Kamla murdered. Dattani's politicization of sexuality in the play is framed by the investigations of the female researcher Uma. Uma and Suresh are a middle class couple, serving the nation as a teacher and police officer. Their encounter with the community of cross-dressing performers, the *hijras,* points to alternative sexuality as criminality and as curiosity.

Most *hijras* are voluntarily or coercively castrated males who have sexual relations with other men. Castration and homosexuality, two features taken as definitive markers of their identity, are criminal offences under the Indian Penal Code. Additionally, their aggressive mannerisms and forceful demands for money for performances have facilitated their categorization as potentially violent, making it easier for the police to criminalize the community. This criminalization is highlighted in the first scene of Dattani's play, which depicts Anarkali, a *hijra* suspected of murdering a member of her group, in police custody. Uma's research into "class- and gender-related violence" takes her to the prison where she hopes to meet and interview Anarkali. Uma's sociological investigation is facilitated by access to the prison since she is the wife of the Superintendent of Police and daughter-in-law of the Deputy Commissioner. Despite these connections she is uncertain about the response from the subject of her investigations. State categorization and popular perception of *hijras* as non-human is evident in Constable Munswamy's surprise at Uma's use of the feminine pronoun to refer to Anarkali: "She! Of course it will talk to you. We will beat it up if it doesn't" (7). This dehumanization is ensured by keeping Anarkali in the male section of the prison where she is under constant threat of physical and sexual violence. Under the circumstances, sexual services are her only means of bargaining for life, although even these are no guarantee against violence.

Commissioned by the BBC as a radio play as part of a season marking fifty years of Indian independence in 1997, the occasion of the play's first broadcast ironically reiterates denial of human rights to sexual minorities. As in the case of Douloti, the tribal woman forced into prostitution in Devi's story titled after her, the prostitutes, and *rudalis,* there is no 'independence' from heteropatriarchal exploitation for these communities sixty years into India's postcoloniality. Dattani cleverly juxtaposes Anarkali's enforced prostitution in a state institution against another *hijra's,* Kamla's, consensual sexual liaison with a politician's son. Kamla's murder at the behest of the minister, Anarkali's implication in the crime, and her imprisonment on a murder charge are evidence of the state's power to criminalize sexual alterity even while actively consuming it.[8]

If Devi and Ganguli present the state as a feudal heteropatriarchy, Dattani represents it is as a disciplinary apparatus. The police's active efforts to enforce sexual codes while covertly abetting and facilitating exploitation of sexual minorities are suggested in Anarkali's invitation to Constable Munswamy to exchange cigarettes for sex: "If you had a beautiful sister, you will give her a cigarette for a fuck, no?" (11). Uma's exploration of the lives of the *hijras* as "cases" originates in her disciplinary affiliations with sociology. In postcolonial disciplinary hierarchies sociology is developmentally useful, therefore this research is underwritten as socially productive. Daughter of the Vice Chancellor of Bangalore University and the wife of a police officer, Uma is connected to the state's mechanisms of classification, categorization, and containment masked through the promotion of benign academic programs in universities, such as anthropology, sociology, social work, and women's studies, enjoying a relative but by no means complete autonomy from the state. This connection deserves emphasis because Dattani's play exposes the ethnocentric motivations in apparently benevolent discipline specific sociological and anthropological research on communities such as the *hijras.*[9]

Indeed ethnography is the primary mode of investigation of *hijra* subculture.[10] Serena Nanda's classification of them as "the institutionalized third sex" is the classic study on the subject. Nanda's book is thorough in its investigations, meticulously argued, and based on months of careful observation and conversations with members of the community. However, her discussion of the state apparati, especially the police and judicial machinery, presents them as protectors of the *hijras*. The police are alternately "sympathetic," "understanding," even "loving." There is ample indication in the interviews that the police are regular customers of *hijra* prostitutes and the threat of police brutality looms large over them, but Nanda's belief in the accommodative nature of the Indian social fabric and state apparati leads her to overlook the obvious evidence. In contrast, Zia Jaffrey's account of *hijras* in Delhi and Hyderabad, written as a travelogue rather than ethnography, offers a realistic appraisal of the state's interaction with this marginal community. Retired police officers are Jaffrey's primary contacts with the *hijras*. Coercion and suspicion mark the *hijras'* relations with the police in the erstwhile princely state of Hyderabad, the primary site of Jaffrey's research, where a major scandal involved a royal prince's sexual relations with a *hijra* prostitute. The police officers Jaffrey meets in this city inform her that even when used by the police as informers, the *hijras* are under constant surveillance and investigation.

On more than one occasion Jaffrey's narrative reads like an investigation and trial of members of the community. Like the upper-class researcher in

Dattani's play whose access to the community is predicated on her proximity to channels of state power, Jaffrey's police contacts lead her to the *hijras* to gain knowledge about them. The silencing of the subaltern is complete when the police narrate their history. Dattani's play, in contrast, allows the *hijras* to speak in their own voice. Uma's second visit to the police station when she manages to interview Anarkali is a "successful" one. The interview begins with the researcher introducing herself, drawing on the disciplinary ethics of exchanging information with the primary informant. Anarkali's insouciant response to the introduction subverts Uma's attempt at egalitarianism:

> UMA: I am doing my paper on class- and gender-related violence.
> ANARKALI: What do you want me to do? Shall I come to sing and dance when you pass your exam?
> UMA: I have told you a little bit about myself. Now tell me something about you.
> ANARKALI: What is there to tell? I sing with other hijras at weddings and when a child is born people give us money otherwise I will put a curse on them. (Laughs.) As if God is on our side. (Smokes.) I did not do anything to Kamla. She was my sister. (12)

Anarkali mentions her sisterly relations with Kamla to quell Uma's doubts that she may have had a hand in the murder, stating that it is natural to quarrel with one's sister. She also tells Uma: "If you were a hijra, I would have made you my sister." Uma invokes the familial term in a different sense when she says that they can be sisters despite her not being a *hijra,* inviting Anarkali's canny observation of the differences in their class and social position: 'Where are you and where am I?' The idea of a cross-class, cross-gender, and cross-cultural sisterhood invoked in academic circles is a discredited cliché in feminist thought. Uma's invocation of it in this conversation puts her research agenda into question: "One day you will understand. Anarkali, I would love to be your sister, if you will be mine." Anarkali seizes this moment of empathy and begs Uma to save her, but on hearing that she's here "to gather some information for . . . [her] paper," she attacks the hypocrisy inherent in her feminist sisterhood paradigm: "Then say that. Don"t pretend to be my sister" (13).

Uma's investigations later lead her to a part of the city where the community has a house of its own. Here she is privy to the *hijra* household's internal workings primarily because the members assume that she is a social worker. Like the scene in Ganguli's play where the prostitutes are depicted in their living quarters, this scene offers a glimpse into the lives of the *hijras.* There is some indication that they are involved in homosexual prostitution since neither Champa, the head of the house who considered Kamla her "daughter," nor Anarkali, who looked upon her as a "sister," approved of Kamla's affair with the politician's son, which would have made her an unproductive member of the community besides endangering her life.

Enforced and voluntary prostitution are the kinds of work essential for the survival of this marginalized community. However, in Dattani's play there is no hierarchy of work as there is in Ganguli's dramatization. Rather the *hijras'* sexual labor is refracted through the lenses of law enforcement and social reform that characterize other kinds of work including the activities of the police and the feminist researcher. The sequence of events detailed in the play precludes any attempt by the researcher to speak for the subaltern. Indeed all such attempts are exposed as vested interests that are in direct contrast to the volatile but extremely supportive community and kinship ties among the *hijras*.

IMAGINING KINSHIP, FORGING COMMUNITY

The covert and overt presence of the state in the lives of subaltern communities in rural and urban locations is evident, first, as a feudal heteropatriarchy and, second, as a disciplinary apparatus. Sexual labor is a crucial means of survival for these exploited groups. However, Devi, Ganguli, and Dattani also describe two specific ritualistic forms of gendered labor—mourning and celebration—as the basis of idealized non-biological relationships in the plays. This idealization is achieved by contrasting occupational connections with kinship bonds including filial, sibling, and marital alliances.

In the story and the play versions of *Rudali,* Sanichari meets Bikhni at a fair while looking for her grandson, who has run away from home. The two recognize each other as childhood playmates and compare their life stories. Like Sanichari, Bikhni feels abandoned by her son, who has moved in with his wife's parents. Once the two decide to live together in Sanichari's house, they also pool their meager financial resources. On the brink of starvation, they opt for ritual mourning or *rudali* work at Dulan's suggestion. Bikhni's role is central in securing them this employment since she contacts the prostitutes as coworkers. Sanichari's reluctance to take up ritual mourning as work stems from the history of her impoverished circumstances when she did not have the luxury of mourning successive deaths in her family. She feels cursed at the lack of the tears appropriately marking female sentimentality. In Devi's story, Dulan explains to her the difference in circumstances: "Budhua's ma, I'm not asking you to shed the tears you couldn't shed for Budhua. These tears are your livelihood—you'll see, just as you cut wheat and plough land, you'll be able to shed these tears" (70). Devi succinctly describes the "professional" attributes that were in great demand after people saw Sanichari and Bhikni's "performance" at Bhairab Singh's funeral. These make them so successful in the trade that they can dictate their terms:

Just for wailing, one kind of rate.
    Wailing and rolling on the ground, five rupees
one sikka.
    Wailing, rolling on the ground
and beating one's head, five rupees two sikkas.
    Wailing and beating one's breast,
accompanying the corpse to the cremation ground, rolling
around on the ground there—for that the charge is six
rupees. ("Rudali" 75).

Ganguli retains Devi's comparative valuation of mourning as labor when Dulan tells Sanichari: "This is crying for money, crying as a business. Just do it the way you would grind wheat or carry bricks for the sake of a daily wage" (129). There is, however, no indication of the specific monetary correlates of different aspects of ritual mourning as gendered performance in the play as there is in the story.

Murderous conflicts and intense rivalry between members of the upper-caste households lead them to outdo each other in hiring famous *rudalis*. Both the story and play offer a devastating critique of family relationships centered on the landowning families' dependence on others to mourn for the dead. One of the first deaths Sanichari and Bikhni mourn is that of a landlord murdered by his son, a fact that the rest of family is aware of but chooses to ignore. These combative high caste relationships serve as a foil to the bond between Bikhni and Sanichari, whose quasi-domesticity is founded on shared resources and mutual concern. Their 'ideal' relationship is desexualized in the story although there is enough indication in the play that the director has adapted the original to suggest physical intimacy between the two women.[11] For instance, in one scene Bikhni plaits Sanichari's hair and asks her to try on a pair of earrings. Sanichari's embarrassed response to the gesture includes an admission that there were very few times when anyone cared enough to get her something. The scene ends with a critique of heteronormativity sustained by women's rivalry when Sanichari quotes the cliché, "a woman's worst enemy was other women," to which Bikhni responds by saying, 'that's all stuff made up by men' (Ganguli 123). The sexual implications of the intimacy shared by the two women are hinted in an altercation with a neighbor:

MISRI: Having fun, eh, Sanichari?
SANICHARI: Oh, yes, loads of fun. Tell you what, Misri—leave your
           husband. And come live here with us. Then all three of
           us can have lots of fun . . .
MISRI: Why are you talking rubbish, Sanichari! You have a filthy
       mind! I just came here to ask after your friend, and you start
       insulting me! (Ganguli 124)

The intimacy is reiterated when simple acts of sharing food and going to sleep together reveal Sanichari's attachment to Bikhni, further expressed as injunctions on her journey to her native village. Whereas Devi foregrounds Sanichari's fear for her livelihood when she learns that Bikhni is dead, Ganguli's stage direction reads, "She turns and begins to fold the black clothes and place them on the cot. Harsh sobs tear through her. Gradually the intensity of the weeping eases. She gets up slowly, and begins to fold the clothes again" (146). The black clothes worn by Bikhni and Sanichari for *rudali* work connect the latter's grief to a sense of personal loss and insecurity about her economic condition. There is added poignancy in that for the first time in her life Sanichari mourns the death of a close one with tears. The women's affective and productive relationship comments on the greed, exploitation, and emotive absence characterizing upper caste familial relations.

A similar absence characterizes intimacy between the burgeois couple Suresh and Uma and the filial relation between the minister and his son, Subbu, in Dattani's play. Dattani's critique of the family is as vehement as Devi's and Ganguli's. However, unlike these authors' direct focus on caste, Dattani indirectly negotiates caste differences in his presentation of the *hijras*. Studies indicate that the *hijras* consider themselves a separate caste deriving from syncretic religious affiliations (the *hijra* genealogy is traced to references of "the third sex" in ancient Hindu texts and to eunuchs guarding harems in the courts of Muslim rulers) and their worship of a particular Hindu deity, Bahuchara Mata. Serena Nanda's interviews with the community reveal that while they function like a caste—a group organized around traditional occupations including performance, begging, and prostitution—they do not follow any caste rules on purity or pollution regarding interdining or intermingling. Nanda also refers to their familial relationships within "houses" as "fictive kinship" (40–45). In contrast Reddy argues that "kinship and elaborations of familial ties are *central* axes of hijra and koti identity" (185).

Dattani presents this kinship among people who perceive their community as a caste unto itself as more authentic in comparison to other relationships. The comparisons are evident from the beginning of the play. Asking Uma about her research, Suresh mocks Anarkali's claim that Kamla was her sister and magisterially declares that the *hijras* are "all castrated, degenerate men." He fends off Uma's questions on the Anarkali and Kamla case by making love to her. This scene is juxtaposed with one where Anarkali refers to herself as the constable's sister, asks for a cigarette from him, propositions him, and concludes the dialogue with the punch line "You are not a sister fucker?" Besides blatantly abusing the constable to his face, Anarkali re-cites sibling relations as sites of coercive sexuality.[12] As indicated earlier, the demystification of Uma's feminist sisterhood paradigm is also a comment on the affectionate but tempestuous relationship between Anarkali and her "sister" Kamla. Although the *hijras* offer a strident critique of Uma's research, her childlessness and her status as an adopted child mark her affinity to them. This also elicits their pity and concern. The head of the *hijra* house to which Anarkali belongs blesses Uma in the traditional manner and gives her a charm that will help her conceive.

This house also provides a glimpse into the kin and familial ties of the members. For the head, Champa, its members are like her "daughters," and although she is angry at Anarkali for aspiring to her position, she is also quick to come to her defense when Uma accuses her of murdering Kamla: "We had fights. But Anarkali and me—we are not killers" (Dattani 28). Champa bails Anarkali out of prison despite knowing that the latter was responsible for scarring Kamla to prevent her from visiting the minister's son. These sibling-like relations among the *hijras*, heavily marked by the violence constantly experienced by the community, mirror and refract the relations between Subbu and his father, the minister. Subbu and Kamla's love story—beginning as a homosexual relationship riddled with domestic disapproval from both sides, and ending in Kamla's murder and Subbu's suicide on the day of his arranged marriage—contrasts with Uma and Suresh's marital 'bliss', referenced by Uma's emotional and sexual withdrawal from her husband, and possible reasons for their childlessness.

Like Ganguli, Dattani depicts the economics of non-normative domesticity through the ritualistic gendered labor performed by the *hijras*. Of the three occupations practiced by members of the community (prostitution, begging, and performance), prostitution is mentioned in the jail scenes and Kamla's relationship with Subbu. While the *hijras* are not directly represented as beggars, Constable Munswamy equates them with beggars in a scene in which street children approach Uma's car to ask for money:

MUNSWAMY: Madam, be careful. The hijras will come running now.
UMA: There are no hijras. Children! Just children.
MUNSWAMY: Same thing. Beggars only, no? (Dattani 18)

Kamala's murder and her lover's suicide at the end of the play reiterates the lack of recognition for and active persecution of those in same-sex relationships in India. While *hijras* have yet to be recognized as a minority community, the state has made token gestures for the protection of other caste-specific minorities. In 1955 the Government of India passed the Untouchability (Offenses) Act, which was amended in 1976 and renamed the Protection of Civil Rights Act. Its most recent form is the Scheduled Castes and the Scheduled Tribes (Prevention of Atrocities) Act, 1989, which is much more stringent than previous provisos (Rao, "Understanding" 300). Here the legislation has been more progressive than in the case of homosexuality, yet lacunae in its implementation have ensured that atrocities against lower castes, especially low caste women, have continued unabated. The preceding discussion of *hijras*, prostitutes, and *rudalis* makes a case for the urgency of feminist recognition. Such recognition and subsequent activism will facilitate the process of legitimizing alternative forms of kinship and assist in securing legal rights for those persecuted for their gendered and sexualized labor practices and orientations. At the same time, as post-*Fire* urban feminist imaginings emphasize, potential alliances with sexual minorities require vigilance about the identity categories gay, lesbian, and queer that may not completely encompass the lived realities of intimacy and sexual expression in India.

The basis for this performative political imagining is already present in these caste- and sexually marked communities. The *hijras* have a nationwide body known as the All India Hijra Kalyan Sabha (Hijra Welfare Organization) that regularly makes demands on the state for inclusion in democratic processes, besides following quasi-judicial procedures deriving from structures of local democracy operating in India. Their *panchayats* or annual gatherings serve as social occasions, meetings for settling issues concerning the community at large, and forums for disciplinary action against offending members. In the same way low caste, or *dalit*, women have formed the National Federation of Dalit Women to mobilize for their rights and representation in the body politic of the nation-state. They presented a Declaration on Gender and Racism at the World Conference Against Racism held in Durban, South Africa, in 2001, highlighting the sexual violence and oppression faced by lower-caste women. These organizational initiatives are a necessary supplement to the politics of indictment articulated in the two plays if the freedom to perform gender and reimagine kinship is to move from the realm of imagination to that of the possible.

RECASTING FEMINISM

To actualize a politics of equality for sexual minorities it is also necessary to create awareness about the multiplicity of indigenous and Western-influenced sexualities. Post-*Fire* there has been a plethora of publications on sexual minorities in India including anthologies by Brinda Bose and Subhabrata Bhattacharya, Arvind Narrain and Gautam Bhan, Hoshang Merchant, Ashwini Sukthankar, and Ruth Vanita and Saleem Kidwai. Some of these emphasize the history of same-sex relationships through a reading of ancient Indian scriptures, archives, and popular literature and culture, but do not direct as much attention to performance traditions among communities where non-normative sexual preferences are sanctioned. Similarly, feminist discussions of caste devote scant attention to female subjectivity outside heteronormative familial structures. These startling omissions in discussions of caste, gender, and sexuality in India lead to drama as an archive and mode of action that challenges and addresses these exclusions by radical forms of social and sexual imagining.

Feminist analyses of sex-, gender-, and class-based oppression have also addressed caste based female socialities, consciousness of oppression and agency, its reflection in literature, the politics of redressing discriminatory laws, and affirmative action policies recently implemented with renewed vigor by the Indian government.[13] The existing framework of class and caste analysis already supports discussion of alternative socialities and sexualities. If caste in India is a form of "embodiment" or an "intimate form of sociality" it may hold the possibility for other intimate forms of low caste socialities that are as yet unrecorded by those recasting feminism to highlight the forms of violence experienced by *dalit* women (Rao 3–14). The questions addressed in this chapter arise from situations in which 'feminized' (marking shifting boundaries of sex, gender, and acceptable sexual and gendered attributes) citizen-subjects, like the *dalit* women in Devi's story and Ganguli's play, and *hijras* in Dattani's play, seek alliance and companionship. How do we theorize the violence experienced by those belonging to these caste-mediated socialities whose potential alliances may also be based on alternative sexual preferences? And why indeed do we need to focus on violence? If caste is an apparatus that regulates sexuality, does this regulation assume that only intercaste heterosexuality needs to be regulated to maintain social hierarchies, or is homosexuality also proscribed within this regulatory mechanism? Can we assume that because homosexuality is non-procreative it does not pose a threat to the caste-regulated sociosexual mechanisms? In either case how do we introduce sexuality as an axis in discussions of caste and gender: as regulated by high caste forms of control or more 'liberated' by being outside the purview of caste based hegemony?

Answers to some of these questions may be found in V. Geetha's homology between Periyar's anti-caste self-respect movement and the women's movement that offers a way of mutually imbricating caste and sexuality by not exclusively focusing on caste related sexual violence or an unrealistic estimate of low caste sexuality as free of social normativity and hence inherently liberatory. Geetha analyzes the self-respecters' politicization of marriage and challenging of sexual relations that sustained caste patriarchy.[14] Issues of pleasure and sexuality were important to men self-respecters, who did not see conjugality or motherhood as determinate experiences (197). Viewing themselves as "citizens of the future," their alliances were based on ideas of women's bodily autonomy and of comradeship in love. The self-respect movement and the women's movement imagine "a utopic citizenship" and a politics of identity that "pitches its arguments in the future." One of Geetha's most important observations is that "a politics of identity need not always work from within already existing subaltern positions. It can also pitch its arguments into the future and in the present which is an anticipation of that future" (199, 202).

The plays analyzed in this chapter can be read along with other Indian dramatists' attempts to 'queer' the Indian stage with indigenous sexualities that are a necessary supplement to the largely urban politics of identity and sexuality deriving from Western categories of sexual identifications. Representations of multiple sexualities were available to Indian theatre-going audiences through Satish Alekar's *Begum Barve,* Vijay Tendulkar's *Mitra's Story,* Vijaydan Detha's story about a lesbian couple adapted for stage, and Rustom Bharucha's Hindi adaptation of Manuel Puig's novel *Kiss of the Spiderwoman.* Not all of these were progressive representations or received as radical statements. Alekar's play about a transvestite's desire to be a 'real' woman used the theatrical conventions of the Marathi stage where men played the roles of women. Tendulkar's play, performed in the early 1980s, staged lesbian sexuality as demonic and destructive. Detha's story "Dohri Joon" ("A Double Life") about two rural women living as a couple was published in 1979 and performed as "Beeja-Teeja" by college students in New Delhi in the early 1980s (Vanita and Kidwai 318). Bharucha's Hindi adaptation of Puig's novel was staged in the early 1990s. Through these proscenium productions that reached audiences in urban locations such as Ahmedabad, Calcutta, Delhi, and Thane, dramatists had already broken the silence regarding performed genders and proscribed sexualities. At least from the late 1970s onwards these nuanced presentations of familial, religious, class, caste, and communitarian contexts influencing alternative sexual expression prepared the ground for Ganguli's and Dattani's dramatization of queer subalternity in the 1990s.

This chapter proposed that ways of expressing gender in performance reveal the mutual imbrication of caste and sexuality to create a discursive and social space for those who are stigmatized by both. It follows then that democratic futures for sexual minorities will involve considering the legal and economic consequences of alternative sexual and familial choices. Feminists' articulations of "atrocities" and "violence" visited upon the body of the *dalit* woman have prepared the ground for such a future. Such articulations can go beyond their immediate references to analyze the stigmatization and destitution of marginalized communities through the axes of sex work, gendered labor, and alternative domesticities. Postcolonial drama in many Indian languages (including English) has anticipated, in a small and hitherto ignored way, Indian feminists' political imaginings as well as a performative resignification of these imaginings to include gender and sexual justice. In representing new socialities and sexualities—work-based communities, non-biological kinship, and non-discriminatory citizenship—drama and theatre in India consolidates its already existing alliances with feminist activism and imagines potential alliances with queer activism.

Part III
Nigeria

5 Resistant Citizenship
Reading Feminist Praxis and Democratic Renewal in Nigeria through Femi Osofisan's *Morountodun*

> I accept that entity, Nigeria, as a space into which I happen to be born, and therefore a space within which I am bound to collaborate with fellow occupants in the pursuit of justice and ethical life, to establish a guaranteed access for all to the resources it produces, and to thwart every tendency in any group to act against that determined common indicator of a rational social existence. [. . .] Clearly, that space, Nigeria, cannot be the duty and the burden of the writer and the intellectual alone. Indeed, our function is primarily to project those voices that, despite massive repression, continue to place their governments on notice.
>
> (Wole Soyinka, *The Open Sore of a Continent* 134–35)

As if anticipating Soyinka—twenty years before he called Nigeria an "open sore" on the African continent—Nigerian drama provides an accessible archive and index to the script of resistance against docile citizenship by projecting voices that placed the government on notice. To continue with the metaphor, state-sponsored and autonomous women's mobilization in Nigeria during this period is a scarcely remembered postscript to this resistance. Femi Osofisan's *Morountodun,* conceptualized and developed during the period of Nigeria's second attempt at a transition to democracy (1979–1983), and performed at the Universities of Ibadan and Ife, illuminates trends in the feminist movement, dramatic production, and national politics in the country. In this play Osofisan turns the spotlight on democratic imaginings by revisiting the Agbekoya peasant rebellion of the 1960s and foregrounding the contribution of women in revolutionary movements. While Osofisan's play does not originate in a revisionist historical impulse, there is a conjuncture between his emphasis on revolutionary praxis and Nigerian feminists' efforts to seek participation in the country's second experiment with democratic renewal. The play can thus be seen as a performance event drawing from and commenting on amendments proposed to alter gendered structures of political power in Nigeria. Reading the play in this manner enables an inquiry into the reality and vision of postcolonial nationalism in Nigeria: first, the revolutionary project (whether secessionist, resource redistributive, or pro-democracy) as indelibly gendered and sexualized; second, cultural production and the women's movement in Nigeria articulating "postcolonial desire," or the "act of imagining, living and negotiating a social reality based on democracy, cultural pluralism, and social justice" (Ampka 10).

The umbrella organization for women's welfare in the country is the National Council of Women's Societies (NCWS), founded in the immediate post-independence moment. Over the decades the NCWS has arrogated to itself the role of a facilitator for grassroots women's developmental concerns. It is supported in its projects by the state since its policies, outlined by upper-class women in entrepreneurial and bureaucratic positions, are largely accommodative of status quoist models of women's development. In contrast, cultural mobilization, research, and activism by feminists and theatre practitioners at Ahmadu Bello University merit attention for the role played by intellectuals in critically transformative social action. An autonomous anti-establishment feminist movement in Nigeria in the late seventies and early eighties can be traced to the organization Women in Nigeria (WIN), that arose out of a study group and a conference held at Ahmadu Bello University, Zaria.

With the concerns that motivated both state-related and autonomous Nigerian feminists in the late seventies and early eighties as an analytical lens, this chapter first looks at the cultural intertexts to Osofisan's use of the figure of Moremi, the legendary heroine of Ile-Ife, to represent the events of the Agbekoya peasant uprising.[1] Next, it addresses subaltern democracy by interrogating recent theorizations of citizenship, democracy, and resistance by Mahmood Mamdani and Achille Mdembe to indicate how the revolutionary and the national scripts reflect each other in obscuring women's actual and potential contribution in postcolonial national and democratic reconstruction. The final section examines the university as the site for alternative conceptualizations of this reconstruction by reading some scenes from *Morountodun*, a sample of critical commentary on it, and an essay by the playwright as reflecting awareness of second-wave feminist concerns in Nigeria. This interrogation into the literary, cultural, and political influences on the play lead towards a theorization of university-based dramatic productions, feminist mobilization, and in some cases a fortuitous conjunction of the two, as forms of 'citizenship education' in Nigeria in keeping with the idea of citizen-audiences sketched out in the Jamaican and Indian contexts.

MATERIALIST MYTHOGRAPHY

Osofisan's play, first performed at the University of Ibadan in 1979 and then at the University of Ife in the 1980s, evokes Moremi in the actions of the female protagonist, Titubi, later renamed Morountodun. The playwright's materialist mythography can be located in the interweaving of the individual and the social in the peasant movement it depicts and Titubi's attendant transformation from bourgeois to revolutionary consciousness. As indicated in the director's address to the audience, the play is a dramatization of the 1969 Agbekoya peasant uprising during the Biafran war. The Agbekoya revolt was considered a minor, regional peasant uprising against unfairly high taxation on agricultural produce, but by late 1968 it had become a coalition of "relatively enlightened peasants, and some middle class professionals and urban elites" (Adeniran 369). The play begins, in characteristic Brechtian anti-naturalistic fashion, with the actors in the dressing area getting ready for the performance. While the director is trying to marshal the actors, Titubi, market leader Alhaja Kabirat's daughter, walks in with a group of women to protest against the representation of the peasant rebellion in the play within the play. With the arrival of the police Titubi finds herself facing Superintendent Salami, who taunts her by asking "if you really want to save your fat-arsed class, why haven't you offered your services to crush this peasant rebellion?" (137) Humiliated and cornered she offers her services to the state. By volunteering to infiltrate the peasants she attempts to become a modern-day Moremi. The opening scene of *Morountodun* thus establishes the connection between the Brechtian form and the materialist content of the play.

After she joins the peasants as an agent of the state, Titubi's subsequent development in revolutionary consciousness leads to her repudiation of the cultural heroism associated with Moremi: "I knew I had to kill the ghost of Moremi in my belly. I am not Moremi! Moremi served the State, *was* the State, was the spirit of the ruling class. But it is not true that the State is always right..." (185). Titubi's initial collaboration with the state followed by her solidarity with the revolutionary cause is a historically accurate representation of the revolt; her transformation dramatically inverts the "common sense" logic which dictates the improbability of sustained cross-class alliances in Nigeria (Olaniyan 78).

Two dramatic productions may have had an impact on Osofisan's transformation of the Moremi legend in depicting the evolution of a pro-establishment bourgeois woman into a revolutionary. Duro Ladipo's Yoruba Opera, *Moremi*, first premiered in July 1965, had already laid the groundwork for a dramatic rendition of the Moremi legend. In Ladipo's rendering, Moremi is a wealthy cloth dealer, a market woman who risks her life and sacrifices her son to discover the secret of the Ibos' success in their attacks on the Yorubas. It is symptomatic of Ladipo's pro-democracy position that the Yoruba ruler's decisions are always made in consultation with a body of "Citizens" who propose that Moremi should be appointed the Market Commandant. In a further reinforcement of the democratic ethos, Moremi's ascendancy over the market women does not preclude her consultation with them to protect the market from falling into Ibo hands. As a leading representative of the citizens, particularly the market women, Moremi's elevation to a tragic heroine works through a contrast with the weak and ineffectual King Alayemore. Her promise to sacrifice her son to the goddess Esinmirin in return for success in the chosen endeavor further elevates her as a tragic heroine. Yet this action reinforces the sacrifice of the individual for the social in the Yoruba worldview enacted in Ladipo's opera. Moremi becomes an agent of reconciliation between the two warring tribes since she enjoins upon the Yorubas not to kill the Ibo king but to accord him a place of honor. This aspect of the opera would undoubtedly have had special resonance for the audience at the moment of its recorded performance in 1971, soon after the end of the Biafran war.[2]

The intertextual references traced here lead to Osofisan's play *The Chattering and the Song* (1976), produced at the University of Ibadan. Focusing more on individual choices with the Farmer's Movement as a backdrop, this play is ostensibly a love triangle between the university-educated intellectuals: Sontri, Mokan, and Yajin. Yajin's rejection of her betrothed Mokan and choice of the committed intellectual Sontri, an artist revolutionary who composes songs for the Movement, is presented as a romantic rather than a class preference. Through a complex plot framed by riddling games in the opening and concluding scenes, Osofisan explores two major issues that he later uses in a different form in *Morountodun*: the role of women in the revolution; and the function of art in struggles for social justice. The embedding of the individual in larger social processes is minimal in this play where the Farmer's Movement serves merely as a reference point to illuminate the dynamics of the characters' romantic and sexual choices.

The Marxist playwright Bode Sowande attempts a synthesis of the individual and the social to evoke the mood of national despair referenced by the farmer's revolt in *Farewell to Babylon,* produced in Ibadan in 1978. Osofisan's *The Chattering and the Song* may have been an intertext for Sowande's dramatization of the revolt. Whereas Ladipo's opera, a possible source for Osofisan's *Morountodon*, directs attention to women's role in national regeneration through Moremi, Sowande points to gender as the central problematic in elite and peasant efforts at national reconstruction through a Moremi-like figure in *Farewell to Babylon*. In this play Moniran is an agent of the state but a covert supporter of the farmers' rebellion, much like Mokan in Osofisan's *The Chattering and the Song*. Moniran's diagnosis of the fragmented national consciousness, "two nations in one," is based on the elite nationalist perception of the farmers having formed a "state within a state" (Sowande 63, 67). Both popular and elite mobilization presented in Sowande's play instrumentalize female sexuality. Thus Moniran's covertly anti-establishment plans as well as the peasant leader Dansaki's plans involve using Jolomi as a pawn in the game of power. As a sexualized woman amid apparently desexualized revolutionaries, Jolomi disrupts the quasi-religious sanctity of the Circle or the inner core of revolutionaries. She comes to embody the blurred boundaries between sexualized unproductivity and a desexualized socially productive military or maternal corporeality.

These intertexts to *Morountodun*—Ladipo's Yoruba opera *Moremi*, one of Osofisan's early plays *The Chattering and the Song* on the Farmer's Movement (not specifically identified as Agbekoya), and Sowande's university-based production of the farmer's revolt—gesture towards a female revolutionary nationalist consciousness. One of the most important aspects of the performance of the Moremi legend in Ladipo's opera and elite and popular forms of nationalism in Sowande's play is the disjunction between the individual and the social in the nationalist cause. Sowande's materialist aesthetics often lapses into an overdose of Marxism, somewhat redeemed by reflexivity about the almost complete masculinization of the revolutionary and ideological ethos. Ladipo's opera by the very nature of its genre draws upon folklore, ritual, dance, and music to present the Moremi legend.

A somewhat more sophisticated materialist analysis—one that is irreverent and poignant at different moments, rather than consistently strident—is characteristic of *Morountodun*. Features that evoke local performance traditions are also evident, particularly in the scenes where Titubi spars with Superintendent Salami or joins in the songs, dances, riddles, and games of the peasant women. Moremi, the tragic cultural heroine, becomes a means of inscribing the peasant's revolt into a nationalist mythography that has hitherto written out the gendered, sexual, and economically underprivileged from its annals. Thus the figure of Moremi provides a way of analyzing the nature, scope, and limits of postcolonial pro-democratic nationalism. Responding to a rigid revolutionary nationalism that demands a sublimation of the sexual for the social, *Morountodun* depicts how gender and sexuality define the limits of this prescriptive agenda. My analysis of *Morountodun* in this chapter describes the incomplete imagination of subaltern democracies founded on revolutionary movements.

THE STATE AND THE SUBALTERN

To discuss the limits of subaltern political imaginings it is essential to outline why Osofisan felt the need to dramatize the revolutionary movement with reference to a particular peasant movement of the sixties. *Morountodun* can be contextualized through historical and political accounts of Nigeria's second transition to democracy describing 'performances' of the state and bearing on Osofisan's play as a performance event. This enables a thick description of the circumstances that help determine whether cultural productions can assist in 'citizenship education'. The immediate impetus for Osofisan's play can be found in the Nigerian socio-political landscape of the late seventies, making *Morountodun* a significant performance event of this period. Analyzing the rise and fall of Nigeria's second transition to democracy, referred to as the "Second Republic," Toyin Falola and Julius Ihonvbere observe that the oil boom of the seventies led to the neglect of agriculture and rural areas. The consequent contradictions in the economy impacted most seriously on agriculture and rural-urban relations; these were evident in "rising unemployment, particularly of university and graduate students, social violence, armed robbery and inter- and intra-class struggles" (97–98, 105). Falola and Ihonvbere's account of agriculture and the food crisis during the Second Republic holds the military regimes' and the democratically elected government's capitulation to Structural Adjustment Policies, imposition of World Bank farm projects, and enforced displacement of the peasantry from their landholdings, responsible for the deteriorating agricultural situation.

While the state's record in ensuring the well-being of the food producers of the nation fell drastically short of its stated intentions, the public declaration of those intentions constituted another performance of sorts. The Murtala-Obasanjo military regime, preceding the democratically elected Shehu Shagari government, relied on "propaganda and rhetoric" instead of addressing the structural problems responsible for declining food production. General Obasanjo introduced Operation Feed the Nation (OFN) with much fanfare; it was "initiated and executed on television and bill-boards by well-dressed and rosy-cheeked army generals and top bureaucrats." The Nigerians, ever quick to subvert official acronyms, renamed the program "Obasanjo Finish Naira (OFN) or Operation Finish Naira (OFN)" (Falola and Ihonvbere 122–24).[3] A similar performance was undertaken by the Shagari government in connection with the Green Revolution, its successes declared through the media and in official speeches. Despite excessive bureaucratization and massive corruption, Shagari presented the program as a success. Not only did the Nigerian public counter these claims by labeling Shagari "share-the-garri" and the Green Revolution as "Greed Revolution," but they also recognized it as an image-building exercise. As one commentator observed, "Shagari grew food on television, he provided qualitative education and shelter on television, he fought inflation and unemployment on television . . ." (qtd. in Falola and Ihonvbere 128, 134).

Given the discrepancy between this political act and material conditions, it is not surprising that Osofisan comments on these events by staging a play in *Morountodun* performed by agents of the state entrusted with maintaining law and order. Towards the middle of the play when Titubi's mother, Alhaja Kabirat, makes her second appearance at the police station to inquire into the whereabouts of her daughter, Superintendent Salami mocks her: "This recurring question. 'My daughter! My daughter!' It's like a scene in a play. Do you like the theatre, Alhaja? Me, I'm simply crazy about it. Ask Corple, he's our Secretary in the Police Drama Club. I'm President." Salami and the Corporal make fun of her by staging the Moremi legend in which, true to form, they represent an exaggerated agony at the loss of state authority: "We lament the land. We weep for the lack of peace, for the violence in the air. We weep that rebels beyond our power fall upon us at will and make mockery of our manhood. Our towns are unsafe. Food no longer reaches the markets, taxes are unpaid. All over . . ."(175).

Another satirical performance, this time subversive rather than parodic, occurs when the peasant women supporting the revolutionaries recollect the visit of the Governor to try and persuade the insurgents into laying down arms. He tries to convince them to accept an unjust yet docile citizenship by handing the revolutionaries over to the authorities: "We shall deal with them. And above all you must pay your tax, it's the only way we can help you [. . .] Pay your tax! Pay your tax!" (180). These dramatic exhortations are a version of Shagari's hyperbolic declarations of his intentions to improve the economic situation. A typical political speech lists the ills plaguing the country and calls on divine aid: "I intend to revamp the economy and continue to pilot our nation on the path to political stability as well as provide increased development in order to improve the quality of life and security of the individual. I will need the guidance of God in order to achieve these objectives" (qtd. in Falola and Ihonvbere 117). Such declarations elicited a sharp response from cultural activists: Sowande's play about the Farmer's Movement was performed in 1978, and Osofisan's play, which gives the movement the historically recorded label Agbekoya, was first performed in 1979 and then in 1980. In the same year, acting on state orders, the Nigerian police allegedly killed farmers and their families while evicting them from lands sold to a foreign construction company. The incident of the massacre of peasants at Bakolori is dramatized by Tunde Fatunde in *No Food, No Country* (1985).[4] Osofisan's representation of the peasants' politicization and the conscientization of the bourgeoisie into supporters of the revolution is thus part of this vehement cultural response, albeit one that is implicated in the very processes he hopes to critique. Perhaps this realization led to the playwright abstaining from the representation of university-educated intelligentsia as the vanguard of peasant revolutions depicted in *The Chattering and the Song*.

As described although not enacted in *Morountodun*, the peasants' armed struggle for an equal distribution of resources is the result of a failed process of negotiation with the state and its representatives. The peasant elder, Baba, recapitulates the torturous process that led them to decide that they had no recourse except violence:

> We said we couldn't pay the tax, that harvests were poor, that we could hardly feed our children. And what happened? The government said, all right, we'll change the tax collectors. [. . .] They merely reshuffled the Council, and made you, Alhaji Buraihmoh, its new chairman. You came here demanding our cooperation, and when we refused, you brought the police back. (167)

Alhaji's punishment involves a forfeiture of his harvest and being detained as a hostage till the "class war" is over (171). The redistributive justice that is explained and executed is in contrast to methods adopted by the state and in keeping with the logic of organizations such the Yoruba-dominated

Oodua People's Congress which emerged as a pro-democracy group in the 1990s and involved "vigilantes' understanding of community security" (Nolte 84). A spate of armed robberies in Nigeria in the 1970s was severely punished by much-publicized executions of the robbers. Osofisan's play *Once Upon Four Robbers* is an indictment of the cheapening of human life into a grisly spectacle by these modes of state (in)justice.

Besides execution, imprisonment is another common mode of state justice. Marshal and some of his supporters declare their intention to destroy one of the central symbols of state repression, the Central Police Station. Marshal's evocative description of the horrors of the prison housed in this building is reminiscent of Ngugi wa Thiong'o's theorization of the prison as the central metaphor for postcolonial space: "All the filthy cells and dungeons in which our people groan their life out. And fine young men are broken, beyond recognition, into blabbering idiots. The torture chambers and solitary confinements where men are changed to rat and roach" (*Penpoints* 60). The prison as a colonial institution symbolized the authorities' fear of open spaces; the fear is pervasive in postcolonial authoritarian regimes. Because the masses can use open spaces for collective mobilization, protests, both theatrical and political, are violently suppressed. Marshal's planned mode of action in the play includes the destruction of the prison in "one huge conflagration" so that "true freedom can begin at last" (191). As a colonially inherited mode of administering state justice, imprisonment is put to maximum use in authoritarian as well as democratic postcolonial states.

Mahmood Mamdani's complex argument about "the regime of differentiation (institutional segregation) as fashioned in colonial Africa—and reformed after independence—and the nature of the resistance it bred" offers further insights on this issue (7). Mamdani's primary and key example of institutional segregation is apartheid in South Africa; this dictates his focus on the two-pronged division (between town and country and between ethnicities) enforced by the colonial state on the colonized and the systems of governance inherited by postcolonial states.[5] The prison can be taken as the postcolonial variant of institutional segregation in a "deracialized" and "detribalized" nation-state, whether authoritarian or nominally democratic, as was the case in Nigeria from 1979 to 1983. As Osofisan's play depicts, the threat of imprisonment characterizes the limits where docile subjecthood (good peasants are asked to pay their taxes) becomes resistant citizenship (revolutionaries who "mislead" the docile peasantry).

Achille Mdembe's detailed identification of the correlates of *commandement* in the postcolony connects to Ngugi's and Mamdani's accounts of colonial and postcolonial segregation. Some of the features of *commandement* in the African postcolony that Mdembe outlines are: a differential system of laws and rights for different sections of the population; a regime of privileges, rights, and immunities including the right to introduce and raise taxes; a collapse of the distinction between ruling and civilizing in colonial times that translates into "an *imaginary* of the [postcolonial] state making it the organizer of public happiness"; and the institutional machinery of the postcolonial state as demanding submission rather than being based on a conception of public good (29–33). Although Mdembe's macro political analysis collapses the distinctions between the historical trajectories of African nations, some of these characteristics of the postcolony are directly applicable to the structures of governance in postcolonial Nigeria. Additionally, his elaboration of the postcolonial "compromise" as consisting in the "redistribution of utilities that partially underpinned the legitimacy of postcolonial government and also made the relations of inequality and coercion morally tolerable" (51) resonates with my proposition that the subaltern democratic project is resource redistributive.

Mdembe's arguments on postcolonial citizenship and subject status can be seen as supplementing Mamdani's focus on colonial modes of governance. Two key chapters from their books illustrate the shifts and continuities. In the introduction to *Citizen and Subject* Mamdani speaks about the colonial policy of indirect rule and its effects on the institutionalization of segregation. Mdembe's "On Private Indirect Government" can be read as a diagnosis of this impasse: the financial indebtedness of many African states to international creditors such as the IMF and the World Bank has led to the undermining of the state's "fragile material base" and erosion of the systems of privileges and clientelistic relations constituting the compromise that gave it some "social cohesion" (73–75). Mdembe's prescriptive diagnosis of the postcolony in its attention towards the "salary-earner," "citizen," and "client" as "reciprocally reproducing one another," is limited in its applicability for peasant citizen-subjects. His diagnosis is also affected by a propensity to sympathize with the state by granting it the status of a victim rather than a perpetrator of injustice for certain sections of the population. For Mdembe, because of the "general insolvency and material deprivation" the state is "unable to make necessary decisions on who is to get what, and to determine the social compromises vital [. . .] to the very production of public order" (75).

At least in Nigeria, there has been little attempt on the part of the state to remedy these conditions of insolvency and material deprivation.[6] Marked by divisions between ethnicities and also between the town and the country, the peasants are the prototypical subjects of the Nigerian nation-state. The Agbekoya peasant insurgency was concurrent with the ethnic divisions reinforced by the Biafran war as outlined in the "rapid summary" provided by the Director at the beginning of *Morountodun:*

> The play, as you will soon see, starts in the year 1969, the month of September. That year, if you will remember, the civil war was raging in the east of the country, but this play has nothing to do with that. It deals with another war, the one that was later to be popularly known as the Agbekoya uprising, in which ordinary farmers, in the west of the country, rose up and confronted the state [. . .] Farmers dying,

policemen falling, soldiers going and not returning. Were they not all our kinsmen? If we could not speak about the war in the east, because of still decrees, would we also be silent about the one in the west. And suppose another one should start in the north? Well, we decided not to be silent. We decided to go and rouse people up by doing a play on the subject. (130)

Contrary to the Director's assertion, the play does not remain silent about the war in the East. Its use of the Moremi legend refers as much to Titubi's growing awareness of and shift in class allegiances as to the history of conflict between ethnicities in Nigeria, of which the Biafran war was a recent instance.

If Moremi's story refers to inter-ethnic conflict, the peasants as prototypical subjects of the Nigerian nation-state discuss the contrast between the city and country. The most obvious point of contrast is between glut and deprivation. Marshal's scathing comment about the lack of compassion of city people and their leaders is that "the well-fed dog has no thought for those who are hungry" (163). The trial of Lawyer Isaac and Alhaji Buraihmoh, two city dwellers who were chosen by the peasants as their representatives, is for their "betrayal of the cause," lending credence to Mamdani's assertion that the ethnic definitions of most postcolonial peasant movements in Africa "took on the dimensions of a civil war inside the ethnic group," or were sometimes "a violation of kinship norms." This leads to the question, "if the struggle against the local authority of indirect rule state is necessarily ethnic ... what then is the democratic potential of popular insurgency in the ethnic civil war?" (Mamdani 197–203). Or rather, if the imagination of democracy in inter-ethnic conflict (Biafran civil war) was characterized by secession and independent governance, what was the aim of the intra-ethnic 'civil war' between city and country dwellers?

A lack of convergence of interests between city- and country-dwelling members of the same ethnic group also leads to the central problematic of lack of consensus among peasant groups. This dissensus can be used to discuss the construction of peasant communities in social struggles, and to understand the contradictory ways in which these communities are reorganized. Mamdani's examples of such peasant communities include the Sungusungu from Tanzania and the Ruwenzururu on the mountains of the Uganda-Zaire border.[7] In both movements it was the poorer peasants who formed the backbone of the armed struggle. Mamdani's oral sources revealed that affluent peasantry among the Ruwenzururu and the Sungusungu dissociated themselves from the struggle by moving away from the region or bribing state personnel. The poorer peasants in Zaire formed highly decentralized alternative organizations at the village level. The village-wide popular assemblies controlled a popular militia (the Sungusungu) and dispensed popular justice. Vigilante work carried out by the members in small groups could include unmarried women but married women were always excluded. In contrast, the Ruwenzururu partially included married and unmarried women, who were encouraged to attend the lower assembly of the "reformed state structure," but the popular assemblies (which exercised judicial and legislative powers) were predominantly male (Mamdani 206–7).

While Osofisan does not depict the Agebkoya movement as founded on the complete exclusion of women, married or unmarried, he does indicate the patriarchal and hierarchical nature of organization on at least two different occasions in the play. At the peasants' trial of the Alhaji, Baba and Marshal try to persuade Mosun to save herself the sight of her father's (Alhaji's) possible execution. Besides sparing her any emotional trauma she might suffer from attending the trial, Marshal also decrees that the women and children among the peasantry will stay with relatives and friends in the city to "save them from the continuous panic of our movements each time the government forces attack." Mosun's response to both these injunctions is to openly confront the leadership with the accusation that they "wish to create privilege in our ranks." This questioning enables her to stay on with the male revolutionaries, who are at the forefront of the struggle. Titubi is also allowed to accompany them as nurse and caregiver for the injured. Her status as an outsider, a person from the city, differentiates her till she protests about how much she is expected to contribute to the movement to "qualify" as one of them. Baba's response is an inclusive one: "Forgive us. The outsider who shares our salt and our suffering is already a kinsman." Towards the end of the play, intervening in the conflict between Baba and Marshal about the decision to continue the armed struggle or to give peace a chance, the women respond to Marshal's condescending rhetorical question, "Are we to argue this out in front of the women?" by the collective declaration: "We want to hear this too, Marshal" (164–65, 190).

Largely due to the conditions in Nigeria at the time the play was conceived and performed, the as-yet-unattained democracy detailed by Osofisan is primarily resource redistributive in its ideology. This is evinced in the recurrent contrast between the affluence of city life and the deprivations faced by the peasant communities in rural areas. At the level of class, gender, and methods of continuation of movement politics, there is very little agreement among the peasants since the conclusion of the play presents two differing perspectives on the imagination and actualization of subaltern democracy. In the light of Baba's acknowledgment of "outsiders" as "kin" we can see the contours of the revolutionary community forged out of interclass alliances. Marshal intends to continue the struggle to strike at the very heart of state power by attacking the police station but Baba is willing to give the state an opportunity to redeem itself, to "give the truce a chance" (191). In this uneasily negotiated truce lies the possible transformation of the revolutionary community to a national community premised on democratic rather than vigilante processes, making it legitimate to question the purported aims of Nigeria's second attempt at democracy.

SCRIPTING DEMOCRACY, POSTSCRIPTING WOMEN

An answer about the aims of the democratic process probably lies in the draft forwarded in 1975 by the Constitution Drafting Committee comprising the "fifty wise men" drawn from various professions including politicians, academics, medical personnel, engineers, and civil servants. The constitution that was being prepared was supposed to provide a blueprint for a modern, democratic Nigerian nation-state. It is symptomatic of the gender biases of these founding fathers and the military regime, which appointed them to their onerous task, that the committee did not include a single woman, not even a token elite representative who could be said to represent the interests of women in Nigeria. Ironically, this was also the period when feminist mobilization was at its peak in the country. While the supposedly autonomous but actually state-supportive organization, the National Council of Women's Societies (NCWS), had been active in various projects from the sixties onwards, a feminist movement representing a younger generation of women vehemently critical of the state's gender policies arose out of a conference held at Ahmadu Bello University in Zaria in 1982. The strategies employed to sideline women from processes of constitutional democracy are evident by juxtaposing feminist analyses of Nigerian democracy with *Morountodun*. I am offering an understanding of second-wave feminist mobilization in Nigeria through a symptomatic reading of the playscript and its postscripts, including critical commentary and authorial meditations.

Commenting on women and pro-democracy politics in Nigeria, Pat Williams contends that the position of women has not improved significantly either since 1960 when the county achieved independence or since 1976 when they were granted universal adult suffrage. Holding women, in some measure, culpable for their co-optation in and contribution to male-dominated politics, Williams notes their token representation under the Shagari government when three women were appointed federal ministers. Usually women's participation in politics has been restricted to the women's wing of the political parties, as was the case during the transition years 1979–1983. Williams's observations indicate an awareness of the cultural, economic, and religious constraints on the participation of women in politics. She also indicts economically successful women for their indifference to political processes (219–42). Osofisan presents this political indifference in Titubi in the opening scene of the play and in the subsequent scenes through Alhaja Kabirat, whose only concern is the state of the market and the possible disruption of her profitable trade owing to revolutionary violence.

From its inception in 1958 as an umbrella organization for women's concerns in Nigeria, the NCWS—which predominantly includes women like Alhaja Kabirat—claims to have had a special relationship with market women as representatives of the "grassroots." The NCWS's emphasis was on transforming women into "citizens" who could advance social growth;

its members were prominent female citizens in Nigeria who viewed the advancement of women in Nigeria as their mission and goal. Sola Ojewusi's mammoth celebratory history of the NCWS mentions without a hint of irony that its battle against "discrimination" included recommending to the government the removal of tax exemption for women. Ojewusi acknowledges that this may seem like "anti-women advocacy" but mentions that to the NCWS this was a "patriotic" step since the organization saw the payment of taxes as one of the responsibilities of women in nation building. In the context of the state's goal of creating docile citizens versus the revolutionary program of resistant citizenship, women like Alhaja Kabirat and her daughter, Titubi (before she is converted to the revolutionary cause), whose interests were represented by bodies like the NCWS, realize the advantages of docility in safeguarding their class interests.

The NCWS's advocacy of patriotic tax-paying citizenship militates against the established tradition of Nigerian feminist activism since colonial times.[8] NCWS's stand on the military regime's politically questionable move of not having any woman on the Constitution Drafting Committee is illustrative of a conflict-bypassing ideology. It asked for more women in public offices, but specified that these should be filled with men and women of discipline, integrity (reflected in their stable and happy family lives), and honest means of livelihood. The criteria for inclusion of women into the democratic process as outlined by the NCWS remain as vague as did the promises of the military dictatorship and the democratically elected government. Just as genuine democratization of the revolutionary cause entails an integration of women into the struggle and reformed political structures arising out of that struggle, the complete realization of democracy in Nigeria would have involved adequate female representation in the CDC. On this view Marshal's grudging permission to Mosun allowing her and Titubi to accompany the revolutionaries, and the military dictatorship's decision to appoint subcommittees representing the interests of women to the CDC, are both token gestures. In Femi Osofisan's dramatic script of resistant citizenship as well as the CDC's national script of docile citizenship, the concerns of women are appended as a negotiable postscript.

These gestures were, however, not uncontested. The charitable and missionary attitude of the NCWS towards the constituency of grassroots women that it claims to represent has been attacked by the autonomous women's organization Women in Nigeria. The history of the setting up of this organization is part of a larger narrative of the university as a site for citizenship education. To recapitulate the argument thus far: the neat dichotomization of the individual from the social premised on female sexuality was detrimental to the national cause; gendered exclusions were evident in the imagination of subaltern democracies; these reflected the marginalization of women from the process of democratic participation at the national level.

CITIZENSHIP EDUCATION

Wole Soyinka's semi-autobiographical memoir *Ibadan: The Penkelemes Years* is perhaps the best account of the destruction of university autonomy in the "*penkelemes* or peculiar mess" of postcolonial Nigerian politics. Soyinka's detailed recounting of repeated attacks on the university as an institution illustrates that "in the opinion of the political party governing the state, the academic sector is the main obstacle to its total control of popular thought" (240–41). Following his narration we learn how Lagos University, like Ibadan and Ife before it, slid into the "seemingly mandatory rite of passage—the academic *penkelemes*" thus proving the claim that the university as a "national institution" had as its destiny "an arena of perverse theatricality" (Soyinka 316–18). The memoir is also striking for the self-representation of a cultural and political icon whose activities as a drama practitioner and as one given to dramatic anti-establishment spectacle, constitutes resistant citizenship.

There are many examples of resistant citizenship emanating from universities in Nigeria in the period under discussion. With respect to gender politics, the feminist organization Women in Nigeria (WIN) initially started as a study group to grow into a wider interdepartmental women's social sciences group at Ahmadu Bello University, Zaria. In her exhaustive study on gender, class, and women's organizations in Nigeria, Ifi Amadiume describes WIN's growth "out of university campus politics to an independent national organization," and sets up an explicit contrast between the NCWS and WIN. Even though WIN's urban-based membership is elite in composition, its stance, unlike that of the NCWS, is distinctly anti-establishment. While it has been responsive to criticisms of elitism and has shifted its focus from academic and urban concerns to work at the grassroots level, Amadiume identifies lack of ideological self-definition as a serious problem confronting the organization (*Daughters* 69). Responding specifically to this charge Ayesha Imam, one of WIN's founders, characterized its difference from existing women's organizations, including the NCWS, as conscious "political ideology" based on the principle of transforming both "gender *and* class" relations in society (291). Imam also mentions WIN's primary aim to raise public awareness about gender and class relations on specific issues, including the economy, the census, sexual harassment, women's reproductive health, the proposed transition to civilian rule, and women's legal rights. One means of "public education" adopted is popular theatre, and the group defines much of this political activity as "a general defense (and extension) of democratic, legal, citizen's rights" towards articulating "a gender identity that is national in its orientation" (Imam 293–95).

This feminist initiative emanating from the university is part of the cultural and political legacy of Nigerian universities' combative engagement with the governments in power. Given that universities in Nigeria (as in Jamaica and India) are state creations and at least a small number of the student population is likely to join the echelons of the government upon completion of their degrees, the university as an institution is deeply implicated in the programs and policies of the state. Do we then dismiss all consciousness-raising efforts emanating from universities, dramatic, feminist, or a conjunction of the two, as always compromised? This chapter has indicated that Nigerian universities offered significant cultural responses to the national situation around the time of the Second Republic. It has presented how the imagination of democracy was concurrent with the exclusion of women from the subaltern and elite nationalist projects. Nigerian feminism, some of it originating in the academic and institutional space of the university, forcefully responded to this exclusion. The university at this specific moment in Nigerian political history was the site of both a social movement and a cultural response. Thus if *Morountodun* dramatizes a revolutionary movement subscribing to a resource redistributive ideology and a negotiated female participation in the imagination of democracy, we can safely propose that the cultural rejoinder is ahead of the social movements for democracy and women's rights. Although it is advisable to be modest in making revolutionary claims in relation to state-funded institutions, it is also useful to remember that although WIN originated as elite feminist mobilizing, it attempted, and to a certain extent succeeded, in conjoining the cultural and the social, through the "national" gender identity it sought to articulate.

Critical commentary on *Morountodun* demonstrates an awareness of women's role in the national processes, and interprets Osofisan's cultural representation as a simplistic reflection of a pre-existing social movement. Saint Gbilekaa observes that since this play was commissioned to commemorate the 'International Year of Women' (an observation I have not been able to confirm; my research suggests that the play premiered at the Arts Theatre, Ibadan in 1979), Osofisan has tried to project the role of women in the predominantly masculinist Nigerian society. And further, that Osofisan "debunks the contemporary myth that restricts the role of our womenfolk to the kitchen and their husband's bedrooms" (Gbilekaa 106). Such an optimistic reading is not borne out by either the position of women in the Agbekoya revolutionary movement politics enacted in the play or the contemporary socio-political landscape in which it was performed. Sandra Richards's exhaustive commentary on *Morountodun* focuses on the feminist message of the scene where the women play a riddling game with Titubi in an attempt to make her confess her love for Marshal. "Particularly for those interested in feminist theory," Richards writes, "this brief interlude may suggest ways of linking what are often perceived as divergent ideologies." The Yoruba festival practice of *gelede* (associated with a founding foremother, thus a celebration of womanhood and motherhood) evoked in the scene "may be used as a tropological paradigm enabling the merger of the spiritualism of feminism with the dialectics of its material proponents" (Richards 110–11). The scene does not corroborate Richards's reading of it as a merger of indigenous feminism and revolutionary materialism, although it does indicate that the mode of social action described by Osofisan is not predicated upon a dichotomizing of the individual and the social enacted upon the gendered and sexualized body of the woman. To that extent, *Morountodun* is more feminist than some of its intertexts discussed early on in this chapter.

Some evidence of the harmonization of the individual with the social is to be found in the conclusion of the play when Marshal decides to continue the armed struggle after renaming Titubi "Morountodun" or "I have found a sweetness" and accepts her love. However, the time to think of the comforts of home and a family has not yet arrived since his martial masculinity is predicated upon a temporary repudiation of marital domesticity. Marshal's 'sacrifice' for the revolutionary cause involves a conscious choice; but the consequences of these choices are not heroism or victimhood as in the case of the female protagonists in *Moremi* and *Farewell to Babylon*. Osofisan's open-ended dramaturgy invites audience response to the conclusion of the play in keeping with the Brechtian mode of "changing its disposition from dormancy to action" (Abubakar 185). If the play does indeed have a feminist message reflecting the attempts to create a women's movement independent of state apparati, it consists in the stage direction concluding the play when Moremi and Titubi stand facing each other, the former an agent of the state and the latter, having rejected what Moremi symbolized, adopting an oppositional consciousness necessary for a revolutionary transformation of society: "Lights come on in the auditorium. Onstage, on opposing platforms, Moremi and Titubi are caught in harsh spotlights, looking at each other" (192). Reading this stage direction in terms of the state-supported status quoist 'feminism' of the NCWS versus institutional initiatives to educate citizens in progressive gender and class consciousness towards a social movement, concretized by WIN in the late 1970s and early '80s, the play carries a special resonance.

As a performance event Osofisan's retrospective look at a significant peasant movement in postcolonial Nigerian history in *Morountodun* and its relation to second-wave feminism in Nigeria can be compared to Dennis Scott's revisiting of colonial Jamaican history in *An Echo in the Bone* and its relation to the women's movement in Jamaica. Originating in the academic and institutional space of the university, these works, although not feminist themselves, reveal an awareness of feminist consciousness in academic and extra-academic initiatives in universities to develop into the women's movement in postcolonial Jamaica and Nigeria.

However, at one of his most dejected moments after the performance of *Morountodun* at Ife, Osofisan offers a less than optimistic interpretation of the play. The playwright's essay on the staging of *Morountodun* at the University of Ife can be seen as a dialogue with Soyinka, who had invited him to direct the play. The difficulties Osofisan faced in finding actors and actresses, his battle with university authorities on ingrained perceptions about his "radical" dramaturgy and "dictatorial" directorial style, and the audience's lack of understanding of the central symbolism, lead to his musings as he looks over Ife town. He wonders whether his artistic and political convictions find an echo in the audience: "Moremi, who started it all, was indeed of these hills and forests, and of the silent and sedative music of terra cotta. Students in jeans and skin-tone creams have taken over; the future is Titubi's. Do these people clapping inside there now, applauding the play, do they really understand?" ("Radical" 216).

That the political message of the play be effectively conveyed is a matter of concern for the playwright, particularly since *Morountodun* was presented as the Convocation Play at the University of Ife. Foluke Ogunleye is of the opinion that the political messages of the Ife Convocation plays have sometimes had populist spinoffs, since the artists whose work has been presented have attempted to conscientize the community through these performances. If the Convocation Play is seen as a link between the university and the wider community, Osofisan's concern at the appropriate transmission of his intentions, and even his apparent pessimism about the lack of revolutionary fervor in the present generation of women, does not detract from the message. It would be erroneous to label his concern as a symptom of authorial anxiety epitomizing a desire for an ideal audience. For the playwright, "*Morountodun* has become a part of history, it will roam now with or without me" ("Radical" 217). In the final analysis then the play is a significant cultural text that is responsive to the women's movement in its dramatization of a historical episode in which participatory democracy was envisaged as equitable resource redistribution. Viewed as an "anticipatory project," this dramatization points to women's involvement in the imagination of such a democracy, during the revolutionary moment of the Agbekoya and the democratic moment of the Second Republic.[9] That neither moment realized its potential bespeaks the poverty of socio-political imagination in Nigeria's postcolonial history. Such poverty is in stark contrast to the richness of the cultural imagination that could, at the very moment of the failure of the Second Republic, dramatize this possibility.

6 "Daughters Who Know the Languages of Power"
Community, Sexuality, and Postcolonial Development in Tess Onwueme's *Tell It to Women*

A critical evaluation of postcolonial governance and an active or tacit support of programs initiated by the government characterize the continuum of Nigerian cultural activism: from the tradition of university-based anti-establishment theatrical production to the work of theatre for development (TfD) practitioners, associated with universities or independent nongovernmental organizations. The latter often, though not exclusively, promote grassroots developmental programs in close cooperation with state agendas and policies. Tess Onwueme's prolific dramaturgy, specifically her attention to women's cultural resistance to developmental programs formulated by leaders and bureaucrats in Nigeria, offers a critique of state power in the university-based anti-establishment theatrical tradition of Wole Soyinka, Femi Osofisan, and Bode Sowande. It also reflects her current location as a Nigerian diasporic intellectual well aware of insidious forms of neocolonialism. Based in the American academy as Distinguished Professor of Cultural Diversity and Professor of English at University of Wisconsin, Eau Claire, Onwueme is self-reflexive about Western-influenced feminist agendas that reinforce the postcolonial state's neocolonial policies.

Onwueme's play *Tell It to Women* (1992/1997) is based on the dramatist's representation of the nexus between the state and neocolonial 'feminism'. Represented as 'unnatural' sexuality between women destructive to the family and the nation, this conflation has been largely ignored in critical assessments of Onwueme's work by Omofolabo Ajayi, Chidi Amuta, and Olu Obafemi. Accepting the limited but significant value of cultural activism, this chapter forwards community as a point of relation between the locally directed social agenda of some Nigerian theatre practitioners and Onwueme's diasporic diagnosis that presents indigenous women's agency as a political remedy to what Wole Soyinka has referred to as the "open sore" of corrupt postcolonial governance. Soyinka's apt metaphor for the relation between the body and the body politic is useful for examining Onwueme's discussion of the postcolonial state through the sexuality of its representatives to answer the following questions: How is women's sexuality overdetermined by the imposition of social developmental programs enlisting the aid of cultural activists? Can theatre and drama be useful in initiating a dialogue on alternative sexualities in Africa? Is it possible for local traditions to be the basis of a postcolonial communitarianism that embraces alternative sexualities, particularly since there is already some evidence to indicate that these are traditionally validated through the identities 'male daughters' and 'female husbands'? The answers to these questions cannot be posited from a single theoretical position, since Onwueme rejects both postcolonial nationalism and Western feminism as offering solutions to the problems facing Nigeria. While the dramatist presents sexual identity politics as separatist and irrelevant to Nigerian society, she suggests ways of working through identities to other forms of communities, especially women's social and political organization, that can significantly and positively influence Nigerian development.

This chapter begins by situating Onwueme's work in the context of Nigerian experiments in social theatre. These experiments illustrate the conjunction of local and global agendas on national development. In particular I discuss a TfD outreach effort against female genital mutilation to introduce the debates on African women's sexuality between Western and non-Western feminists. The narrative of victimization in these debates is one of the predominant ways in which African women's sexuality has been addressed in international forums. My discussion of TfD also frames the analysis of the complex structure of Onwueme's play, its connections with socially progressive dramaturgy such as Ngugi wa Thiong'o's significant work in community drama, and the modalities involved in presenting sexual identity politics as symptomatic of the unbridgeable chasm between indigenous women's communities and Westernized feminists.

MOVING TOWARDS DEVELOPMENT

Tell It to Women exists in two versions (published in 1992 and 1997) and has been performed twice in 1992 in the US. Its detailed stage directions and dialogues sometimes read like narrative descriptions. Much of the original framework has been edited in the second edition that is a curtailed version of the three-hundred-page original. Structured in five "movements," the play describes literal as well as metaphorical transitions: Ruth and Daisy arrive in the village with promises of governmental largesse; in response the women of Idu send Yemoja to the city as their representative; finally, the rural community reaches the city *en masse* and takes over Ruth and Daisy's government-orchestrated program meant to celebrate 'authentic' Nigerian life. These actions also represent a movement towards modernization in its deleterious and beneficial aspects. The play was conceptualized during a period when, in the wake of the UN Decade for Women (1975–1985), international funding was forthcoming for community outreach initiatives related to development, a period which also marked the curtailment of activities of collectives like the Jamaican theatre group Sistren, whose cultural programs did not overtly fit this narrowly defined paradigm. Often the source of funding prescribes the focus of specific TfD projects in which, as in Onwueme's play, city-based professionals temporarily travel to rural communities to facilitate their progress from underdevelopment to modernization. I focus on the second edition of the play to contend that *Tell It to Women* is a commentary on the neocolonial policies of the postcolonial military regime and internationally funded cultural activities used to reinforce these policies.

The second movement of the play begins with Yemoja's nightmarish recollection of the city women's arrival in Idu. Her nightmare glosses the power relations between TfD practitioners and the local communities with whom they interact, as well as the retrospective mode of most TfD reports, including the one analyzed here. On my reading, the play's metatheatrical references to the rural welfare policies launched by Ibrahim Babangida's military regime through the First Lady Maryam Babangida's "Better Life for Rural Women" illustrate TfD's supposedly participative dramaturgy. These developmental projects, marked by a bourgeoning taxonomy—community theatre, theatre for integrated rural development, theater for development, and more recently, theatre in development—consistently invoke Ngugi's work in participative dramaturgy at Kamiriithu Cultural and Educational Centre, Kenya. Ngugi's foreword to the second edition of Onwueme's play underscores the connection I am trying to establish between the various kinds of cultural work emerging from Africa and African diasporic locations: "For Ruth and Daisy, progress is directly related to their notion of a Western-based, global sisterhood and their needs as middle-class African women. [. . .] Rural culture represents the past which they want to put behind them" (8) Ngugi's belief in the usefulness of cultural experiments in grassroots development leads him to state that "real national" theatre lies "where the majority of people resided: in the villages, in the countryside and in the poor urban areas" (*Penpoints* 39). At Kamiriithu theatrical productions were seen as a means of continuing the education of those of the villagers who had enrolled in the adult literacy project started at the center (Bjorkman 51–52).

Since the Kamiriithu experiment is cited as a model in many accounts of TfD, it is essential to distinguish this experiment from TfD, particularly in their relations with the state, since many TfD productions involve students and teachers located in theatre departments in Nigerian universities. According to Ngugi, the intellectual and the artist are responsible for concentrated opposition to the state and an alignment with the people towards a commitment to social change. While most accounts of TfD such as Iyorwuese Hagher's and Frances Harding's carefully consider relations between university-based intellectuals and local communities, the class and power differentials influencing the interaction, and the predominance of male activists in the drama groups, they are less concerned about the state's co-optation of culture and cultural workers, which could dilute a commitment to social change. Workshop reports indicate that the facilitators prefer to work on concerns that the community deems important. However, this is more an expressed ideal rather than the ground reality. Since donor agencies often indicate areas such as health, literacy, and employment-generating activities for funding developmental initiatives, there is a possibility that local activist groups seeking resources for TfD outreach projects prioritize the donor agency's focus over the needs and cultural specificities of the target community. TfD activists' autonomy and their professed aim of discovering and addressing concerns important to the target community are compromised in such situations.

The project I describe as a case in point was a collaborative venture between Chuck Mike's Performance Studio Workshop (PSW), a "Lagos-based laboratory for alternative communication, social development, community empowerment and the perpetuation of mutual understanding between people through culture and performance art," and the TfD cell of the University of Ibadan (61). From the project report it appears as if the program was predetermined by the donor agencies and governmental diktat.[1] The 'dramatis personae' included members of the Inter-African Committee on Harmful Traditional Practices, the Association for Reproductive and Family Health, as well as the PSW members and students. Not listed among the dramatis personae but present at the opening ceremony were representatives of the Ford and MacArthur Foundations. Clearly, preparing and presenting a 'Mini Dramatic Information Blitz on FGM [Female Genital Mutilation]' in the Yoruba Church, Olosunde was closely connected to national and international perspectives on what constitutes African development.

When members of the Performance Studio Workshop and students from the University of Ibadan's Theatre for Development unit visited Olosunde in 1996 to make the villagers aware of harmful African practices such as female genital mutilation that were ostensibly hindering their progress towards modernization, their audience comprised mostly men and children. The arrival of TfD participants in Olosunde was as intrusive as the arrival of the city women in Idu detailed by Onwueme at the beginning of *Tell It to Women*. The play begins with the village women waiting for the university-educated intellectuals, Daisy and Ruth, who are expected in Idu as "[o]ur daughters raised from this very soil supplying answers to our questions" (23). The first and longer version of the play published in 1992 signposts Onwueme's critique of a universal feminism through the frame narrative of a group of American students' research project on African women. This version begins with a reassessment of the feminist movement and concludes that feminism has failed. Another stage of the research project involves traveling to Africa, where the assumptions of Western feminists are contrasted with indigenous African 'feminism'. The two versions coalesce with the arrival of Ruth and Daisy, a bureaucrat and a researcher, whose rhetoric of gendered oppression and feminist liberation alienates their rural audience.[2]

The "stumbling Yoruba" of the TfD experiment led by Performance Studio Workshop's female Program Officer, who outlined the purpose of the gathering and reassured the villagers that the PSW and the invited guests were not politicians or "developers with elaborate goals," is similar to Ruth's and Daisy's efforts at communication with the women of Idu through the rural women's representative Yemoja's partially successful attempts at translation:

> RUTH: The watchword for contemporary woman is EQUALITY. Time has come for redressing the female on the paradigmatic scale of being in equality with her male counterpart. (*Yemoja mutters the words "contemporary" and "paradigmatic" jerkily and inaudibly, as she nervously tries to understand the concept herself.*)
> YEMOJA: She says, she says . . . that . . . that ehm . . . yes . . . she says there is no reason why men and women should not be dressed in the same way. The men and women are equal and . . . and . . . that. . . . (*Tell* 34)

Although these hollow claims of feminist solidarity cannot be equated with the genuine developmental goals of the TfD practitioners, there is a schematization in the process involving TfD activities that makes a sustained involvement with the community difficult, if not impossible to achieve. Hagher's outline can be taken as representative of most such workshop efforts involving one or several days spent with the local community, collection of data, and conceptualization of the issues around which the play is to be made (109). *Tell It to Women* presents a reversal of this process where the urbanites Ruth and Daisy take Yemoja to the city—ostensibly as a trainee for the showcasing of development but actually as an exploited domestic worker.

The TfD organizers' conclusion was that there was "very little sign of development or intention to develop amongst these women" (75) is comparable, in condescension if not vehemence, to the way Daisy talks about the villagers in *Tell It to Women*: "What on earth would improve the lives of these people who are so fixed in the past? Don't you realize that for them the present died in the past?" (17). In Onwueme's dramatic rendition of the schematized and opportunistic program, the main reason the village women are willing to listen to the "Oyibo" (Westernized) women from the city is in the hope that these women will become facilitators of governmental schemes of community development. Adaku's expectations echo others': "And now, our own daughters who know the languages of the powers on their fingertips, our own daughters stretch the arms of 'Gomenti'[Government] to the extent that now they remember us! . . . they say 'Gomenti' has given them a package for us." Even when they cannot understand the language the city women use, the villagers stay quiet for fear of annoying the people in power. Daisy's mother-in-law Sherifat is of the opinion that if they 'do not nod [. . .] heads to whatever they say, they will take back what they are going to give us (*Tell* 29, 42). Unquestioning acceptance is not submission, for these women later subvert the rehearsals of development when they take over the official inauguration of the Better Life for Rural Women program.

The failure of this patronizing developmentalism is similar to that of the PSW and University of Ibadan team, whose record indicates that the outreach effort was largely unsuccessful: "In summary, from the laziness and lethargy perceived there, not much was expected from the villagers. The group's impression of Olosunde was of a petty-minded people who would hold on to minor conflicts at the cost of their development" (Mike 78). Their opinion was confirmed when a follow-up visit indicated no "developmental" changes had taken place. Ruth's disparagement of the villagers in *Tell It to Women* echoes the patronizing tone of the PSW report: "These rural women—always scapegoating . . . always blaming their failings on someone. Always! Always . . . Someone must be responsible for their failings" (68).

This description of the PSW experiment indicates the similarities between its stated aims and the apparent claims of the developmental project represented in Onwueme's play. While the PSW experiment was only one among the few 'failures' and many 'successes' in TfD outreach, it indicates the hazards of imposing pre-identified agendas on communities already suffering the brunt of governmental apathy and systemic corruption such as those depicted in *Tell It to Women*.

RESEARCHING THE SEXUAL

The PSW experiment also foregrounds the stakes in feminists' focus on genital mutilation as the primary means of analyzing African women's sexuality. There is a pre-existing framework of research on FGM, which African feminist scholars used for their arguments on same-sex relations between women. A brief outline of the debate on FGM and its implications for a discussion of African women's sexuality highlights the feminist arguments offered in the 1980s and 1990s as a prelude to the problems encountered in discussing African sexualities outside the heteronormative framework.

The debate on female genital mutilation is crucial to Chandra Talpade Mohanty's argument against the representation of third-world women as 'victims'.[3] Refuting Western feminists' ascription of victim status to third-world women, Mohanty devotes a brief section of her classic essay "Under Western Eyes" to Fran Hosken's book on human rights and female genital mutilation in Africa and the Middle East. Hosken's condemnation of the practice is based on the 'privileged premise' that its goal is to "mutilate the sexual pleasure and satisfaction of the woman" (Hosken qtd. in Mohanty 24). Mohanty briefly comments on same-sex relations in her assessment of publications like Hosken's that purport to deal with feminist concerns in the third world. According to Mohanty, none of these works focuses on lesbian politics, thus defining women's resistance "as cumulatively reactive, not as something inherent in the operation of power" (24).

The concerns central to research in African sexualities that led to conflicting feminist surmises on FGM in the 1980s and 1990s have been documented in feminist literature and film by Alice Walker and Pratibha Parmar, among others. These recur in a different form in discussions of sexuality and sexual orientation in other forums. A 1989 article by the Nigerian-British author Buchi Emecheta mentions intimacy among young girls growing up in Nigeria that may be labeled 'lesbian' in the West but are "natural gestures" among girls of a certain age. Framing her discussion in the context of "a society where one's life belongs to the community," she expresses a non-threatening view of homosexuality as an adolescent phase:

> Girls wrestled. Girls danced together. Girls lay together holding and touching each other during the cold harmattan. Nobody stopped us. We thought it was natural.
> Of course when you got married, your whole desire and comfort, confidences and hopes were channeled to your husband. Most of us remained sexually virgins but we knew how to play with each other as young girls. To us it was nothing. To us it was one human being comforting another. For instance in my culture, we do not kiss, but we do hug each other, we hold hands openly, all natural gestures for us. Nobody ever made it into a 'problem'—lesbianism—as you do in the West. ("Natural Gestures")

This position was reiterated in the 2004 African Literatures Association (ALA) Conference at the University of Wisconsin, Madison, where one of the theory panels, titled 'Institutions, Contexts, Politics', included Gaurav Desai's paper on 'Queer Theory and Alternative Sexualities'. The heated argument that followed Desai's presentation was led by a person in the audience who angrily denied the existence of any homophilic traditions in African cultures. According to her, African girls are trained to become "whole women," dutifully fulfilling the roles of daughters, wives, and mothers. This distinctly hostile and untheoretical attitude in a session meant to advance new approaches to African politics, literature, and culture was revealing of attitudes to homosexuality and resistance to queer readings of African texts.[4]

This incident illustrated that the significant work being done in exploring, documenting, and reading alternative sexualities in specific national or pan-African contexts encounters entrenched attitudes that are difficult if not impossible to overcome. I am not forwarding alternative sexual preferences as a way out of patriarchal dominance in traditional societies including those in Africa, since we need to be on guard against an uncritical celebration of alternative forms of sexual expression that can replicate structures of dominance and oppression. Feminist critics such as Molara Ogundipe-Leslie have expressed somewhat contradictory views on the lack of research on homosexuality, especially lesbianism, in African contexts. Recognizing the urgent need for discussion on alternative sexualities, Ogundipe-Leslie nevertheless subscribes to the opinion that sexuality is a "private" matter in most African societies.

However, there is substantial documentation and acknowledgment of same-sex relationships which indicates the existence of multiple forms of sexual expression in postcolonial Africa that are not necessarily identifiable under the categories 'gay', 'lesbian', or 'queer'. This body of work includes single-authored books and collections by Ada Azodo and Maureen Eke, Marc Epprecht, Neville Hoad, Stephen Murray and Will Roscoe, and William Spurlin. A refusal to acknowledge these sexualities under the pretext of ideal African womanhood in an idyllic African society is a cultural denial symptomatic of intolerance that goes beyond homophobia. Onwueme dialectically presents a stridently patriarchal perspective against radical feminism in the person of Daisy's husband, Okei. Okei's diatribe is similar to the anti-theoretical thrust of the public skirmish at the ALA conference:

> This is what you feminists, especially, have reduced the academy to: cultism. Our institutions are no longer citadels of learning, but factories of hot-burning ultra-violent words: showrooms and parade grounds for new jargons and jaw-breaking words to bamboozle willing minds. You're daily competing for spinning out new jargons and jaw-breaking words like overdressed, expensive-looking dolls are no more than toys for mammies and baby-less mothers. So you swing from structuralism to poststructuralism to Marxism to feminism to postfeminism, to deconstruction to postdeconstruction and genderism and lesbianism and the new ethnicity and all in the name of oppositionality and epistemologies of closets of nothings. (*Tell* 92)

This vicious invective would be amusing in its references to academic fashions selected, worn, and discarded like garments from the Sedgwickian epistemological closet but for the entrenched misogyny and homophobia. As in the debates on genital mutilation where one of the common charges was Western feminists' hastiness to label genital surgery as oppressive, 'cultural insiderism' makes it difficult for non-Africans working on African literature and culture to enter into the debate on a level playing field. Writing on homosexuality in his article "Out in Africa" Gaurav Desai has observed that:

[j]ust as Western feminism finds itself in a 'nervous condition' vis-à-vis its negotiations with non-Western practices such as incision and clitoridectomy [FGM], an antihomophobic politics finds itself unable to open up gay-affirmative spaces without running the risk of being culturally insensitive.

According to Desai, the question that needs to be asked is: "Could sensitivity to the needs and desires of *some* subjects mean risking insensitivity to the needs and desires of others? If so, to which subjects and voices must such a politics pay heed?" (140).

While Onwueme's work demonstrates adequate recognition of the existence of socially validated same-sex domestic arrangements in Nigeria in the form of "woman-woman marriage," the "subjects and voices" to which her "politics pay[s] heed" is an African matrilineality that discusses sexual expression in these relationships in much the same way as Emecheta's dichotomy between Western modes of sexual and social arrangements versus indigenous community-validated structures:

Now, I know that in the West two women may live together as a couple, but this is something I have never come across on Nigeria. What we did have, however, were cases of women marrying other women—but this was not a sexual union. It happened when a rich woman could not produce a son. Instead she would pay a dowry for the younger girl and marry her. The girl would be encouraged to take a lover and the child of such a union would belong to the rich woman. The younger woman was usually treated well; she would help her mistress in her trade and in most cases would inherit from the older woman. ("Natural Gestures")

While the city-based women in Onwueme's play are guilty of assumptions of African women's victimhood and ethnocentrism about indigenous modes of organization that are the grounds of Mohanty's critique, their lesbianism is the fundamental signifier of difference in the play. As "daughters" who know the languages of power, Ruth and Daisy's interest in the village women is malignantly individualistic in contrast to the apparently benign universalism Mohanty analyzed as Western feminist colonization of the non-Western world. Onwueme depicts a neocolonial 'feminism' through Ruth and Daisy's lesbian relationship, discussed in four of the five movements in the play. Although this is not the play's area of focus, the suggestion that Western feminist influence necessarily leads to lesbianism is symptomatic of a disturbing trend that demonizes anything other than domesticity and motherhood as sources of women's social and cultural power. While it is facile to see radical feminism as the only form of resistance to patriarchal oppression, it is equally dangerous to represent non-normative sexual practices as a Western disease symptomized by disrespect for indigenous cultures and infecting family life. Onwueme's representation not only parodies radical feminist hubris, but also presents Ruth and Daisy's relationship as anti-life, anti-tradition, and anti-African.[5] The playwright's critique of feminist imperialism thus runs the risk of reinstating the community as the basis of an indigenous life-affirming (heterosexual) feminism.

In her study of women's organizations in Africa, British-Nigerian sociologist Ifi Amadiume seems to subscribe to a similar communitarianism. Amadiume contrasts community-oriented African women leaders working with traditional African matriarchal models of power who she names "daughters of the Goddess" with "daughters of Imperialism," that is, women in partnership with the contemporary state and the global model of power (*Daughters* 3). Here too the issue of African women's sexuality is framed within the FGM debates. Though Amadiume begins by denouncing the propensity among international feminist and postcolonial governmental schemes to conceptualize genital mutilation as a single issue unconnected to other dimensions of power affecting women's lives, her assessment demonstrates a marked development and change in direction: she barely mentions the issue in *Male Daughters and Female Husbands* (1987), although she does indicate that she has interviewed local women about FGM; in *Daughters of the Goddess* (2000) she offers a sophisticated interpretation of the practice based on medical research, local customs, legal and political dimensions, literary sources, and activist accounts.

Like Mohanty, Amadiume summarizes feminist views on circumcision in her anthropological study, particularly the way in which it has become a metaphor for African women's sexual subordination. Amadiume suggests that the practice may be seen as a point of patriarchal incursion into the largely matriarchal Igbo community of Nnobi, the site of her research. Since FGM is no longer widely prevalent in Nnobi, Amadiume does not feel the need to address the matter in detail, and confines her opinion to a footnote. In her recent work one notices more detailed observations on circumcision, including the reminder that any activist efforts against it would have to function at multiple levels involving education of women, the community, and medical informational campaigns leading to the "social, religious, and cultural transformation of certain communities, rather than overturning or uprooting this base by rapid legal decrees" (*Daughters* 157). Amadiume's judgment of the "money-guzzling bureaucracy" producing "facts and figures, brochures and campaign materials" on FGM targets local bureaucracy and international agencies such as the World Health Organization. The demystification is essential for, as we have seen in PSW and University of Ibadan's TfD students' propaganda against FGM in Olosunde, often the campaigns are imposed on local communities under the rubric of "developmentalism."[6]

Amadiume's analysis of the programmatic schemas on FGM indicates her awareness of female erotic autonomy. From a denunciation of lesbianism as a Eurocentric political stance and sexual preference that is irrelevant

140 *Feminist Visions and Queer Futures in Postcolonial Drama*

to matrifocal Ibo communities, her analytical framework has expanded to acknowledge (if not give credence to) a lesbian perspective on FGM: "[L]esbian women would be justified in attacking these practices from their own points of view." Since the practice is related to women's position in society and is a social justice issue, Amadiume urges continual vigilance: "Women should resist being categorized into simplistic but damaging genitalia-based dichotomies in the politics of otherness" (*Daughters* 155, 157) Given the history of the FGM debates and the neat dichotomization of third-world women as victims of harmful traditional practices versus first-world feminists as concerned activists exposing these practices through research and publications, the warning is a timely one.

AFRICAN *AND* LESBIAN

Traditional conceptions of gender and sexuality, modern ways of expressing sexuality, and the contrast between them are significant ideological concerns in *Tell It to Women*. According to Adaku, a female elder of the Ibo community in Idu village, traditions are "things to do with the spirit, moral values and the community" and modernization is an "Oyibo [Western] disease" (38–39). When Adaku mentions that in Oyibo land "men marry men and women marry men," Sherifat replies that the "Idu people have that too." Adaku is quick to explain the difference: "Do not confuse the two. Idegbe marries another woman to take her place in the family. HER wife is free to take any man who will give her children to continue the name of the lineage. Then Idegbe can go out and marry her own husband" (38). The rural women's representative Yemoja, an articulate, independent-minded, educated young woman who is ill treated and abused as a servant in Daisy's home, comments on Daisy and Ruth's liaison in unambiguous terms. The grounds for criticism of alternative sexuality in Onwueme's play are social as well as biological. While Adaku presents the existence of marriage between women as a tradition justified by the responsibility of continuing the "name of the lineage," Yemoja's condemnation of Ruth's and Daisy's individualistic self-gratificatory sexuality is implicitly contrasted with this responsibility to the community.

Onwueme's representation of rural women as a strong, close-knit group with undisputed powers in the political economy of Idu does not preclude a recognition of patriarchal oppression within the community. When reminded that she is not a 'daughter' but a 'wife' and hence has limited rights, Yemoja's comments on the traditional relations between the daughters and wives are an assertion of indigenous feminism as well as a critique of the hierarchical nature of the community. Yemoja condemns a system that valorizes predetermined social roles for women and insists on typecasting them within these roles. Her voluntary separation from her husband to go to the city is a move away from some of these socially obligated roles. Yet towards the end of the play she is reinstated into domesticity when her husband expresses pride in her new leadership role. Thus while articulating a critique of patriarchy Onwueme puts the responsibility for a separatist feminism on the two 'lesbians', Ruth and Daisy. If the playwright's purpose is to present a stark contrast between two divergent ways of life, the articulation of an indigenous feminism is accomplished only at the cost of a predatory Westernized feminism. Excesses of the successive Nigerian governments make Onwueme's critique of postcolonial agendas of development a necessary one, yet cultural commentary that posits homosexuality as a symptom of postcolonial corruption risks foreclosing dialogue on alternative sexualities.

Daisy's and Ruth's privileged class positions, ensured by their education and their ranks in the structure of governmental power, enable them to set programmatic agendas for rural women which are in fact exercises in monetary and social self-interest. These privileges also give them the freedom (or license according to the rural women) to express their sexuality in non-defined terms. Onwueme spotlights Daisy's and Ruth's sexuality and refracts it through the lens of gender and sexual roles defined by the community. One aspect of the communitarian ethos that distorts this critical perspective on the alliance of radical feminism and postcolonial developmentalism is an existing tradition of women's social power based on their class position that enables them to opt out of gender roles (and possibly heterosexuality). Discussing the "evidence of 'class' differentiations on the basis of wealth in indigenous society," Amadiume mentions the "possession of wives by 'male daughters', that is, first daughters, barren women, rich widows, wives of rich men and successful female farmers and traders," the kind of women whom she collectively refers to as "female husband." The tradition partook of patriarchy since in "the practice of 'female husbands' women benefited from the accumulation of wives in the same way as did men" (*Male Daughters* 31, 45). These relations were inegalitarian as rich women used the institution to increase "labour force, wealth and prestige." The incorporation of certain class-stratified categories of women into maleness gave them a position of authority. Hence, as in the case of the difference between daughters and wives, the institution of a female husband establishes a tradition of inegalitarian relations between women that is also reflected in the city women's exploitation of rural women.

Amadiume would have us believe that indigenous relations of power such as those between female husbands and their wives or those between lineage daughters of the clan and lineage wives (in classificatory terms the daughters were 'husbands' to the wives and were addressed as such) were completely devoid of sexual expression. While it is difficult to comment on the authenticity of this desexualized perspective, there is some ambivalence about the expression of sexuality in these relations in Amadiume's detailed ethnography. Perhaps it is neither possible nor desirable to arrive at a definitive assessment about sexual relations between two women 'married' to each other according to the Igbo traditions. A more productive reading of these relations may be one that engages with a theorization of gender and sex, such as that offered by Amadiume, not in order to prove the existence of covert sexuality in socially validated same-sex alliances, but to point to 'community' and 'postcolonial development' as the dominant notes in the cacophony of hostile voices drowning out the expression of an African *and* lesbian identity.[7] Amadiume states in the introduction to *Male Daughters, Female Husbands* that she does not give any credence to black lesbians' interpretations of African women's relationships as 'lesbian', for any such interpretation of woman-woman marriages would be "totally inapplicable, shocking and offensive to Nnobi women, since the strong bonds and support between them do not imply lesbian sexual practices." For her this would be an imposition of Western prejudices and assumptions as in the "search for power, or more positive models and images of powerful women, there is a limit to how far facts can be bent or our own wishes and fantasies imposed" (*Male Daughters* 7). A response to this position must address the question: how do we initiate a discussion about African women's identities to achieve a candid, non-pejorative assessment of sexuality within same-sex alliances? To arrive at a theorization of same-sex relations in postcolonial Africa we must first come to terms with the community-centered traditions that may in fact be the basis and models of these relations, and move beyond these to a historical notion of the community defined by changes and transformation of sexualities as much as it is by economic models of development.[8]

POSTCOLONIALISM AS COMMUNITARIAN ACTS

We can understand some of these traditions by reading Onwueme's play as indelibly marked with the communitarian ethos that is also the impulse for Amadiume's research. In the concluding movement the playwright's focus shifts from sexuality to a showcasing of cultural-economic development:

> Slowly, the women begin some tunes with the drums, the gong and other instruments while Yemoja speaks. At the same time, the women begin to pile up the artifacts and produce: yams, hand-woven cloths, garri, oil, and so on, for which they have proverbial fame and prowess in their villages. (188)

The village women arrive *en masse* in the city followed by their menfolk, and this "good gathering of the entire community" becomes the occasion for Onwueme's recasting of postcolonialism as community agency.

The author's strident attack on developmentalism targets performances of power by First Ladies in the Better Life Program launched in the 1990s by the Babangida military regime. More than one commentator has observed

Illustration 6.1 Idu women raise their voices and gesticulate in protest at the showcasing of development in *Tell It to Women*. Photo courtesy Tess Onwueme.

that the high-profile program whose achievements were celebrated with the launching of the National Commission for Women involved a skilled performance of sorts (Mama 64; Amadiume, *Daughters*).

The play's undisguised attack on these policies initiated in the name of grassroots women implicates cultism associated with the First Lady, "Her Excellency," corruption at all levels of the governmental machinery involving co-opted bureaucrats like Daisy, and the university-based researcher Ruth. The showcasing of culture by these elite women is challenged and resisted by the village women, whose denunciations of "these modern girls" also involve self-condemnation for allowing themselves to be duped. Adaku voices this condemnation: "We sold out . . . we sold ourselves . . . we sold our pride for the promise of this, their better life. . . . I mean momentary, material crumbs. We made ourselves look weak and cheap." For Adaku the ultimate form of degradation is that the village women have allowed themselves to be used to "create a new dance-step" that does not bring any "respect" or "credit" to them (*Tell* 172, 173). The final movement involves a reclamation of their traditional dance step, representing their move from instrumentalization to agency. Much like the enactment of state power, the agency of the rural women is in the realm of performance, a shifting metaphor in Onwueme's play that encompasses the co-opted and resistant aspects of Nigerian drama at large.

The scenes in the last movement, intended as comments on the relations between the state and the community as well as on indigenous women's politicization, represent a concentration of focus somewhat lost in the

144 *Feminist Visions and Queer Futures in Postcolonial Drama*

Illustration 6.2 Idu women dance their resistance in a new dance step in the last movement of *Tell It to Women*. Photo courtesy Tess Onwueme.

domestic drama involving homosexuality that comprises the middle section of the play. Onwueme's primary commitment, evident in all her work, is to expose the excesses of state power. Some of the issues she has dealt with in her other plays include: precolonial political traditions of matriarchal power; the plight of the Ogoni people in the oil-rich Delta state in Nigeria; and an unequal distribution of global resources between countries of the North and the South. In this chapter I have argued that studying the playwright's critique of postcolonial developmentalism in Nigeria should also involve a scrutiny of her critique of Western feminist imperialism, since both these concerns are articulated simultaneously. Such an analysis is useful in locating sites of postcolonial agency. My argument that Onwueme conflates a postcolonialism gone wrong with a sexual desire gone wrong reveals that the same unified notion of community that is the target of state-supported TfD activities operates in Onwueme's oppositional dramaturgy. However, the community also emerges as a site of moral and social strictures on Westernized women as agents of development. If TfD errs in devaluing the agency of its target communities, in Onwueme that agency is presented as one compromised by no meeting ground between differing versions of women's empowerment.

Continuing the conversation on female sexuality within already existing paradigms of victimhood, or of women as targets for development, leads to foreclosing the long-overdue exchange on alternative sexualities in postcolonial African nation-states. Literary and dramatic texts like *Tell It to Women* can be useful in initiating such an exchange. Yet how do we reconcile this progressive agenda with the polarization of identity categories between African *or* lesbian that makes a non-pejorative consideration of African *and* lesbian a difficult if not impossible task? One of the earliest articles on the representation of homosexuality in African literature, by Chris Dunton, concludes by referring to the "abstention among African writers, and even among the most searching and responsive of these, from a fully characterized and nonschematic depiction of homosexuality between Africans. [. . .] A non-schematic treatment of the subject in that [the African] context would, after all, have no need to acknowledge Western modes of self-representation" (445).

Early on in this chapter I established that international funding and state policies on development often dictate the community-based (though not necessarily community-participative) activities of TfD. Onwueme's play reveals that the bureaucratic machinery and the university-educated intelligentsia are equally implicated in this imposed model of development. A powerful response to these impositions is possible from a more inclusive notion of community than is present in the PSW report or in Onwueme's play. Can the strong female bonding and women-centric traditions within local communities lead to development that embraces economic security along with sexual freedom, particularly since there is already evidence to indicate that these are validated in traditionally institutionalized forms of sociality such as 'male daughters' and 'female husbands'? For Onwueme, an author who derives inspiration from a culture that sees social gender as separate from biological sex, this perspective would not involve disconnection from the communitarian ethos but rather an extension of postcolonial resistance to demand economic and sexual justice. Onwueme's play initiates a dialogue in this direction by referencing African traditions of social alliances between rural women and sexual alliances between urban women, leading one to hope for a conjoining rather than a polarization of the two. Taking responsibility for continuing the dialogue on African homosexualities, despite academic, cultural, and social resistance, we can make the text speak for the recognition of multiple sexual identities in Africa.

Epilogue

As this book was in its final stages, the Indian media reported a series of events reflecting confused thinking over gendered and sexual rights in the country. First, the reopening of a case against Inspector General Rathore, accused of molesting a fourteen-year-old girl in 1994, that led to a six-month imprisonment and a nominal fine, made a mockery of adequate and speedy justice to the victim's family. This travesty of justice led a 'mentally disturbed' student from the National Institute of Design to slash Rathore across his face with a knife as he was going to court for a hearing in early February 2010. In the same month, Sri Ram Sena leader Pramod Muthalik, who had called for a ban on Valentine's Day in India, had his face blackened by youth in Bangalore just as he was getting ready for a public debate on the issue. And finally, lest there be any sense of lingering optimism in the high court ruling reading down Section 377 of the Indian Penal Code against "unnatural" sexual offences used to persecute gay men in India, a professor at Aligarh Muslim University, suspended after some students recorded him on camera as having consensual sex with a rickshaw puller, was found dead in his house in April this year.

These recent instances point to virulent forms of gendered and sexual injustice. Anglican Christianity in Nigeria, Rastafarianism and the Christian Church in Jamaica, and Hinduism and Islam in India are some of the institutionalized religions advocating restrictions both on women's sexual autonomy and on non-normative sexuality on religious and moral grounds. In 1998, right-wing leaders of the Shiv Sena called for a ban on the screening of Indo-Canadian filmmaker Deepa Mehta's 'lesbian' film *Fire* in Indian cinemas. These ideologues claimed that lesbian sexual desire was not in keeping with Indian cultural traditions. In 2003, some British newspapers reported the controversy regarding the appointment of Jeffrey John, an openly gay Anglican priest, as bishop in the Church of England, spearheaded by Archbishop Peter Jasper Akinola of Nigeria, who denounced the consecration of gay bishops as a satanic attack on God's church. This controversy led to John quitting his post and brought to the forefront the estrangement of African churches from their metropolitan Anglican headquarters. In 2004, Brian Williamson, an openly gay man and a gay rights activist from Jamaica, was found murdered in Kingston.

How realistic then is it to expect gender and sexual justice in postcolonial nations where even sartorial choices and a celebration of heterosexuality face the wrath of traditionalists?

Feminist Visions and Queer Futures has pointed out how the rights of women and sexual minorities are violated under the watchful eye and sometimes with the active collaboration of postcolonial states. The book posits the non-negotiability of the rights of subaltern groups marked by race, class, gender, or sexuality as a precondition for postcolonial democracy. Examining cultural and social activism in conjunction with each other, it also suggests drama as public pedagogy and citizenship education as a means of combating institutionalized religious and state-sanctioned undermining of gendered and sexual justice.

Plays by Dennis Scott, Femi Osofisan, Jan Natya Manch, and Tess Onwueme continue to be performed in educational institutions, which are often sites of feminist activism. My research into the history of the institutions that provided a hospitable environment to these radical and often subversive performances originated, in part, due to the difficulty of obtaining performance records of and responses to the plays. Undertaking this research on postcolonial universities was also, in retrospect, a way of remaining connected to the University of Delhi in the years away from India. To say that strong ties of intellectual inquiry and scholarship characterize my kinship with this university would not be an exaggeration. Implicitly asking what role, if any, can the postcolonial university, dependent though it is on the state for its continued existence, play in furthering cultural and social agendas, one of the aims of this book is to place center stage university-based social and cultural activism: the University of West Indies furthered as well as questioned the gender ideologies of Jamaica's experiment with democratic socialism; educational institutions in India such as the University of Delhi often take their cue on gender concerns from the state, but are also sites from where these ideologies are interrogated; an autonomous feminist organization that initially started as a discussion group at Ahmadu Bello University in Nigeria has successfully highlighted and suggested measures for curbing social violence against women.

There are crucial lessons to be learned from the struggles and successes of the feminist movements originating from universities, which can also ground transformative thinking and action about the provision of social justice to sexual minorities. The areas of emphasis will necessarily differ according to the postcolonial context. Elsewhere I have written about the possible impact of recent publications on alternative sexuality on the teaching of literature in the Indian classroom ("Emergent Sexualities"). Collaborative and independent work by scholars on documenting indigenous sexual traditions in literature, history, and popular culture along with substantive curricular revisions have gone some way in changing misogynist and homophobic attitudes in students at the University of Delhi. At the University of

West Indies, the focus is less on documenting indigenous traditions than on research into popular cultural and religious discourses to account for rampant violence against women and gay men, including examining the claim that Jamaica is or among the worst offenders in this regard. The exceptionality of Nigeria, where such efforts are not anchored in a particular educational institution—although there has been research into indigenous sexual traditions as well a questioning of homophobia flourishing under Church patronage—underscores the need for pedagogic initiatives. Marc Epprecht's efforts in sexuality education at a local Nigerian university indicate that Nigerians "may be more open to consideration of scientific evidence and international best practices around sexual diversity, rights, and health than is commonly assumed in the literature" ("Teaching").

These initiatives suggest it is crucial to change the terms of discourse(s) in which any expression of sexuality outside heterosexual conjugality is demonized as Western, immoral, irreligious, unnatural, and deserving of violent repression. Curtailing social violence and promoting justice involves (but should not be limited to) securing legal protection despite the colonial legacy of discriminatory legislation in postcolonial times. Because the effort will involve interdisciplinary collaboration, we need to be very clear about the role the teaching of literature can play in this effort.

My primary disciplinary training is in English and Comparative Literature, and I accept the limited nature of an intervention involving reading contemporary literature and culture to chart a shift in the terms of representation over the past two decades, since this broadly is the period when gender and sexuality concerns emerged in postcolonial public spaces largely due to women's activism. Dramatists who allied with such activists staged opposition to popular cultural representations perpetuating gendered stereotypes. These performances help build spectatorial communities at universities where curricular changes are already encouraging nuanced readings and interpretations of gender. However, curricular transformations need not be a precondition for teaching literature through a methodological and theoretical approach that is aware of multiple vectors of power, oppression, and resistance, among them caste, class, race, gender, and sexuality. There is a significant body of work on canonical Euro-American and postcolonial literature, which can be pressed into service for a postcolonial counter-discourse. Many teachers of literature are almost completely responsible for creative writing activities and publications in their respective institutions. These forums can be used to begin conversations in contexts where there no other venues are available. I offer these discipline-specific suggestions not to suggest that we abandon a commitment to interdisciplinary collaboration in our academic and extra-academic efforts but to point to quotidian acts that prepare the way for structural changes.

I have had the good fortune of teaching at institutions with a commitment to gender issues. Many of my senior colleagues' unobtrusive commitment to feminist teaching and the more apparent feminist thinking of my young colleagues gives me reason to be hopeful about the changes in social perceptions and provision of justice for *all* marginalized groups. These will be achieved only by constant and persistent struggle in the face of state ideologies, religious fundamentalism, social and cultural norms, and internalized strictures against difference. One cannot discount the personal and professional costs of this struggle while being hopeful of such consciousness arising out of educational institutions.

Notes

NOTES TO THE INTRODUCTION

1. For a useful overview of postcolonial Indian theatre see Aparna Dharwadker's *Theatres of Independence: Drama, Theory, and Urban Performance Since 1947*.
2. Linda Nicholson's account of the second-wave begins with a questioning of the distinction "first wave/second wave" as a way of organizing the history of feminism ("Introduction" 1–3). See also Nancy Fraser's brilliant reconstruction of the history of debates about difference in second-wave US feminism in *Justice Interruptus*. The wave metaphor has been critiqued by Kimberly Springer for excluding the historicity of race in feminist organizing. Jennifer Purvis points to its generational, familial language to discuss relations between the waves, and hence its heterosexual underpinnings.
3. The Delhi High Court's ruling in June 2009 reading down Article 377 criminalizing "unnatural sexual acts" is the result of decades of organizing by women's and gay rights groups. Those who oppose decriminalization of homosexuality have sought a repeal of the judgment by appealing to the Supreme Court of India.
4. My account of how these ideas have impacted on postcolonial theatre practitioners has been characterized as "homage to Brecht, Grotowski and Boal—a canon of drama studies—all male, two of them of a very particular European hue—whose significance for the project of the book, especially of the first two, is [. . .] overplayed in the introduction where discussing their theoretical frames becomes the kind of end in itself." I hope to have sufficiently indicated that many postcolonial dramatists conceive of their work in agreement with, modification of, or in opposition to Boal's, Brecht's, or Grotowski's principles. For the influence of Brecht's ideas on Indian and Nigerian drama, see Aparna Dharwadker's *Theatres of Independence*, Abdullahi S. Abubakar's essay on Brechtian influences on Femi Osofisan's drama, and the essays in Osofisan's *The Nostalgic Drum*. For Grotowski's contested relationship with Indian and Caribbean drama, see Rustom Bharucha's "Goodbye Grotowski" in *Theatre and the World* and Honor Ford-Smith's discussion of Grotowski's influence on Dennis Scott in "Performing Nation". There is a very easy concordance between Boal and the drama I discuss because of a shared postcolonial or 'third world' context.
5. In *Theatre of the Oppressed*, Boal assigns to the "Joker" a permanent structure of performance in all his plays. This structure is divided into seven main parts: dedication, explanation, episode, scene, commentary, interview, and exhortation. A high level of stylistic innovation is possible using the "Joker" since the existence of a single perspective in this figure prevents the anarchy,

which may otherwise arise when various styles are intermixed in a single performance. Boal clarifies: "With the 'Joker' we propose a permanent system of theater (structure of text and cast) which will contain all the instruments of all styles and genres. Each scene must be conceived, aesthetically, according to the problems it presents" (176). This explanation forcefully answers Brecht's charge of "simplicity" as aesthetic poverty in poor (working class) theatres by extending the applications of Brechtian alienation effect.

NOTES TO CHAPTER 1

1. Honor Ford-Smith, Scott's student and later Staff Tutor at the Jamaica School of Drama, acknowledges his support and encouragement in the formation of the grassroots women's theatre group, Sistren Theatre Collective. Ironically, unlike Sistren's work, Scott's own drama has received scant attention in post-colonial drama studies. Ford-Smith's research on Scott supplements studies like Judy Stone's in *Theatre: Studies in West Indian Literature* and Helen Gilbert and Joanne Tompkins's in *Post-colonial Drama: Theory, Practice, Politics*. These studies do not offer a detailed discussion of the impact of Scott's plays on Caribbean drama. One possible reason could be the lack of performance records. See also Ford-Smith's poignant account of the destruction of the Scott archive at the Jamaica School of Drama in the 1990s in "Performing Nation: The Pedagogy and Politics of Post-Colonial Jamaican Performance."
2. Scott's notes on community drama workshops at the JSD and the unpublished article on theatre in development indicate these influences. These notes are in the personal collection of Honor Ford-Smith.
3. See Phillip Sherlock and Rex Nettleford's excellent history of the UWI.
4. In *Antigone's Claim* Judith Butler has explored the contradictory claims of the state versus kinship obligations through a reading of Antigone's rebellion in giving a burial to her brother, Polynices, against Creon's edict declaring Polynices traitor to the state. Postcolonial readings of Antigone include Caroline Rooney's discussion in *African Literature, Animism and Politics*. See in particular the chapter "Clandestine Antigones and the Pre-post-Colonial" where Rooney argues that Antigone's "figure—a sister-brother conjunction of a radical democracy—may serve as the bearer, the signifier, of 'traditional' or pre-colonial cultural values and valued cultures that hope to survive colonialism in post-colonialism" (151).
5. The Nine-Night ceremony is a celebration concluding the nine-day period of funeral activities by singing, dancing, ring play, games, and storytelling. Ford-Smith mentions that "contemporary nine nights incorporate food and aspects of dance hall culture particularly speaker banks, deejays and music" ("Performing Nation" 199).
6. Butler's signification of kinship as "social arrangements that organize the reproduction of material life, that can include the ritualization of birth and death, that provide bonds of intimate alliance both enduring and breakable, and that regulate sexuality through sanction and taboo" is helpful in this context (*Antigone's Claim* 72).
7. For purposes of comparison I consulted the manuscript of *Dog* generously provided by Honor Ford-Smith with the permission of Mrs. Joy Scott. The play was published in the Macmillan Caribbean Writer's series collection *You Can Lead a Horse to Water and Other Plays*, edited by Judy Stone. There are no substantial differences between the unpublished and published versions, except for the spelling and punctuation of some words.

8. It is useful to remember David Scott's caveat on the "normalized centrality of a specific identity," especially the possibility that "the emergence of an increasingly vocal Indo-Caribbean critique of Afro-Caribbean hegemony has very much to do with the presumed privilege of Afro-Caribbean identity that Independence installed. The story of the postcolonial state in the Caribbean, in other words, is normalized as the story of the empowerment of peoples of African descent, as peoples whose 'authentic suffering' has guaranteed them a special and permanent dispensation" (*Refashioning* 204).
9. The metaphorical invocation of the unborn child as an optimistic or nihilistic symptom of the future is common to African and Caribbean drama. Walcott's *Ti-Jean and His Brothers* concludes with the hero Ti-Jean giving the gift of life to the *bolom*, an unborn fetus. Wole Soyinka's *Dance of the Forests* uses the figure of the *abiku*, an unborn child trapped between the world of the living and the dead, to discuss the predicament of Nigeria after independence from colonial rule.
10. In an issue of *TDR* focusing on Grotowski's legacy, Richard Schechner observes that along with Stanislavsky and Brecht, Grotowski was one of the "three most influential theatre people of the past century." Schechner also mentions that "[h]is influence is pervasive, but . . . more a tone, a flavor, or scent than anything fixed" ("Grotowski" 11). Since Grotowski's plays are not as widely performed as Brecht's, although the influence of his ideas is "pervasive," he is not acknowledged as influential a figure as say Brecht is by postcolonial theatre practitioners and critics.
11. Sistren Theatre Collective's performances directed attention to the female-headed family as the norm during the 1970s. Gay men and lesbian women also articulated alternative versions of the family and community through an underground newspaper, *The Jamaica Gaily News*, published from 1977 to 1984. This connection is further discussed in my article "'Our Own Gayful Rest': A Postcolonial Archive."

NOTES TO CHAPTER 2

1. This chapter refers to two versions of the play: the first is edited by Rhonda Cobham and exists only in manuscript form; the second is the published version. The parenthetical references in this chapter list the MS as "Sistren and Ford-Smith." The published script is a revised and altered version, directed by Rawle Gibbons, and included in Erika Waters and David Edgecombe's anthology of Caribbean drama. This is cited as *"Bellywoman"* in the parenthetical references and indexed under "Sistren Theatre Collective" in the Bibliography. Grateful thanks to Honor Ford-Smith for allowing me to use the unpublished manuscript.
2. Sharon Green and Karina Smith analyze the decline of the group's work with local communities in Jamaica in the 1980s and 1990s as a dilution of its grassroots mandate. While this is attributed to a combination of factors including political changes in Jamaica and migration of many group members, Smith also suggests that the collective's work is compromised because of its alignment with national and international development policies. Green's and Smith's essays lack an engagement with the plays to test their claims. I understand that this is not their primary focus but surely these ideas could have been tested against Sistren's plays developed in the 1980s and 1990s as well as reports of community outreach activities documented in the *Sistren Newsletter*.
3. See Pat Ellis's work on women's organizations and the Caribbean women's movement, which includes a reminder that there are many who question

whether there is or ever has been a women's movement in the Caribbean (*Women* 2).

4. Hertencer Lindsay's explanation of these rituals in the director's notes to *QPH* describes *Ettu* as a ritual celebrating the life of the dead, danced by old women in their sixties and seventies, as observed by her in Jamaica's Hanover district. Lindsay specifies that the "shawling" in the play acknowledges each woman and celebrates her life. There is a reference to *Kumina* drumming in the play, and it is useful to keep in mind the director's clarification that *Ettu* is not the same as *Kumina* since the former does not involve a conscious effort to get the ancestors to join in and possess the people (8).

5. Adrian Jackson, translator of most of Boal's work, explains in the introduction to *Games for Actors and Non-Actors* that Image theatre, Invisible theatre, and Forum theatre are the three main categories of the Theatre of the Oppressed. In Image theatre participants "make still images of their lives, feelings, experiences, oppressions: groups suggest titles or themes, and then individuals 'sculpt' three-dimensional images under these titles, using their own and other's bodies as 'clay'" (xix). Invisible theatre occurs when the public is a participant in the action. Spect-actors or spectators as actors are involved in the scene without knowing that this is theatre rather than real life. They are involved as participants in the discussion following the performance (xx). Forum theatre is "a theatrical game in which a problem is shown in an unsolved form, to which the audience, again spect-actors, is invited to suggest and enact solutions. . . . In its purest form, both actors and spect-actors will be people who are victims of the oppression under consideration; that is why they are able to offer alternative solutions, because they themselves are personally acquainted with the oppression" (xxi).

6. Michelle Cliff's novel *No Telephone to Heaven* (1987) brings together many of the incidents in the plays discussed in Chapters 1 and 2. For instance, Christopher's murder of the rich landowner Mr. Charles, when the latter dismisses his request for a piece of land on which to bury his grandmother, echoes Crew's murder of Mr. Charles in *An Echo in the Bone*. The novel also contains Harry/Harriet's account of the Kingston almshouse fire supposedly caused by arson as dramatized in *QPH*. Cliff presents political rivalry between the two parties contending for power in Jamaica as directly responsible for such acts of violence leading to the death of destitute old women. The novel's rupture of the heterosexual conceptualization of the nation-state by performances of deviant womanhood and deviant sexuality by feminist, gay, lesbian, and bisexual citizen-subjects resonates with my argument in this chapter.

7. In her work on dancehall lyrics Cooper coins the term "heterophobia" as "a politically neutral label for a whole range of anxieties that plague all people in all cultures: phobias that are reducible to the singular *fear of difference*. Differences of race, ethnicity, gender, class, age and sexual orientation all generate phobias." For Cooper heterophobia "incorporate[s] the current definitions of homophobia" by going to "the heart of the problem of cultural difference" (*Sound Clash* 25). I agree with Cooper that differences of race, ethnicity, gender, class, age, and sexual orientation generate phobias but I am not sure either of the purpose of a term such as "heterophobia" or of the work it performs by incorporating other terms such as 'women', 'black', 'queer' that have a long history of activism.

8. Carl Stone has critiqued Manley's brand of economic and cultural populism in a retrospective look at the decade of the seventies in *Class, State, and Democracy in Jamaica*. Stone has decisively analyzed the "political sociology" of the seventies and proposed "clientelism" as the key factor governing the practice of democracy in Jamaica. According to Stone, "patron-clientelism

Notes   155

   ... is the exchange of economic and social favors to a poor and socially fragmented population in return for party support" (*Democracy* 91–92). For a review and a "re-positioning" of this important concept, see David Scott's essay "Political Rationalities of the Jamaican Modern."
9. Gloria Wekker's discussion of Afro-Surinamese women's patterns of socialization and sexuality is set against the "dominant model" on how to be a woman "engaged in by white, middle-class women, in which the rhetoric of 'political choice', feminist chauvinism, conformity between partners along a number of dimensions, including socioeconomic status and age, and predominantly childlessness, played central parts." Against this, Wekker provides the contours of a "submerged model" where women "differed greatly in age from their women partners, typically had children, and apparently maintained heterosexual relationships." Such nonstigmatized fluidity of female sexual relationships makes for a different kind of Caribbean socius than exists in Jamaica. There are few discussions of lesbianism in Jamaica apart from Makeda Silvera's article "Man Royals and Sodomites: Some Thoughts on the Invisibility of Afro-Caribbean Lesbians," Silvera's novel *The Heart Does Not Bend*, based on life experiences in Jamaica, Tara Atluri's monograph on sexism, homophobia, and misogyny in Barbados, Cayman Islands, and Jamaica, and Staceyann Chin's memoir *The Other Side of Paradise*.
10. Mair delivered this as the J. P. Naik Memorial Lecture at the Center for Women's Development Studies. The occasion of this lecture aids connections between educational structures, dramatic activities, and feminist mobilization in postcolonial India, Jamaica, and Nigeria.

NOTES TO CHAPTER 3

1. Grateful thanks to Moloyashree Hashmi for collections of Janam's street plays, issues of the journal *Nukkad Natak Samvad* (*Street Theatre Dialogue*), unpublished scripts of Janam's plays, a copy of Sherna Dastur's film on Safdar, and for patiently explaining the nuances of the performances over lengthy interviews. Thanks also to Sudhanva Deshpande, Brijesh Sharma, and other members of Janam, who allowed to me sit in on their rehearsals during December 2003 and January 2004 and invited me to Janam's performances in June 2009.
2. Safdar's writings on theatre in articles, drama reviews, and political pamphlets emphasize the political nature of street theatre but do not see it in complete contradiction to proscenium theatre. Firmly believing that both kinds of theatre belong to the people he nevertheless makes a distinction between "the proscenium theatre which has been appropriated by the escapists, the anarchists, and the revivalists and the street theatre which stands with the people," even while calling upon his colleagues in mainstream theatre to assist in developing and enriching street theatre (*Right* 13–15).
3. For an account of Safdar's involvement with film and cinema, see Qamar Hashmi's biography of Safdar, *The Fifth Flame*. Safdar was script and dialogue writer of a television series and eight documentary films in the late 1970s and early 1980s. From 1986 onwards Safdar was also associated with Mediastorm, a collective of eight women filmmakers, all graduates from the Mass Communication Research Center at Jamia Millia Islamia University (Mala Hashmi Interview 2004).
4. As a spectator of these performances from the mid-1990s to the present, some of these techniques I have noticed are: minimalist setting for on-stage

and street performances, deliberate lack of emphasis on costumes and props, a vignette-based rather than linear presentation of the issue being discussed, direct addresses to the audience during the performance, and a thematic consistency in representing the state as a corrupt entity by referencing misuse of authority vested in the police, judiciary, and medical personnel.
5. V. Padma's essay "Let Me Live: Cry the Baby Girl, in the Cradle and in the Womb, *Pacha Mannu,* An Interventionist Theatre Experience" is an excellent account of the "effect" of theatre activism in generating "social affect" against female infanticide in Tamil Nadu. See also the brief section on women's activist theatre in the epilogue to Nandi Bhatia's work on colonial and postcolonial theatre in India.
6. Janam's plays are written and performed in Hindi. I have translated all the quotations used in this chapter into English from the Hindi originals.
7. Much of the history of the autonomous women's movement in India centers around famous 'cases' or legislative battles that come to be invested with public and activist emotion. Examples include: the Mathura case; the Shahbano case, which involved securing the right to maintenance for divorced Muslim women under criminal rather than personal laws; and most recently, the Ruchika rape case, which has galvanized the call for early jurisdiction in rape trials.
8. Raka Ray's *Fields of Protest: Women's Movements in India* offers an excellent account of the women's movement in India though Sachetana, a Calcutta-based women's organization, and the FAOW, based in Bombay.
9. The anti-rape campaign of the early 1980s politicized only violence against women, although rape of men and boys in custody was also rampant. Feminists called for a widening of a definition of rape in the 1990s to include sexual offences involving nonvaginal penetration. This is discussed later in the chapter.
10. Vibhuti Patel mentions the molestation of filmmaker-director, Madhushree Dutta, who was assaulted by the railway police while traveling in a train in 1991. When the police initially refused to register her complaint, Dutta used her contacts in the media to publicize the incident although she received threatening phone calls from the police pressurizing her to withdraw the report she had filed (Patel 158). Dutta's has been one of the strongest media voices to protest violence against women. She has also worked with the Calcutta-based feminist group Sachetana to direct feminist street plays in the 1980s.
11. There is an uncanny similarity between the dramatic and non-dramatic presence of the police in public spaces. During the January 2004 commemoration of Safdar's death anniversary through a series of performances in Sahibabad, I assumed that the young man standing next to me in police uniform was a constable. A moment later he barked out an order, scattered the audience seated on the ground, and made his way to the central area to take his role in a play on rampant systemic corruption and abuse of authority being performed by the Kirori Mal College Players.
12. Some years ago, a middle-aged man abducted Divya, my neighbors' seven-year-old daughter, while she was playing in the neighborhood park with her friends. Despite being alerted about the incident almost immediately, the Delhi police had not taken any measures to prevent the child being smuggled out of the state and possibly raped or sold into prostitution. Her loud cries alerted some of passengers in a bus and caused the abductor to abandon her at the Inter-State Bus Terminal in Delhi. She was handed over to the police and escorted home later in the night.

Notes 157

13. The grand claims that accompanied the setting up of these programs at select universities in India failed to materialize. A directory prepared by the Association of Indian Universities indicates that these programs remained "essentially research centers or centers for collection of books, with no interaction with other sections or departments of Universities" (11). Reliant on limited funding from the University Grants Commission, Women's Studies is marginal to the curricular life of these universities. Far from being integrated into the main curriculum of various disciplines, its influence has been limited to the extra-curricular Women's Development Centers set up in various participating institutions.
14. While Sakshi and IFSHA are non-governmental, non-party-based organizations, AIDWA is connected to the Communist Party of India (Marxist).

NOTES TO CHAPTER 4

1. Analysis of trends in Indian drama from the 1970s to the 1990s reveals three dominant traditions: street theatre experiments inspired by the legacy of the left-oriented Indian People's Theatre Association that believed in the populist function of theatre and drama; a "theatre of the roots," which rejected the proscenium stage and focused on a reinterpretation of traditional performance forms for contemporary urban and nonurban audiences; and contemporary proscenium theatre based in urban metropolitan centers directed specifically at theatre-going audiences.
2. Sunder Rajan's summary of feminist positions on prostitution helps contextualize the status of sex work in India: a radical or abolitionist view sees prostitution as criminal; a tolerationist view decriminalizes it, but in practice the prostitute continues to bear the brunt of oppressive legal strictures; a liberal view demands complete decriminalization and views all forms of state intervention as a violation of the rights of the prostitute to practice her profession ("Prostitution" 117–46).
3. The four castes in Indian society are: *brahmans* (priestly caste), *kshatriyas* (warriors including kings and chiefs), *vaishyas* (the merchants and moneylenders), and *shudras* (menial and agricultural laborers including those engaged in 'unclean' occupations such as tanners and night soil carriers). The upper castes include *brahmans*, *kshatriyas*, and *vaishyas*, who maintain their social hegemony by occupational and professional advantages. The Indian government officially follows a policy of "reservations" or affirmative action including educational and occupational opportunities for the lower castes.
4. Butler refers to Victor Turner's notion of drama as ritualized social acts to posit gender as an "act," though not a singular one since it "requires a performance that is *repeated*" (*Gender* 178). For Butler drag is an example of performative resignification of sex/gender categories *par excellence*, since it reveals the construction of these categories. Butler's critics point out that gender performativity need not always be subversive, leading to her famous clarification in *Bodies That Matter:* "[T]here is no necessary relation between drag and subversion . . . drag may well be used in the service of both the denaturalization and reidealization of hyperbolic heterosexual gender norms" (125).
5. See my article "Emergent Sexual Identities in Indian Women's Writing."
6. See the essays "Contract Labour or Bonded Labour" and "An Eastside Story: Construction Labourers in West Bengal" in *Dust on the Road: Activist Writings of Mahasweta Devi* for accounts of sexual exploitation of women brick

workers and women's recruitment into prostitution and bonded labor in West Bengal and Bihar.

7. The *panchayat* is a five-member elected council at the village level with the power to make decisions concerning the use of resources allocated by the government, maintenance of records, common village facilities, and settlement of minor civil disputes.

8. The Indian government has introduced measures to enfranchise the *hijras* by allowing them to choose their gender while voting. Thus the state categorizes them as potential vote banks while denying them human rights and social dignity. The *hijras* have countered this denial by fielding candidates in national and local politics. Kamla Jaan, a *hijra,* was elected mayor of Katni in Madhya Pradesh in 1999 and functioned in that office from 2000 to 2003 before being divested of the position. The grounds for her removal included contesting an electoral seat reserved for women while being registered in the electoral rolls as a man (Chakravorty 368). This indicates the state's investiture of power and authority to gendered categorizations.

9. See Vinay Lal's essay for a critique of the sociological literature on the *hijras* and an account of the various modes of the state's classification of them as paradoxical markers of auspiciousness and impotency, as male or female in census records, but not "homosexuals."

10. Gayatri Gopinath's analysis of queer sexualities in a transnational frame, although it does not discuss *hijras,* critiques "a failure to trouble the conventions of her [the anthropologist's] overdetermined status as White, first world ethnographer in the 'field'" (114). Gopinath's analysis connects to Geeta Patel's call to "decolonize" the figure of the *hijra* from ethnographic literature and queer theory (416).

11. Kalpana Lajmi's filmic translation of Devi's story provides yet another interpretation of this quasi-kinship. A startling revelation occurring towards the end of the film is that Sanichari is the child Bikhni abandoned to make a career with a local theatrical company. Yet even this filial revelation does not erase the clearly sexual moments of intimacy in the film, especially the scenes where Bikhni does Sanichari's hair or draws her into a sensuous dance.

12. Testimonies published by RAHI (Recovery and Healing from Incest, a support center for women survivors) indicate the pervasiveness of incest in middle and upper class families in India. Dattani's work with RAHI led to a play about sexual abuse of children. With this extra-dramatic context, Anarkali's comment to the Constable goes beyond the use of "sister fucker" as a common term of abuse in most Indian languages to become a comment on sexual hypocrisy.

13. See the essays by V. Geetha, Gopal Guru, Gail Omvedt, Anupama Rao, Sharmila Rege, and Susie Tharu in the anthology *Gender and Caste,* edited by Anupama Rao.

14. The Self-Respect Movement was a radical anticaste movement led by E. V. Ramasamy Periyar in 1925.

NOTES TO CHAPTER 5

1. The legend of Moremi is about a market woman born in Ile-Ife who volunteered to be taken captive by the Ibos to learn the secrets of their raids against the Yorubas. The Yorubas' victory over the Ibos leading to peace in Ile-Ife is attributed to Moremi. For a brief account of the Moremi legend, see Samuel Johnson's *The History of the Yorubas: From the Earliest Times to the Beginning of the British Protectorate.*

2. Literary representations of the inter-ethnic conflict include Buchi Emecheta's novel *Destination Biafra* (1982) and Flora Nwapa's *Never Again* (1992).
3. For an analysis of 'acronymizing' as a subversive process that undermines statist propaganda in the African postcolony, see Achille Mdembe's *On the Postcolony*, especially the chapter "The Aesthetics of Vulgarity."
4. Fatunde acknowledges intellectual, material, and moral indebtedness to Bala Usman's political analysis of the Second Republic, Femi Osofisan and the Department of Theatre Arts at the University of Benin, and Women in Nigeria (WIN). His depiction of state repression and the political response it elicited in the form of the Bakolori Farmer's Union (BAFU) also contains the structures of a peasant democracy incompletely imagined in Osofisan's play. This "government of workers, poor farmers, students and soldiers" includes a people's militia, people's secretaries of agriculture, education, and a female people's secretary of health (Fatunde 77–79).
5. Mamdani characterizes systems of postcolonial governance as "conservative" and "radical." The "conservative" states did away with racism but kept ethnicity in place ("deracialization"); the "radical" states did away with both, following an agenda of "deracialization" as well as "detribalization," but substituted centralized forms of control over local authorities. Thus the prototypical subject in the conservative state bore an ethnic mark, but that in the radical states was simply the rural peasant. Mamdani sees Nigeria as a radical state where postcolonial governance tried to reform the "decentralized despotism" of the colonial governance (exercised through local authorities). The country's oscillation between civilian and military regimes is one between centralized and decentralized despotism in which "each regime claimed to be reforming the negative feature of its predecessor" (26).
6. Chinua Achebe's *The Trouble with Nigeria* (1984) and Wole Soyinka's *The Open Sore of a Continent: A Personal Narrative of the Nigerian Crisis* (1996) discuss the nature of Nigerian nationalism, the crisis of Nigerian leadership, and the misuse of political power in the post-independence era.
7. At the peak of its activity from 1962 to 1980, the Ruwenzururu was a response to deprivation of land, language oppression, and job discrimination throughout the colonial period. After negotiations with the post-independence Ugandan state, its leader Isaah Mkirani set up a "reformed state structure" between 1964 and 1966. The Sungusungu was active between 1980 and 1983; it organized over fifty thousand square kilometers of land in rural northwestern Tanzania with a population of over five million peasants (Mamdani 1996).
8. One of the most important events in the history of women's mobilization is the 1929 Women's War. Nina Mba provides an excellent account of the war in her book *Nigerian Women Mobilized: Women's Political Activity in Southern Nigeria, 1900–1965*. A response to the taxes imposed by the British colonial authorities, the movement was known as the Women's War by the local population and the Aba Tax Riots by the colonial authorities. Mba's meticulous documentation of the causes, spread, reach, and impact of the war leads her to conclude that it was "very much a feminist movement in the sense that women were very conscious of the special role of women, the importance of women to society, and the assertion of their rights as women *vis a vis* the men. They consistently drew attention to their sexual identity through their dress, body gestures, and songs" (91). T. Obinkaram Echewa's novel *I Saw the Sky Catch Fire* (1992) is a postcolonial fictional reconstruction of the Women's War.
9. Ato Quayson uses this term in *Calibrations: Reading for the Social*. For Quayson the social is "always an object produced out of interrogation and

thus has to be *read for*." He "strategically" separates "*the social* from *society* (context, history etc.) . . . to make clear that the social that is being read for across the literary is part of an anticipatory project." The key point in Quayson's theorization of the social, relevant to my reading of drama and feminist movements, is his assertion that "[i]f the social that is read for in any text is of any value, then it also implies that the insights derived from local texts may also be translated into different contexts and times" (xxxi).

NOTES TO CHAPTER 6

1. A contrasting view is presented in Awam Amkpa's *Theatre and Postcolonial Desires*. Amkpa provides a brief history of the People's Studio Workshop (PSW) and its links to other similar efforts in Nigeria.
2. Amina Mama has outlined the difficulties faced by researchers in conveying the concept of gender to local audiences while arguing for strengthening civil society through participatory action research. The difficulties are compounded by the fact that in many Nigerian languages there is "no translation of the term 'gender', whose current English usage derives much from feminist scholarship of the 1970s" (66–67). A feminist pedagogy whereby questions were posed and understood in concrete and local terms enabling people to "respond by narrating incidents that indicated their level of engagement with gender" is comparable, though by no means similar, to the participatory methods of TfD. Feminist groups in Nigeria and elsewhere have employed these methods to reach out to local communities, sometimes under governmental patronage but often functioning as autonomous NGOs. The point I wish to make in relation to Onwueme's play is that a neat polarization between Western-educated intelligentsia's flawed feminist ideology and indigenous women's feminist consciousness does disservice to efforts like the one outlined by Mama.
3. For an outline of the motivations that led the author to write the essay, its impact on feminist studies, its appropriation by postmodernists arising from an incomplete understanding of its premises, and the articulation of a "transnational anticapitalist feminist politics," see Mohanty's "'Under Western Eyes' Revisited: Solidarity through Anticapitalist Struggles."
4. It is not my intention to set up an adversarial relationship between critics of South Asian origin (Desai and myself) and those from Africa who deny African homosexuality such (Emecheta and the member of the audience who objected to Desai's paper). Emotional responses may foreclose a long-overdue discussion on African sexualities, and the national affiliations of critics should not be an issue in what is after all a significant social concern. Thanks to Joseph McLaren for pointing out that this is one of the ways in which my account of the ALA session might be interpreted.
5. Onwueme clarified her representation of Ruth and Daisy. She said that since alternative sexual preferences exist, the writer runs the risk of falsifying reality if these are not discussed in literature.
6. Amadiume defines "developmentalism" as a "pattern of language" that recurs "in claims by local elites, development advisers and workers, donor agencies, and global women's conferences to give relevance and legitimacy to leadership over rural and peasant women" (*Daughters* 8).
7. Commentators on same-sex love and eroticism in postcolonial societies have drawn attention to the problem of describing African forms of sexual expression through Western vocabularies of identity politics. For instance the Hausa *yan daudu* in northern Nigeria are a community of cross-dress-

ing performers many of whom are in same-sex relationships while fulfilling their social commitments as husbands and fathers. They do not subscribe to the global vocabularies of identity categories (homosexual, gay, lesbian, or queer) and would hesitate from identifying themselves in these terms. Additionally since some of them take on gender roles divorced from their biological sex (male) it would not be correct to say that they engaged in same-sex relationships. Some who are in a relationship with a man of the same social status or have taken on a feminine gender role and enter into relationships with other "womanlike" *yan daudu* use the local term for lesbians to refer to themselves (Gaudio).

8. Recent anthropological, sociological, and historical work from India, Africa, and the Caribbean has demonstrated that indigenous queer existence is intrinsic to the cultures and societies of these regions. Gloria Wekker's ethnographic research on the *mati* tradition among working class Creole women in Surinam is indicative of one such attempt to present sexual desire between women outside the framework of Westernized identity politics and labels. Kendall's investigations on love between women in Lesotho is marked by a similar circumspection in affixing the Western categorizations 'lesbian' and 'bisexual' to women whose interactions involve heterosexual marriage as well as intense emotional, social, and sexual bonding with women.

Bibliography

Abah, Oga Steve. *Performing Life: Case Studies in the Practice of Theatre for Development.* Zaria, Nigeria: Shekut Books, 1997.
Abubakar, Abdullahi S. "A New Concept of Actor/Audience Interaction and Audience Participation in Modern African Theatre: An Example of Osofisan." *Research in African Literatures* 40.3 (2009): 174–85.
Achebe, Chinua. *The Trouble with Nigeria.* London: Heinemann Educational, 1984.
Adeniran, Tunde. "The Dynamics of Peasant Revolt: A Conceptual Analysis of the Agbekoya Parapo Uprising in the Western State of Nigeria." *Journal of Black Studies* 4.4 (1974): 363–75.
Afzal-Khan, Fawzia. "Exposed by Pakistani Street Theater: The Unholy Alliance of Postmodern Capitalism, Patriarchy, and Fundamentalism." *Social Text* 19.4 (2001): 67–91.
———. "Street Theatre in Pakistani Punjab: The Case of Ajoka, Lok Rehas, and the Woman Question." *TDR* 41.3 (1997): 41–61.
Agnes, Flavia. "The Anti-Rape Campaign: The Struggle and the Setback." *The Struggle against Violence.* Ed. Chaya Datar. Calcutta: Stree, 1993. 99–150.
———. "Law, Ideology, and Female Sexuality: Gender Neutrality in Rape Law." *Economic and Political Weekly* 2 Mar. 2002: 844–47.
Ahmad, Aijaz. *In Theory: Nations, Classes, Literatures.* London: Verso, 1992.
Ajayi, Omofolabo. "Who Can Silence Her Drums?: An Analysis of the Plays of Tess Onwueme." *African Theatre: Women.* Eds. Martin Banham, James Gibbs, and Femi Osofisan. Oxford: James Curry, 2002. 109–21.
Alekar, Satish. *Begum Barve.* Trans. Shanta Gokhale. Calcutta: Seagull, 1994.
Alexander, M. Jacqui. "Erotic Autonomy as a Politics of Decolonization: An Anatomy of Feminist and State Practice in the Bahamas Tourist Economy." Alexander and Mohanty 63–100.
———. "Not Just (Any)Body Can Be a Citizen: The Politics of Law, Sexuality and Postcoloniality in Trinidad and Tobago and the Bahamas." *Cultures of Empire: Colonizers in Britain and the Empire in the Nineteenth and Twentieth Centuries, A Reader.* Ed. Catherine Hall. New York: Routledge, 2000. 359–76.
Alexander, M. Jacqui, and Chandra Talpade Mohanty, eds. *Feminist Genealogies, Colonial Legacies, Democratic Futures.* New York: Routledge, 1995.
———. "Introduction: Genealogies, Legacies, Movements." Alexander and Mohanty xiii–xlii.
Amadiume, Ifi. *Daughters of the Goddess, Daughters of Imperialism: African Women Struggle for Culture, Power, and Democracy.* London: Zed, 2000.
———. *Male Daughters and Female Husbands: Gender and Sex in an African Society.* London and Atlantic Highlands, NJ: Zed, 1987.

Amkpa, Awam. *Theatre and Postcolonial Desires*. Routledge Advances in Theatre and Performance Studies. London and New York: Routledge, 2003.
Antrobus, Peggy. Letter to Honor Ford-Smith. 26 Sept. 1980. MS. Personal Collection of Honor Ford-Smith.
———. "The Lucille Mathurin Mair Lecture 2000: The Rise and Fall of Feminist Politics in the Caribbean Women's Movement 1975–1995." Mona: Phillip Sherlock Centre for the Creative Arts, U of West Indies, 2000.
Association of Indian Universities and Commonwealth of Learning. "Women's Studies and the Universities in India." *Directory of Women's Studies in India*. New Delhi: Association of Indian Universities, 1991. 10–24.
Atluri, Tara L. *When the Closet Is a Religion: Homophobia, Heterosexism and Nationalism in the Commonwealth Caribbean*. Working Paper Series 5. Bridgetown: Centre for Gender and Development Studies, U of West Indies, Cave Hill, 2001.
Azodo, Ada Uzoamaka, and Maureen Ngozi Eke, eds. *Gender and Sexuality in African Literature and Film*. Trenton: Africa World P, 2007.
Barriteau, Eudine. "Theorizing Gender Systems and the Project of Modernity in the Twentieth-Century Caribbean." *Feminist Review* 59.1 (1998): 22–54.
Batra, Kanika. "'Daughters Who Know the Languages of Power': Community, Sexuality, and Postcolonial Development in Tess Onwueme's *Tell It to Women*." *Interventions: International Journal of Postcolonial Studies* 9.1 (2007): 124–38.
———. "Emergent Sexual Identities in Indian Women's Writing." *South Asian Review* 29.1 (2008): 251–68.
———. "'Our Own Gayful Rest': A Postcolonial Archive." *Small Axe: A Caribbean Journal of Criticism* 14.1 (2010): 46–59.
Beckett, Paul A., and Crawford Young, eds. "Introduction: Beyond the Impasse of 'Permanent Transition' in Nigeria" by Beckett and Young. *Dilemmas of Democracy in Nigeria*. Rochester: U of Rochester P, 1997. 1–14.
Beckford, George, and Michael Witter. *Small Garden, Bitter Weed: The Political Economy of Struggle and Change in Jamaica*. 1980. Morant Bay: Maroon; London: Zed, 1982.
Bentley, Eric. "Dear Grotowski: An Open Letter." Schechner and Wolford 165–171.
Bhabha, Homi. *The Location of Culture*. London: Routledge, 1994.
Bharucha, Rustom. *In the Name of the Secular: Contemporary Cultural Activism in India*. New Delhi: Oxford UP, 1998.
———. *The Politics of Cultural Practice: Thinking Through Theatre in the Age of Globalization*. New Delhi: Oxford UP, 2001.
———. *Theatre and the World: Performance and the Practice of Culture*. 1990. London: Routledge, 1993.
Bhatia, Nandi. *Acts of Authority, Acts of Resistance: Theatre and Politics in Colonial and Postcolonial India*. Ann Arbor: U of Michigan P, 2004.
Bjorkman, Ingrid. *Mother, Sing for Me: People's Theatre in Kenya*. London: Zed, 1989.
Boal, Augusto. *Games for Actors and Non-Actors*. Trans. Adrian Jackson. London: Routledge, 1992.
———. *Legislative Theatre: Using Performance to Make Politics*. Trans. Adrian Jackson. London: Routledge, 1998.
———. *The Rainbow of Desire: The Boal Method of Theatre and Therapy*. Trans. Adrian Jackson. London: Routledge, 1995.
———. *Theatre of the Oppressed*. 1974. Trans. Charles A. and Maria-Odilia Leal McBride. New York: Theatre Communications, 1985.

Bose, Brinda, and Subhabrata Bhattacharya, eds. *The Phobic and the Erotic: The Politics of Sexualities in Contemporary India*. Calcutta: Seagull, 2007.

Brecht, Bertolt. *Brecht on Theatre: The Development of an Aesthetic*. Ed. and Trans. John Willett. New York: Hill & Wang, 1964.

———. "My Audience." *Bertolt Brecht: Poems and Songs from the Plays*. Ed. and Trans. John Willett. London: Methuen, 1990. 116.

Brodber, Erna. *A Study of the Yards of Kingston*. Working Paper 9. Mona: Institute of Social and Economic Research, U of West Indies, 1975.

Butler, Judith. *Antigone's Claim: Kinship between Life and Death*. New York: Columbia UP, 2000.

———. *Bodies That Matter: On the Discursive Limits of 'Sex'*. New York and London: Routledge, 1993.

———. *Gender Trouble: Feminism and the Subversion of Identity*. 1990. New York and London: Routledge, 1999.

———. "Is Kinship Always Already Heterosexual." *Undoing Gender*. New York and London: Routledge, 2004. 102–30.

———. "Performative Acts and Gender Constitution: An Essay in Phenomenology and Gender Constitution." *Performing Feminisms: Feminist Critical Theory and Theatre*. Ed. Sue-Ellen Case. Baltimore: Johns Hopkins UP, 1990. 270–82.

Campbell, Edmond. "Parliament Drama: Theatre Director Checks in on Abortion Debate in Historic Fashion." *Jamaica Gleaner* 13 Mar. 2009. <http://www.jamaica-gleaner.com/gleaner/20090313/lead/lead1.html> Accessed 22 Mar. 2010.

Carr, Robert. "A Politics of Change: Sistren, Subalternity, and the Social Pact in the War for Democratic Socialism." *Black Nationalism in the New World: Reading the African-American and the West Indian Experience*. Durham: Duke UP, 2002. 225–69.

Chakravorty, Bhaswati. "Rights for the Third Gender: Problems of Identity and Recognition." Bose and Bhattacharya 369–90.

Chatterjee, Partha. *"The Nation and Its Fragments."* 1993. *The Partha Chatterjee Omnibus*. New Delhi: Oxford UP, 1999. 1–282.

———. "On Civil and Political Societies in Post-Colonial Democracies." *Civil Society: History and Possibilities*. Eds. Sudipta Kaviraj and Sunil Khilnani. Cambridge: Cambridge UP, 2001. 165–78.

Chin, Staceyann. *The Other Side of Paradise: A Memoir*. New York: Scribner-Simon & Schuster, 2009.

Clarke, Edith. *My Mother Who Fathered Me: A Study of Families in Three Selected Communities of Jamaica*. 1957. Mona: U of West Indies P, 1999.

Cliff, Michelle. *No Telephone to Heaven*. New York: Dutton, 1987.

Cobham, Rhonda, and Honor Ford-Smith. "Introduction." *Bellywoman Bangarang* by Sistren and Honor Ford Smith. Ed. Rhonda Cobham. Unpublished MS. iv–xxxvi. 1978/1982

Cooper, Carolyn. *Noises in the Blood: Orality, Gender and the 'Vulgar' Body of Jamaican Popular Culture*. London: Macmillan Caribbean, 1993.

———. *Sound Clash: Jamaican Dancehall Culture at Large*. New York: Palgrave-Macmillan, 2004.

Cooper, Frederick. "Conflict and Connection: Rethinking Colonial African History." *History After the Three Worlds: Post-Eurocentric Historiographies*. Eds. Arif Dirlik, Vinay Bahl, and Peter Gran. Lanham: Rowman & Littlefield, 2000. 157–90.

Crow, Brian, and Chris Banfield. *An Introduction to Post-Colonial Theatre*. Cambridge and New York: Cambridge UP, 1996.

Cumper, Gloria. *Planning and Implementing the Family Court Project, Jamaica.* Working Paper 27. Institute of Social and Economic Research: U of West Indies, 1981.

———. *Survey of Social Legislation in Jamaica.* Law and Society in the Caribbean 1. Institute of Social and Economic Research: U of West Indies, 1972.

Dattani, Mahesh. "A Dialogue with Mahesh Dattani." Interview with Lakshmi Subramanyam. *Muffled Voices: Women in Modern Indian Theatre.* New Delhi: Shakti-Har Anand, 2002. 128–34.

———. "Seven Steps around the Fire." *Collected Plays.* New Delhi and London: Penguin, 2000. 1–42.

Dawes, Caroll. "Production Notes on *Echo in the Bone.*" Creative Arts Centre. UWI, Mona: May 1974. Scott Papers in the Personal Collection of Honor Ford-Smith.

D'Emilio, John. *Sexual Politics, Sexual Communities: The Making of a Homosexual Minority in the United States, 1940–1970.* 1983. Chicago: U of Chicago P, 1998.

Desai, Gaurav. "Out in Africa." *Postcolonial Queer: Theoretical Intersections.* Ed. John C. Hawley. Albany: State U of New York P, 2001. 139–64.

Deshpande, Sudhanva. "Sahmat and the Politics of Cultural Intervention." *Economic and Political Weekly* 22 June 1996: 1586–90.

———. "Sculpting a Play." 1996. *Theatre of the Streets: The Jana Natya Manch Experience.* Ed. Sudhanva Deshpande. New Delhi: Janam, 2007. 100–16.

Devi, Mahasweta. "Douloti." *Imaginary Maps.* Trans. Gayatri Chakravorty Spivak. Calcutta: Thema, 1993. 19–94.

———. *Dust on the Road: Activist Writings of Mahasweta Devi.* Ed. Maitreya Ghatak. Calcutta: Seagull, 2000.

———. "Rudali." Devi and Ganguli 54–91.

Devi, Mahasweta, and Usha Ganguli. *Rudali: From Fiction to Performance.* Trans. Anjum Katyal. Calcutta: Seagull, 1997.

Dharwadker, Aparna Bhargava. *Theatres of Independence: Drama, Theory, and Urban Performance in India since 1947.* Iowa City: U of Iowa P, 2005.

Diamond, Elin. "Brechtian Theory/Feminist Theory: Toward a Gestic Feminist Criticism." *Unmaking Mimesis: Essays on Feminism and Theatre.* Ed. Elin Diamond. London and New York: Routledge, 1997. 43–55.

Diaz, Angeli R. "Postcolonial Theory and the Third Wave Agenda." *Women and Language* 26.1 (2003): 10–17.

Dunton, Chris. "'Wheyting be Dat?': The Treatment of Homosexuality in African Literature." *Research in African Literatures* 20.3 (1989): 422–48.

Echewa, T. Obinkaram. *I Saw the Sky Catch Fire.* New York: Dutton, 1992.

Edwards, Nadi. "Notes on the Age of Dis: Reading Kingston through Agamben." *Small Axe: A Journal of Caribbean Criticism* 25 (Feb. 2008): 1–15.

Emecheta, Buchi. *Destination Biafra: A Novel.* London: Allison and Busby, 1982.

———. "Natural Gestures." *New Internationalist* 201 (Nov. 1989). <http://www.newint.org/issue201/gestures.htm> Accessed 22 Mar. 2010.

Ellis, Patricia. *Women, Gender and Development in the Caribbean: Reflections and Projections.* London: Zed; Kingston: Ian Randle, 2003.

Epprecht, Marc. *Heterosexual Africa: The History of an Idea from the Age of Exploration to the Age of AIDS.* Athens: Ohio UP, 2008.

Epprecht, Marc, and Sula E. Egya. "Teaching about Homosexualities to Nigerian University Students: A Report from the Field." *Gender and Education*, forthcoming in 2010.

Evans, David T. *Sexual Citizenship: The Material Construction of Sexualities.* London: Routledge, 1993.

Falola, Toyin, and Julius Omozuanvbo Ihonvbere. *The Rise and Fall of Nigeria's Second Republic, 1979–1984.* London: Zed, 1985.
Fatunde, Tunde. *No Food, No Country.* Benin: Adena, 1985.
Findlen, Barbara, ed. *Listen Up! Voices from the Next Feminist Generation.* Seattle: Seal P, 1995.
Fisher, Berenice. "Feminist Acts: Women, Pedagogy and Theatre of the Oppressed." *Playing Boal: Theatre, Therapy, Activism.* Eds. Mady Schutzman and Jan Cohen-Cruz. London: Routledge, 1994. 185–97.
Flaszen, Ludwig. "*Akropolis:* The Treatment of the Text." Grotowski *Poor* 61–78.
Ford-Smith, Honor. "Performing Nation: The Pedagogy and Politics of Post-Colonial Jamaican Performance." Diss. Ontario Institute for Studies in Education, U of Toronto, 2005.
———. Personal Interview. Oct. 2003.
———. *Ring Ding in a Tight Corner: A Case Study of Funding and Organizational Democracy in Sistren 1977–1988.* Toronto: Women's Program, 1989.
Forgacs, David. "Glossary of Key Terms." *The Gramsci Reader: Selected Writings 1916–1935.* Ed. David Forgacs. New York: New York UP, 2000. 420–31.
Foucault, Michel. "Governmentality." *The Foucault Effect: Studies in Governmentality.* Eds. Graham Burchell, Colin Gordon, and Peter Miller. Chicago: U of Chicago P, 1991. 87–104.
Fraser, Nancy. *Justice Interruptus: Critical Reflections on the 'Postsocialist' Condition.* New York: Routledge, 1997.
Freeman, Carla. *High Tech and High Heels in the Global Economy: Women, Work, and Pink-Collar Identities in the Caribbean.* Durham: Duke UP, 2000.
Freire, Paulo. *Pedagogy of the Oppressed.* Trans. Myra Bergman Ramos. New York: Herder and Herder, 1970.
French, Joan. "Women and Colonial Policy in Jamaica After the 1938 Uprising." *Subversive Women: Historical Experiences of Gender and Resistance.* Ed. Saskia Wieringa. London: Zed, 1995. 121–46.
French, Joan, and Honor Ford-Smith. "Women, Work and Organization in Jamaica 1900–1944." Unpublished MS. The Hague: Institute of Social Sciences, 1987.
Gandhi, Nandita, and Nandita Shah. *The Issues at Stake: Theory and Practice in the Contemporary Women's Movement in India.* New Delhi: Kali for Women, 1992.
Ganguli, Usha. "*Rudali.*" Devi and Ganguli 93–156.
Gaudio, Rudolf P. "Male Lesbians and Other Queer Nations in Hausa." *Boy-Wives and Female Husbands: Studies in African Homosexualities.* Eds. Stephen O. Murray and Will Roscoe. New York: St. Martin's, 1998. 115–28.
Gbilekaa, Saint. *Radical Theatre in Nigeria.* Ibadan: Caltop, 1997.
Geetha, V. "Periyar, Women and an Ethic of Citizenship." Rao *Gender* 180–203.
Gilbert, Helen. "Introduction." *Postcolonial Plays: An Anthology.* Ed. Helen Gilbert. London and New York: Routledge, 2001. 1–5.
Gilbert, Helen, and Joanne Tompkins. *Post-Colonial Drama: Theory, Practice, Politics.* London and New York: Routledge, 1996.
Gilroy, Paul. *The Black Atlantic: Modernity and Double Consciousness.* Cambridge: Harvard UP, 1993.
Gopinath, Gayatri. "Homo-Economics: Queer Sexualities in a Transnational Frame." *Burning Down the House: Recycling Domesticity.* Ed. Rosemary Marangoly George. Boulder: Westview P, 1998. 102–24.
Gramsci, Antonio. *The Gramsci Reader: Selected Writings 1916–1935.* Ed. David Forgacs. New York: New York UP, 2000.
Gray, Obika. *Demeaned but Empowered: The Social Power of the Urban Poor in Jamaica.* Mona: U of West Indies P, 2004.

———. "Predation Politics and the Political Impasse in Jamaica." *Small Axe: A Caribbean Journal of Criticism* 7.1 (2003): 72–94.
Green, Sharon L. "On a Knife Edge: Sistren Theatre Collective, Grassroots Theatre, and Globalization." *Small Axe: A Journal of Caribbean Criticism* 11.1 (2006): 105–18.
———. "Sistren Theatre Collective: Struggling to Remain Radical in an Era of Globalization." *Theatre Topics* 14.2 (2004): 273–95.
Grotowski, Jerzy. 1967. "The Actor's Technique." Grotowski *Poor* 205–15.
———. "The Theatre's New Testament: An Interview with Jerzy Grotowski by Eugenio Barba." 1964. Grotowski *Poor* 27–54.
———. *Towards a Poor Theatre*. 1968. Ed. Eugenio Barba. New York: Methuen, 1975.
Guha, Ranajit. "Subaltern Studies: Projects for Our Time and Their Convergence." Rodriguez *Latin* 35–46.
Gutzmore, Cecil. "Casting the First Stone: Policing of Homo/Sexuality in Jamaican Popular Culture." *Interventions* 6.1 (2004): 118–34.
Hagher, Iyorwuese. *The Practice of Community Theatre in Nigeria*. Owerri: Society of Nigerian Theatre Artists, 1990.
Halberstam, Judith. "Forgetting Family: Queer Alternatives to Oedipal Relations." *A Companion to Lesbian, Gay, Bisexual, Transgender, and Queer Studies*. Eds. George E. Haggerty and Molly McGarry. Malden: Blackwell, 2007. 315–25.
Harding, Frances. "Fifteen Years Between: Benue and Katsina Workshop, Nigeria." *African Theatre in Development*. Eds. Martin Banham et al. Oxford: James Curry, 1999. 99–112.
Harrison, Faye V. "Women in Jamaica's Urban Informal Economy: Insights from a Kingston Slum." Mohanty, Russo, and Torres 173–96.
Hashmi, Moloyashree. Personal Interview. Jan. 2004.
———. Personal Interview. July 2009.
Hashmi, Qamar Azad. *The Fifth Flame: The Story of Safdar Hashmi*. Trans. Madhu Prasad and Sohail Hashmi. New Delhi: Viking-Penguin, 1997.
Hashmi, Safdar. "An Interview by Eugene Van Erven." Hashmi *The Right* 139–80.
———. *The Right to Perform: Selected Writings of Safdar Hashmi*. New Delhi: Sahmat, 1989.
———. "Theatre in Pakistan." Interview by Mansoor Saeed. Hashmi *The Right* 130–35.
Harneit-Sievers, Axel. "Introduction." *Constructions of Belonging: Igbo Communities and the Nigerian State in the Twentieth Century*. Rochester: U of Rochester P, 2006. 1–14.
Hawley, John C, ed. *Postcolonial Queer: Theoretical Intersections*. Albany: State U of New York P, 2001.
Hill, Errol. "Introduction." *Plays for Today*. Ed. Errol Hill. Longman Caribbean Writers. Essex: Longman, 1985. 3–19.
Hoad, Neville. *African Intimacies: Race, Homosexuality, and Globalization*. Minneapolis: U of Minnesota P, 2007.
Hodge, Merle. "Young Women and the Development of Stable Family Life in the Caribbean." *Savacou: A Journal of the Caribbean Artists Movement*. Special issue on Caribbean Woman. 13 (1977): 39–44.
Imam, Ayesha. "The Dynamics of Winning: An Analysis of Women in Nigeria (WIN)." Alexander and Mohanty 280–307.
Jaffrey, Zia. *The Invisibles: A Tale of the Eunuchs of India*. New York: Pantheon, 1996.
Jana Natya Manch. "Aartanaad [Echoing Wails]." 1993. *Nukkad Janam Samvad [Street Theatre Dialogue]* 9.37–38 (2007–2008): 84–89.

———. "*Aurat* [Woman]." 1978. *Nukkad Janam Samvad* [*Street Theatre Dialogue*] 9.37–38 (2007–2008): 93–103.
———. "*Police Charitram* [*Characterizing Police*]." 1981. *Nukkad Janam Samvad* [*Street Theatre Dialogue*] 9.37–38 (2007–2008): 90–92.
Johnson, Samuel. *The History of the Yorubas: From the Earliest Times to the Beginning of the British Protectorate.* 1921. Westport: Negro UP, 1970.
Johnson-Odim, Cheryl, and Nina Emma Mba. *For Women and the Nation: Funmilayo Ransome-Kuti of Nigeria.* Urbana: U of Illinois P, 1997.
Joseph, Richard A. *Democracy and Prebendal Politics in Nigeria: The Rise and Fall of the Second Republic.* African Studies Series 56. Cambridge: Cambridge UP, 1987.
Juneja, Renu. "Recalling the Dead in Dennis Scott's 'An Echo in the Bone'." *Ariel* 23.1 (1992): 97–114.
Katyal, Anjum. "The Metamorphosis of 'Rudali'." Devi and Ganguli 1–53.
Kidd, Ross. *The Popular Performing Arts, Non-Formal Education, and Social Change in the Third World: A Bibliography and Review Essay.* The Hague: Centre for the Study of Education in Developing Countries, 1982.
King, Bruce. "Introduction." *Post-Colonial English Drama: Commonwealth Drama Since 1960.* New York: St. Martin's, 1992. 1–16.
Kinser, Amber E. "Negotiating Spaces For/Through Third-Wave Feminism." *NWSA Journal* 16.3 (2004): 124–53.
Ladipo, Duro. *Moremi: A Yoruba Opera.* Trans. Joel Adedeji. Ibadan: School of Drama, U of Ibadan, 1973.
Lal, Vinay. "Not This, Not That: The Hijras of India and the Cultural Politics of Sexuality." *Social Text* 61 (1999): 119–40.
Life and Debt. Dir. Stephanie Black. Tuff Gong Films; New Yorker Films, 2001.
Lindsay, Hertencer. "Director's Notes to *QPH.*" Personal Collection of Honor Ford-Smith. n.d.
Ludlam, Charles. "Let Grotowski Sacrifice Masculinity Too." Schechner and Wolford 141–43.
Mama, Amina. "Strengthening Civil Society: Participatory Action Research in a Militarised State." *Development in Practice* 10.1 (2000): 59–70.
Mamdani, Mahmood. *Citizen and Subject: Contemporary Africa and the Legacy of Late Colonialism.* Princeton: Princeton UP, 1996.
Mair, Lucille Mathurin. "International Women's Decade: A Balance Sheet. Third J. P. Naik Memorial Lecture. New Delhi: Center for Women's Development Studies, 1985.
Manley, Michael. *The Politics of Change: A Jamaican Testament.* 1975. Rev. ed. Washington: Howard UP, 1990.
Mathurin, Lucille. "Reluctant Matriarchs." *Savacou: A Journal of the Caribbean Artists Movement.* Special issue on Caribbean Woman. 13 (1977): 1–6.
Mba, Nina Emma. *Nigerian Women Mobilized: Women's Political Activity in Southern Nigeria, 1900–1965.* Berkeley: Institute of International Studies, U of California, 1982.
Mdembe, Achille. *On the Postcolony.* Berkeley: U of California P, 2001.
Mee, Erin B. "From Movement to Style to 'National Theatre' at the Sangeet Natak Akedemi." *Theatre of Roots: Redirecting the Modern Indian Stage.* Calcutta: Seagull, 2008. 179–222.
Meeks, Brian. "The Political Moment in Jamaica: The Dimensions of Hegemonic Dissolution." *Radical Caribbean: From Black Power to Abu Bakr.* Jamaica: U of West Indies P, 1996. 123–42.
Merchant, Hoshang. *Yaarana: Gay Writing from India.* New Delhi: Penguin, 1999.
Mignolo, Walter. "Coloniality of Power and Subalternity." Rodriguez *Latin* 424–44.

Mike, Chuck, and Members of the PSW. "Performance Studio Workshop: Igboelerin East." *African Theatre in Development.* Eds. Martin Banham et al. Oxford: James Curry, 1999. 61–78.
Miss Amy and Miss May. Dir. Cynthia Wilmot, Pauline Crawford, and Honor Ford-Smith. Sistren Research. Women Make Movies, 1990.
Mohanty, Chandra Talpade. "Under Western Eyes: Feminist Scholarship and Colonial Discourses." 1987. *Feminism without Borders: Decolonizing Theory, Practicing Solidarity.* 2003. 17–42.
———. "'Under Western Eyes' Revisited: Solidarity through Anticapitalist Struggles." *Feminism without Borders: Decolonizing Theory, Practicing Solidarity.* 2003. 221–51.
Mohanty, Chandra Talpade, Ann Russo, and Lourdes Torres, eds. *Third World Women and the Politics of Feminism.* Bloomington: Indiana UP, 1991.
Moi, Toril. *Sexual/Textual Politics.* 1985. New Accents. London: Routledge, 1988.
Mouffe, Chantal. "Feminism, Citizenship, and Radical Democratic Politics." *Feminists Theorize the Political.* Eds. Judith Butler and Joan W. Scott. New York and London: Routledge, 1992. 369–84.
Munroe, Trevor. *Renewing Democracy into the Millennium: The Jamaican Experience in Perspective.* Jamaica: U of West Indies P, 1999.
Nanda, Serena. *Neither Man nor Woman: The Hijras of India.* Belmont: Wadsworth, 1990.
Narrain, Arvind, and Gautam Bhan, eds. *Because I Have a Voice: Queer Politics in India.* New Delhi: Yoda P, 2005.
National Commission of Women. *Report of Seminar on Child Rape, October 7–8, 1992.* New Delhi: National Commission of Women, Government of India, 1992.
———. *The Velvet Blouse: Sexual Exploitation of Children.* New Delhi: National Commission of Women, Government of India, 1997.
Nettleford, Rex M. *Caribbean Cultural Identity: The Case of Jamaica: An Essay in Cultural Dynamics.* Studies on Social Processes and Change. Los Angeles: Center for African-American Studies & UCLA Latin American Center Publications, U of California, Los Angeles, 1978.
———. "To Be Liberated from the Obscurity of Themselves." Interview with David Scott. *Small Axe: A Caribbean Journal of Criticism* 10.2 (2006): 97–246.
Newton, Esther. *Mother Camp: Female Impersonators in America.* Chicago: U of Chicago P, 1972.
Ngugi wa Thiong'o. *Penpoints, Gunpoints, and Dreams: Towards a Critical Theory of the Arts and the State in Africa.* Oxford: Clarendon, 1998.
Ngugi wa Thiong'o, and Micere Mugo. 1976. *The Trial of Dedan Kimathi.* African Writer's Series. Chennai: Heinemann-Worldview, 2001.
Nicholson, Linda. "Introduction." Nicholson 1–5.
———, ed. *The Second Wave: A Reader in Feminist Theory.* New York: Routledge, 1997.
Nolte, Insa. "'Without Women, Nothing Can Succeed: Yoruba Women in the Oodua People's Congress (OPC), Nigeria" *Africa* 78.1 (2008): 84–106.
Nwapa, Flora. *Never Again.* Trenton: Africa World P, 1992.
Obafemi, Olu. "Towards Feminist Aesthetics in Nigerian Drama: The Plays of Tess Onwueme." *Critical Theory and African Literature Today.* Eds. Eldred Durosimi Jones, Eustace Palmer, and Marjorie Jones. London: James Currey, 1994. 84–100.
Ogundipe-Leslie, Molara. *Re-Creating Ourselves: African Women and Critical Transformations.* Trenton: Africa World P, 1994.

Ogunleye, Foluke. "Ife Convocation Plays as Politics: An Examination of Some Past Productions." *African Theatre: Playwrights and Politics*. Eds. Martin Banham, James Gibbs, and Femi Osofisan. Oxford: James Currey; Bloomington and Indianapolis: Indiana UP; Johannesburg: Witwatersand UP, 2001. 18–25.

Ojewusi, Sola. *Speaking for Nigerian Women: A History of the National Council of Women's Societies, Nigeria*. Abuja: All State P, 1996.

Olaniyan, Tejumola. "The Form of Uncommon Sense." *Research in African Literatures* 30.4 (1999): 74–91.

Omvedt, Gail. "The Women's Movement." *Reinventing Revolution: New Social Movements and the Socialist Tradition in India*. New York and London: Eastgate-M.E. Sharpe, 1993. 71–99.

Onwueme, Osonye Tess. *Go Tell It to the Women: An Epic Drama for Women*. Newark: African Heritage P, 1992.

———. *Tell It to Women: An Epic Drama for Women*. Detroit: Wayne State UP, 1997.

Osofisan, Femi. "And After the Wasted Breed? Responses to History and to Wole Soyinka's Dramaturgy." 1992. *Insidious Treasons: Drama in a Postcolonial State*. Opon Ifa Publishers: Ibadan, 2001. 1–23.

———. *The Chattering and the Song*. Ibadan: Ibadan UP, 1976.

———. "Morountodun." *Oriki of a Grasshopper and Other Plays*. Ed. Abiola Irele. Washington: Howard UP, 1995. 127–95.

———. "Radical Playwright in an Ancient, Feudal Town." 1975. *The Nostalgic Drum: Essays on Literature, Drama, and Culture*. Trenton: Africa World P, 2001. 207–18.

Padma, V. (Mangai). "Let Me Live: Cry the Baby Girl, in the Cradle and in the Womb, *Pacha Mannu*, an Interventionist Theatre Experience." *Muffled Voices: Women in Modern Indian Theatre*. Ed. Lakshmi Subramanyam. New Delhi: Shakti-Har Anand, 2002. 215–30.

———. "Re-presenting Protest and Resistance on Stage: Avvai." *Indian Journal of Gender Studies* 7.2 (2000): 217–30.

Padmanabhan, Manjula. "Famous Last Words." *Hidden Fires: Monologues*. Calcutta: Seagull, 2003. 18–23.

Pandey, Gyanendra. "Notions of Community: Popular and Subaltern." *Postcolonial Studies* 8.4 (2005): 409–19.

"Parliamentary Submission." Jamaica Forum for Lesbians, All-Sexuals and Gays (J-FLAG). <http://www.jflag.org/programmes/parliamentary_sub.htm> Accessed 22 Mar. 2010.

Patel, Geeta. "Home, Homo, Hybrid: Translating Gender." *A Companion to Postcolonial Studies*. Ed. Henry Schwarz and Sangeeta Ray. Malden; Oxford: Blackwell, 2000. 410–27.

Patel, Vibhuti. "Women's Action Groups and the State Machinery." *Dossier on Violence Against Women*. Delhi: Women's Studies and Development Center, U of Delhi, 1999. 153–66.

Patton, Cindy. *Globalizing AIDS*. Minneapolis: U of Minnesota P, 2002.

Purvis, Jennifer. "Grrrls and Women Together in the Third Wave: Embracing the Challenges of Intergenerational Feminism(s)." *NWSA Journal* 16.3 (2004): 93–123.

Quayson, Ato. *Calibrations: Reading for the Social*. Public Worlds 12. Minneapolis and London: U of Minnesota P, 2003.

Rad, Amiya, Sudesh Vaid, and Monica Juneja. "Rape, Society and State." *Understanding Violence*. Readings on Women Studies Series 3. Eds. Veena Poonacha. Bombay: Research Center for Women's Studies, SNDT U, n.d. 91–100.

RAHI (Recovering and Healing from Incest). *The House I Grew Up In: Five Indian Women's Experiences of Childhood Incest and Its Impact on Their Lives*. New Delhi: Rahi-Survivor, 1999.

Rao, Anupama, ed. *Gender and Caste*. Issues in Contemporary Indian Feminism 1. Ser. Ed. Rajeswari Sunder Rajan. New Delhi: Kali-Book Review, 2003.

———. "Introduction." Rao *Gender* 1–47.

———. "Understanding Sirasgaon." Rao *Gender* 276–309.

Reddock, Rhoda. "Women's Organizations and Movements in the Commonwealth Caribbean: The Response to Global Economic Crisis in the 1980's." *Feminist Review* 59.1 (1998): 57–73.

Reddy, Gayatri. *With Respect to Sex: Negotiating Hijra Identity in South India*. Chicago: U of Chicago P, 2005.

Richards, Sandra. *Ancient Songs Set Ablaze: The Theatre of Femi Osofisan*. Washington: Howard UP, 1996.

Roach, Joseph. *Cities of the Dead: Circum-Atlantic Performance*. New York: Columbia UP, 1996.

Robinson, Tracy. "Beyond the Bill of Rights: Sexing the Citizen." *Confronting Power, Theorizing Gender: Interdisciplinary Perspectives in the Caribbean*. Ed. Eudine Barriteau. Mona: U of West Indies P, 2003. 231–61.

Rodriguez, Ileana. "Acknowledgements." Rodriguez *Latin* ix–x.

———. "Apprenticeship as Citizenship and Governability." Rodriguez *Latin* 341–66.

———, ed. *The Latin American Subaltern Studies Reader*. Latin America Otherwise: Languages, Empires, Nations. Durham and London: Duke UP, 2001.

———. "Reading Subalterns Across Texts, Disciplines, and Theories: From Representation to Recognition." Rodriguez *Latin* 1–32.

Rooney, Caroline. *African Literature, Animism and Politics*. London: Routledge, 2000.

Rubin, Gayle. "The Traffic in Women: Notes on the 'Political Economy' of Sex." Nicholson 27–62.

Saheli. "Amendments to Rape Laws: Problems and Possibilities." *Saheli Newsletter* Jan.–Apr. 2002: 13–20.

Schechner, Richard. "Exoduction: Shape-shifter, Shaman, Trickster, Artist, Adept, Director, Leader, Grotowski." Schechner and Wolford 462–94.

———. "Grotowski and the Grotowskian." *TDR: The Drama Review* 52.2 (2008): 7–13.

Schechner, Richard, and Lisa Wolford, eds. *The Grotowski Sourcebook*. Ser. Worlds of Performance. London and New York: Routledge, 1997.

Scott, David. "Political Rationalities of the Jamaican Modern." *Small Axe: A Caribbean Journal of Criticism* 7.2 (2003): 1–22.

———. "The Permanence of Pluralism." *Without Guarantees: In Honor of Stuart Hall*. Eds. Paul Gilroy, Lawrence Grossberg and Angela McRobbie. London: Verso, 2000: 282–301.

———. *Refashioning Futures: Criticism After Postcoloniality*. Princeton Studies in Culture/ Power/History. Princeton: Princeton UP, 1999.

Scott, Dennis. *Dog*. Unpublished MS, Scott Papers in Personal Collection of Honor Ford-Smith. n.d.

———. "An Echo in the Bone." *Plays for Today*. Ed. Errol Hill. Longman Caribbean Writers. Essex: Longman, 1985. 73–137.

———. "Theatre in Development: What It Means to Us at the Jamaica School of Drama and in the Caribbean Generally." Unpublished MS, Scott Papers in Personal Collection of Honor Ford-Smith. 1980.

Senior, Olive. *Working Miracles: Women's Lives in the English-Speaking Caribbean*. London: J. Currey; Bloomington: Indiana UP, 1991.

Shepherd, Verene. "Introduction." *Working Slavery, Pricing Freedom: Perspectives from the Caribbean, Africa, and the African Diaspora*. Ed. Verene Shepherd. New York: Palgrave, 2001. x–xxi.

Sherlock, Phillip, and Rex Nettleford. *The University of West Indies: A Caribbean Response to the Challenge of Change.* Macmillan Caribbean. London: Macmillan, 1990.
Silvera, Makeda. *The Heart Does Not Bend.* Toronto: Random House, 2002.
———. "Man Royals and Sodomites: Some Thoughts on the Invisibility of Afro-Caribbean Lesbians." *Piece of My Heart: A Lesbian of Color Anthology.* Ed. Makeda Silvera. Toronto: Sister Vision, 1992. 14–26.
Sistren. 1986. *Lionheart Gal: Life Stories of Jamaican Women.* Ed. Honor Ford-Smith. Mona: U of West Indies P, 2005.
Sistren, and Honor Ford-Smith. *Bellywoman Bangarang.* Ed. Rhonda Cobham. Unpublished MS. Personal Collection of Honor Ford-Smith. 1978/1982.
Sistren Theatre Collective. "*Bellywoman Bangarang.*" *Contemporary Drama of the Caribbean.* Eds. Erika J Waters and David Edgecombe. Kingshill, St. Croix: Caribbean Writer Research Publications, 2001. 77–131.
———. "*QPH.*" *Postcolonial Plays: An Anthology.* Ed. Helen Gilbert. London and New York: Routledge, 2001. 153–78.
Smith, Karina. "Narratives of Success, Narratives of Failure: The Creation and Collapse of Sistren's 'Aesthetic Space'." *Modern Drama* 51.2 (2008): 234–58.
Songs of Freedom. Dir. Phillip Pike. Jahloveboy Productions, 2002.
Sowande, Bode. "Farewell to Babylon." *Farewell to Babylon and Other Plays.* London: Longman, 1979.
Soyinka, Wole. "*Dance of the Forests.*" 1963. *Collected Plays: Volume 1.* Oxford: Oxford UP, 1972. 1–78.
———. *Ibadan: The Penkelemes Years, a Memoir, 1946–1965.* London: Methuen, 1994.
———. "The National Question: Internal Imperatives." *The Open Sore of a Continent: A Personal Narrative of the Nigerian Crisis.* New York and Oxford: Oxford UP, 1996. 109–43.
Spivak, Gayatri Chakravarty. *Death of a Discipline.* The Wellek Library Lectures. New York: Columbia UP, 2003.
———. "Scattered Speculations on the Subaltern and the Popular." *Postcolonial Studies* 8.4 (2005): 475–86.
Springer, Kimberly. "Third Wave Black Feminism?" *Signs: Journal of Women in Culture and Society* 27.4 (2002): 1059–82.
Spurlin, William. "Broadening Postcolonial Studies/Decolonizing Queer Studies: Emerging 'Queer' Identities and Cultures in South Africa." Hawley *Postcolonial Queer* 185–206.
———. *Imperialism within the Margins: Queer Representation and the Politics of Culture in Southern Africa.* New York: Palgrave Macmillan, 2006.
Srampickal, Jacob. "Street Theatre: Protest All the Way." *Voice to the Voiceless: The Power of People's Theatre in India.* London: Hurst; New York: St. Martin's, 1994. 99–153.
Sukthankar, Ashwini. "Introduction." *Facing the Mirror: Lesbian Writing from India.* New Delhi: Penguin, 1999. xiii–xli.
Sunder Rajan, Rajeswari. "Children of the State?: Unwanted Girls in Rural Tamilnadu." *The Scandal of the State: Women, Law and Citizenship in Postcolonial India.* Delhi: Permanent Black, 2003. 177–211.
———. "The Prostitution Question(s): Female Agency, Sexuality, and Work." *The Scandal of the State: Women, Law and Citizenship in Postcolonial India.* Delhi: Permanent Black, 2003. 117–46.
Stone, Carl. *Class, State, and Democracy in Jamaica.* Politics in Latin America Hoover Institution Ser. Stanford: Hoover; New York: Praeger, 1986.
———. *Democracy and Clientelism in Jamaica.* New Brunswick and London: Transaction, 1980.

Stone, Judy, Ed. "*Dog.*" *You Can Lead a Horse to Water and Other Plays.* Oxford: Macmillan, 2005.
———. *Theatre.* Studies in West Indian Literature. Ser. Ed. Kenneth Ramchand. London and Basingstoke: Macmillan Caribbean, 1994.
Swarr, Amanda Lock, and Richa Nagar. "Dismantling Assumptions: Interrogating "Lesbian Struggles for Identity and Survival in India and South Africa." *Signs: Journal of Women in Culture and Society* 29.2 (2003): 491–516.
Taussig, Michael, and Richard Schechner. "Boal in Brazil, France, the USA: An Interview with Augusto Boal." *Playing Boal: Theatre, Therapy, Activism.* Eds. Mady Schutzman and Jan Cohen-Cruz. London: Routledge, 1994. 17–34.
TDR: The Drama Review. Social Theatre. Special Ed. James Thompson. *TDR* 48.2 (2004).
van Erven, Eugene. "An Interview with Safdar Hashmi." *The Right to Perform: Selected Writings of Safdar Hashmi.* New Delhi: Sahmat, 1989. 139–80.
———. *The Playful Revolution: Theatre and Liberation in Asia.* Bloomington: Indiana UP, 1992.
Vanita, Ruth. "*Dosti* and *Tamanna*: Male-Male Love, Difference, and Normativity in Hindi Cinema." *Everyday Life in South Asia.* Eds. Diane P. Mines and Sarah Lamb. Bloomington: Indiana UP, 2002. 146–58.
———. "Thinking Beyond Gender in India." Ed. Nivedita Menon. *Gender and Politics in India.* New Delhi: Oxford UP, 1999. 529–39.
Vanita, Ruth, and Saleem Kidwai, eds. *Same-Sex Love in India: Readings from Literature and History.* 2000. New York: St. Martin's-Palgrave, 2001.
Walcott, Derek. "*Ti-Jean and His Brothers.*" *Dream on a Monkey Mountain and Other Plays.* New York: Noonday, 1970. 88–166.
———. "What the Twilight Says: An Overture." 1970. *What the Twilight Says: Essays.* New York: Farrar, Strauss and Giroux, 1998. 3–35.
Walker, Alice, and Pratibha Parmar. *Warrior Marks: Female Genital Mutilation and the Sexual Blinding of Women.* New York: Harcourt Brace, 1993.
Walker, Rebecca. *To Be Real: Telling the Truth and Changing the Face of Feminism.* New York: Anchor, 1995.
Warrior Marks. Dir. Pratibha Parmar. Alice Walker, Pratibha Parmar, and Efua Dorkenoo. Women Make Movies, 1993.
Wekker, Gloria. "One Finger Does Not Drink Okra Soup: Afro Surinamese Women and Critical Agency." Alexander and Mohanty 330–52.
Weston, Kath. *Families We Choose: Lesbians, Gays, Kinship.* New York: Columbia UP, 1991.
Williams, Pat Ama Tokunbo. "Women and the Dilemma of Politics in Nigeria." *Dilemmas of Democracy in Nigeria.* Eds. Paul A. Beckett and Crawford Young. Rochester: U of Rochester P, 1997. 219–42.
Wolford, Lisa. "General Introduction: Ariadne's Thread." Schechner and Wolford 1–22.

Index

A
Agbekoya. *See* farmer revolts
agency: of the prostitute 99–100; Spivak's definition of 99; indigenous women's 130; community 142–44
Ahmadu Bello University. *See* University
Alexander, M. Jacqui 9–10, 19, 48, 57, 65
Amadiume, Ifi: *Male Daughters and Female Husbands* 10–11, 139–42; *Daughters of the Goddess; Daughters of Imperialism* 126, 139–40, 143, 160 n.6
anthropology: 10, 139, 161 n.8, *see also* ethnography
Auslander, Philip 62

B
Babandiga, Ibrahim 132
Babandiga, Maryam: Better Life for Rural Women Program 20, 132, 135; cultism associated with the First Lady 143
Batra, Kanika 147, 153 n.11
Bhabha, Homi 38
Bharucha, Rustom: adaptation of Manuel Puig's *Kiss of the Spiderwoman* 110; community 88; on Grotowski 21, 151 n.4; on social movements 91; on theatre 92
Boal, Augusto: Arena Theatre of São Paulo 17; exercises and games for actors and non actors 62–3, 154 n.5; fable about the birth of theatre 47; Forum theatre 19, 154 n.5; influence of 15, 19–23, 50, 52, 56–7, 59, 71, 151 n.4; Joker system 17, 19, 151–2 n.4; Legislative theatre 19, 22; spect-actors 18–19; Theater of the Oppressed 21, 50, 56, 62, 65, 151–2 n.5, 154 n.5; rituals and counter-rituals 62–3
Brecht, Bertolt: Epic theatre 16; criticism of 19–21, 151–2 n.5; influence of 13, 15, 17, 23, 25, 39, 42, 45–6, 57, 69, 76, 82, 115, 151 n.4, 153 n.10; on pedagogics 30, 41; on the social function of theatre 18–19, 128; on working class theatre 16, 17, 69
Brodber, Erna: social research 51, 53, 55; on yards 51, 53
Butler, Judith: on kinship 1, 7, 35, 152 n.4,6; on performativity 93–4, 157 n.4

C
caste; as community 6, 93, 106–8; as discriminatory 6, 11, 24–5, 77, 107; as embodiment 109; feminist analyses of 77, 92–3, 109–10, 158 n. 13; system in India 157 n.3
Chatterjee, Partha 4–5
citizenship: citizen-subjects 6, 10, 13, 94, 109, 121, 154 n.6; docile 113, 119, 120, 125; education 114; feminist interrogation of 7, 9–10; normative 4, 7, 22–3, 30, 45, 51; theatrical 19
community: drama 19, 30, 60, 131; socially marginal 24, 46, 93, 101–4, 107–8; spectatorial 3, 14, 30–1, 38–9, 42–5, 148; theories of 5–8, 32–3, 76, 82, 88
Convocation plays 129
Cooper, Carolyn: *Noises in the Blood* 60; *Soundclash* 64, 154 n.7
Cooper, Frederick 6
criticism: of Janam's plays 83, 91; of Tess Onwueme's plays 130;

of Femi Osofisan's plays 115, 127–8; postcolonial drama 12–15; of Dennis Scott's plays 21, 29, 33, 35, 45–6; of Sistren's plays 50, 153 n.2
cultural activism: feminist 48, 57; and the postcolonial state 3, 22, 91; university based 130, 147
Cumper, Gloria, on family courts in Jamaica 9, 51, 54

D

Dattani, Mahesh: as a gay playwright 24, 100; *Seven Steps Around the Fire* 15, 92–6, 100–10; work with incest victims 158 n.12
D' Emilio, John, on the making of a homosexual community 8
democracy: constitutional/parliamentary 11, 25, 57, 108, 113–14, 117, 124; organizational 19, 57, 65; questioning of 65; subaltern/peasant 114, 123, 159 n.4; theories of 4–5, 25, 154–5 n.8; transition to 19, 113–4, 117, 122–4, 127, 129, 159 n.5; radical feminist 7, 152 n.4; theatrical 19
Desai, Gaurav, on homosexuality in Africa 136–8, 160 n.4
Deshpande, Sudhanva 83, 91, 155 n.1
Devi, Mahasweta: "Douloti" 96–9, 101; *Dust on the Road* 157–8 n.6; "Rudali" 96- 100, 104–9.
Diamond, Elin 20

E

Edwards, Nadi 36
Emecheta, Buchi: on the Biafaran war 159 n.2; on sexuality 136, 138, 160 n. 4
Epprecht, Marc 137, 148
ethnography: *dalit* 95; *hijras* 102, 158 n. 10; male wives and female husbands 10, 141; *mati* women 161; *yan daudu* 160–1 n.7

F

farmer revolts: Agbekoya 113–5, 117, 119, 121, 127, 129; Bakolori Farmer's Union 119, 159 n. 4; Sunusungu 122, 159 n. 7; Ruwenzururu 122, 159 n.7
Fatunde, Tunde 119, 159 n.4

Female Genital Multilation (FGM): drama about 133–4; feminist debates about 133, 135–6, 138–40
Ford-Smith, Honor, 2, 9; on Dennis Scott 21, 38, 45–6, 151 n.4, 152 n.2, 5, 7; on Sistren 47–57; 59; 63–4; 152 n.1, 153 n.1
Fraser, Nancy 11, 151 n.2
Friere, Paulo: conscientization 21; literacy 22, 56; pedagogy of the oppressed 50

G

Ganguli, Usha, *Rudali* 24, 92–3, 96–110
gay and lesbian studies 4, 7–8, 95, 136–7, 140, 142, 155 n.9
Gibbons, Rawle 51, 54, 153 n.1
Gilbert, Helen 3, 13–15, 152 n.1
globalization 2, 9, 22, 29, 71–2, 91
Gopinath, Gayatri 158 n.10
Gray, Obika 4, 33, 51
Grotowski, Jerzy: on aesthetics 15, 42–3, 45; *Akropolis* 43; on audience-actor interaction 18, 21, 30; criticism of 18–19, 21, 151 n.4, 153 n.10; influence of 15, 21, 23, 42–3, 45, 151 n.4, 153 n.10; national theatre 17, 45; Poor theatre 15–18, 21

H

Halberstam, Judith 8
Hashmi, Moloyashree (Mala) 73, 76, 83–90, 155 n.1
Hashmi, Safdar 69–73, 77, 82, 88, 90–1, 155 n.2, 156 n.11
heteropatriarchy: as episteme of the postcolonial state 57; feudal 5, 97, 102, 104
hijra: households/families 11, 95, 103; political participation 158 n.8
homophobia 46, 64–5, 137, 147–8, 154 n.7, 155 n.9

I

India: drama 1, 5, 92, 109, 157 n.1; gay rights 151 n.3; women's studies 90, 102, 157 n.13

J

Jamaica: drama 6, 31, 48; gay rights 24, 46, 66, 146, 153 n.13;

women's development 48, 50, 63–4
Jana Natya Manch(Janam) 24, 69–91, 155 n.1, 156 n.6

K
King, Bruce 12
kinship: communal 33–7; non-biological, non-normative 5, 8, 33, 45, 66, 95–6, 106, 110; as interrogation of citizenship 7, 10, 23, 30, 108, 110, 152 n.4; subaltern 4
labor: domestic 56, 99, 134; enforced 39–40, 97–8, 157–8 n.6; industrial 75–6, 78–9; ritualistic 93, 98, 104–8, 110; sexual 44, 92–3, 96, 99–100, 104, 110, 157–8 n.6; voluntary 32; see also work

L
Ladipo, Duro 115–7

M
Mama, Amina 143, 160 n.2
Mamdani, Mahmood 25, 114, 120–22, 159 n.5
Manley, Michael 23, 30, 32, 40–1, 44, 51, 154 n.8
Manushi 9
Marley, Bob 44, 60
Mdembe, Achille 25, 114, 120–1, 159 n.3
Munroe, Trevor 32
Mohanty, Chandra Talpade: on citizenship 9–10, 19; on feminist theory 135–6, 138–9, 160 n.3
Mouffe, Chantal 7

N
nation-state 6, 8, 9, 11, 25, 96–9, 108, 120–2, 124, 144, 154 n.6
neighborhood as community 6, 81, 83, 86, 88, 96
Nettleford, Rex 30, 32, 152 n.3
Newton, Esther 7
Ngugi wa Thiong'o: as dramatist 13, 131–2; on prisons 120
Nigeria: Better Life for Rural Women, see Maryam Babangida; drama 6, 25, 113, 143, 151 n.4; National Council of Women's Societies 114, 124–6, 128; universities in 25–6, 114, 116, 118, 124–30, 132–3, 135, 139, 145, 147–8, 159 n.4

O
Olaniyan, Tejumola 115
Onwueme, Tess, *Tell it to Women* 6, 12, 25, 130–45
Osofisan, Femi: *The Chattering and the Song* 116–7, 119; *Once Upon Four Robbers* 120; *Morountodun* 25, 113–29

P
Pandey, Gyanendra 5
Pandies theatre group 19, 71
performativity: performance and 20, 94; postcolonial 92–5; gender 100, 157 n.4
performances: of active female citizenship 57; of sexual deviancy 11, 100–1, 154 n.6, 160–1 n.7; of state power 96, 117, 142
Performance Studio Workshop (PSW) 133–5, 139, 145, 160 n.2
postcolonial: development 26, 130, 142, 144; drama 1–3, 10, 12–26, 48, 151 n.4;
feminisms 2, 8–12; nationalism 113, 117, 131, 159 n.6; sexual citizenship 50; state 2, 5, 24, 31, 51, 120, 121, 130, 147, 153 n.8
prostitution: child 88, 156 n.12; heterosexual 99, 101, 157–8 n.6; homosexual 99, 102- 4, 106–7; debates 81, 99–100, 157 n.2

Q
Quayson, Ato 159–60 n.9
queer: activism 4, 110; families 35, 45 see also *hijra* households/families; subalternity 25, 110; theory 4, 136, 158 n.10

R
Reddy, Gayatri 101, 106
ritual: *Ettu* 51, 154 n.4; as framework 14, 21, 33–4, 36–7, 45, 50–1, 53, 56–7, 59, 117; *hijra* 92–3, 100–1, 104, 107; *Kumina* 51, 154 n.4; as liberatory 61–2; Nine Night 33–5, 39; *rudali* 92–3, 96, 98, 104–5; as social commentary 3, 20, 22–3, 41, 43; as structure of oppression 56, 62
Roach, Joseph 33

S

Schechner, Richard: on Boal 59; on Grotowski 21, 153 n.10
Scott, David 5, 31–3, 57, 153n, 154–5 n.8
Scott, Dennis: *Dog* 5, 23, 30–1, 33, 35–8, 42–6, 152 n.7; *An Echo in the Bone* 23, 29- 46; influence on Caribbean drama 14, 21–3, 29–30, 48, 51, 69, 147, 152 n.2
sexual identity 25–6, 48, 91, 108–10, 131, 159 n.8
Sistren Theatre Collective (Sistren): *Bellywoman Bangarang* 15, 47, 50–65, 153 n.1; *Lionheart Gal* 56, 58, 60; *QPH* 50–3, 56–66, 154 n.4
Sowande, Bode 116–7, 119, 130
Soyinka, Wole 12, 25, 113, 126, 128, 130, 153 n.9
Spivak, Gayatri Chakravorty 2, 93, 99
Spurlin, William 65, 137
subaltern: democracy 114, 117, 121, 123, 125, 127; cultural politics 3; history 5–6; groups 4, 24, 41, 50, 65, 93–4, 98, 103–4, 109, 147
street theatre 1, 9, 13, 16, 19, 69–91, 155 n.2, 157 n.1
students: as actors 90, 110, 129, 132–3, 139; as audiences 1–2, 69; as vigilantes 118, 146–7, 159 n.4
Stone, Carl: clientelism 4, 154–5 n.8; community 5–6, 33
Stone, Judy 152 n.1
structural adjustment: International Monetary Fund 51, 12; World Bank 118, 121

T

Theatre for Development (TfD): Africa 19, 25, 130–5, 144–5; Caribbean 29
Tompkins, Joanne 13–15, 152 n.1

U

U.N. International Women's Decade 50, 64, 131
University: Ahmadu Bello University 26, 114, 124, 126, 147; of Delhi 1–2, 26, 69, 71–2, 79–80, 90, 147; of Ibadan 116, 126, 133–5, 139; of Ife 126, 128–9; of West Indies (UWI) 26, 29, 31, 42, 48, 51, 152 n.3

V

Vanita, Ruth 12, 95, 108, 110

W

Walcott, Derek 12–13, 29, 38, 153 n.9
Weston, Kath 8
Women in Nigeria (WIN) 9, 114, 124–6, 159 n.4
women's movements: autonomous 9, 25, 72, 78, 83, 88–9, 113–4, 124–5, 147, 156 n.7; party-based/state-sponsored 9, 88, 113, 157 n.4; second wave 9–10, 50, 73, 93, 96, 114, 124, 128, 151 n.2; third wave 3, 9–10, 93; university-based 26
work: cultural 9, 16–17, 23, 29, 45, 48, 52, 63, 66, 69, 71–3, 130–3, 153 n.2; *see also* labor
working class: audiences 21, 75, 90; performers 21, 23, 51; theatre 16–17, 24, 69–70, 151–2 n.5